*In Vino Veritas*

# *In Vino Veritas*

## An Anthology of Drinking in Literature

*Edited and Compiled by*
NICHOLAS O. WARNER

McFarland & Company, Inc., Publishers
*Jefferson, North Carolina, and London*

E.E. Cummings, "I was sitting in mcsorley's. outside it was New York and beauti-." Copyright 1923, 1925, 1951, 1953, (c) 1991 by the Trustees for the E.E. Cummings Trust. Copyright (c) 1976 by George James Firmage, from *Complete Poems: 1904–1962* by E.E. Cummings, edited by George J. Firmage. Used by permission of Liveright Publishing Corporation. • Nicolás Guillén, "Bars." By permission of Nicolás Hernández Guillén. Translation reprinted from *Man-Making Words*. Copyright (c) 1972 by Roberto Marquez and David Arthur McMurray and published by the University of Massachusetts Press. • Langston Hughes, "Cocktail Sip," *The Best of Simple*. Reprinted by permission of Harold Ober Associates Incorporated. "Cocktail Sip" from *The Best of Simple* by Langston Hughes. Copyright (c) 1961 by Langston Hughes. Copyright renewed 1989 by George Houston Bass. Reprinted by permission of Hill and Wang, a division of Farrar, Straus and Giroux, LLC. • Naguib Mahfouz, "Blessed Night," translated by Denys Johnson-Davies, *The Time and The Place*. Copyright (c) 1991 by The American University of Cairo Press. • Carson McCullers, "A Domestic Dilemma" from *The Ballad of the Sad Café and Collected Short Stories* by Carson McCullers. Copyright (c) 1951 by Carson McCullers, renewed by 1979 by Floria V. Lasky, Executrix of the Estate of Carson McCullers. Reprinted by Permission of Houghton Mifflin Harcourt Publishing Company. All rights reserved. Reproduced by permission of Pollinger Limited and the Estate of Carson McCullers. • Brian Moore, "The Lonely Passion of Judith Hearne." Copyright (c) 1956 by Brian Moore. Reprinted by permission of Curtis Brown, Ltd. • Pablo Neruda, "Ode to Wine." *Selected Odes of Pablo Neruda*, edited and translated by Margaret Sayers Peden, (c) 1990 by the Fundacion Pablo Neruda. Published by the University of California Press. *Pablo Neruda* "Oda al vino," *Odes Elementales* (c) Fundación Pablo Neruda, 2012. • Simon J. Ortiz, "Woman Singing." Reprinted by permission of the author. • "I Get a Kick Out of You" (from *Anything Goes*). Words and Music by Cole Porter. Copyright (c) 1934 (Renewed) WB Music Corp. All Rights Reserved. Used by Permission. "I Get a Kick Out of You." Words and Music by Cole Porter. (c) 1934 (Renewed) WB Music Corp. (ASCAP) All rights administered by Warner/Chappell North America Ltd. • Tennessee Williams, *Cat on a Hot Tin Roof*. Copyright (c) 1954, 1955, 1982, 1983 by The University of the South. Reprinted by permission of New Directions Publishing Corp. and Georges Borchardt, Inc., on behalf of the Tennessee Williams Estate.

LIBRARY OF CONGRESS CATALOGUING-IN-PUBLICATION DATA

In vino veritas : an anthology of drinking in literature / edited and compiled by Nicholas O. Warner.
    p.    cm.

ISBN 978-0-7864-6883-6
softcover : acid free paper ∞

1. Drinking of alcoholic beverages—Literary collections.
2. Drinking customs—Literary customs.  I. Warner, Nicholas O., 1950–  editor of compilation.
PN6071.D715 2013
808.8'0355—dc23                                  2012041228

BRITISH LIBRARY CATALOGUING DATA ARE AVAILABLE

© 2013 Nicholas O. Warner. All rights reserved

*No part of this book may be reproduced or transmitted in any form or by any means, electronic or mechanical, including photocopying or recording, or by any information storage and retrieval system, without permission in writing from the publisher.*

On the cover: Hermann Armin Kern, *Wine Drinker in Cellar*, oil on wood panel, 18⅛" × 11¾"

Manufactured in the United States of America

*McFarland & Company, Inc., Publishers*
  *Box 611, Jefferson, North Carolina 28640*
    *www.mcfarlandpub.com*

*For my children*
*Natasha, Katya, Gregory*

"I get no kick from champagne.
Mere alcohol doesn't thrill me at all,
So tell me why should it be true
That I get a kick out of you?"
—Cole Porter,
"I Get a Kick Out of You"

# Acknowledgments

Like many another editor, I found compiling this anthology to be far more complex and time-consuming a task than I had expected. The project entailed not only researching, assembling, and commenting on a wide range of texts, but turning myself into a Sherlock Holmesian copyright sleuth, tracking down often elusive permissions rights over a period of many months. It is a pleasure to thank the people who helped me through this enterprise. At Claremont McKenna College, Dean of the Faculty Gregory Hess generously authorized crucial financial support for this project, while Cindi Guimond helped smooth the way with permissions, reimbursements, and her well-known blend of good sense and good cheer. Leslie Elias-Volz was a model of patience and technical savvy as she worked with me on preparing the manuscript. My research assistant, Chris Ferrer, helped with logistical details. At the Huntington Library and Art Gallery, the rare books staff efficiently and courteously gave me access to original editions for many of the works included in this anthology. To Ernest Kurtz, author of a classic work on the spiritual and cultural aspects of alcoholism—*Not God: A History of Alcoholics Anonymous*—I owe thanks for encouragement in pursuing this project, and for suggesting the topic of the last section, on Spirits and the Spirit. Special and loving thanks go to Alejandra Vargas, who used her linguistic and diplomatic skills to communicate with literary agents in Spain and Cuba; because of her efforts, I was able to include two literary gems in this book—the poems by Nicolás Guillén and Pablo Neruda. As for the dedicatees of the book, no words can suffice; I thank them just for being there.

# Table of Contents

*Acknowledgments* . . . . . . . . . . . . . . . . . . . . . . . . . . . . . . . . . . . . . . . . . . . vi
*Preface* . . . . . . . . . . . . . . . . . . . . . . . . . . . . . . . . . . . . . . . . . . . . . . . . . . . . . 1
*Introduction* . . . . . . . . . . . . . . . . . . . . . . . . . . . . . . . . . . . . . . . . . . . . . . . . 5

## I. CAUSES OF DRINKING . . . . . . . . . . . . . . . . . . . . . . . . . . . . . . . . 23
Li Bo, "Drinking Song" (8th century) . . . . . . . . . . . . . . . . . . . . . . . . . . . 23
Ralph Waldo Emerson, from "The Poet" (1844) . . . . . . . . . . . . . . . . . . 25
Nathaniel Hawthorne, from *The Blithedale Romance* (1852) . . . . . . . . . . . 27
Leo Tolstoy, "Why Then Do Men Stupefy Themselves?" (1890) . . . . . . . 34
Tennessee Williams, from *Cat on a Hot Tin Roof* (1955) . . . . . . . . . . . . . . 46

## II. EFFECTS OF DRINKING . . . . . . . . . . . . . . . . . . . . . . . . . . . . . . 54
William Shakespeare, from *Macbeth* (1605), and *Othello* (1604) . . . . . . . . . 54
Robert Burns, "John Barleycorn" (1782) . . . . . . . . . . . . . . . . . . . . . . . . . 63
Thomas Dekker and John Ford, "Cast Away Care" (1656) . . . . . . . . . . . 65
Daniel Defoe, from *Colonel Jack* (1722) . . . . . . . . . . . . . . . . . . . . . . . . . . 66
James Fenimore Cooper, from *The Pioneers* (1823) . . . . . . . . . . . . . . . . . 69
Charles Dickens, from *David Copperfield* (1849–50) . . . . . . . . . . . . . . . . . 75
Herman Melville, from *Moby-Dick* (1851) . . . . . . . . . . . . . . . . . . . . . . . . 80
Mark Twain, "Edward Mills and George Benton" (1880) . . . . . . . . . . . . 83
Frances Ellen Watkins Harper, from *Iola Leroy, or Shadows
  Uplifted* (1892) . . . . . . . . . . . . . . . . . . . . . . . . . . . . . . . . . . . . . . . . . . . 89

## III. DRINKING AND THE TAVERN . . . . . . . . . . . . . . . . . . . . . . . 92
William Blake, "The Little Vagabond" (1794) and Stephen Crane,
  from *George's Mother* (1896) . . . . . . . . . . . . . . . . . . . . . . . . . . . . . . . . . 92
Charles Dickens, "Gin-Shops" (1836) . . . . . . . . . . . . . . . . . . . . . . . . . . 105
James Joyce, "Counterparts" (1914) . . . . . . . . . . . . . . . . . . . . . . . . . . . 110
Langston Hughes, "Cocktail Sip" (1953) . . . . . . . . . . . . . . . . . . . . . . . 119

Nicolás Guillén, "Bars" (1958) . . . . . . . . . . . . . . . . . . . . . . . . . . . . . . 122
John Keats, "Lines on the Mermaid Tavern" (1818) and E.E.
    Cummings, "i was sitting in mcsorleys" (1922) . . . . . . . . . . . . . . . . . . . . 124

## IV. DRINKING AND THE FAMILY . . . . . . . . . . . . . . . . . . . . . . . . . . . . 128
Walt Whitman, "Reuben's Last Wish" (1856) . . . . . . . . . . . . . . . . . . . . . 128
Émile Zola, from *L'Assommoir (The Dram-Shop)* (1877) . . . . . . . . . . . . . 134
Mark Twain (Samuel Langhorne Clemens), *The Adventures of
    Huckleberry Finn* (1885) . . . . . . . . . . . . . . . . . . . . . . . . . . . . . . . . . . 147
Carson McCullers, "A Domestic Dilemma" (1951) . . . . . . . . . . . . . . . . . 149

## V. DRINKING AND GENDER . . . . . . . . . . . . . . . . . . . . . . . . . . . . . . . 159
George Eliot (Mary Anne Evans), from "Janet's Repentance" (1857) . . . 159
Willa Cather, "On the Divide" (1896) . . . . . . . . . . . . . . . . . . . . . . . . . . 166
Jack London, from *John Barleycorn* (1913) . . . . . . . . . . . . . . . . . . . . . . 178
Brian Moore, from *The Lonely Passion of Judith Hearne* (1955) . . . . . . . . 186

## VI. SPIRITS AND THE SPIRIT . . . . . . . . . . . . . . . . . . . . . . . . . . . . . . 195
Li Bo, "Drinking Alone by Moonlight" (8th century) . . . . . . . . . . . . . . . 195
Emily Dickinson, "I taste a liquor never brewed" (1860) . . . . . . . . . . . . 196
William James, from *The Varieties of Religious Experience* (1902) . . . . . . 198
Pablo Neruda, "Ode to Wine" (1954) . . . . . . . . . . . . . . . . . . . . . . . . . . 200
Simon Ortiz, "Woman Singing" (1969) . . . . . . . . . . . . . . . . . . . . . . . . 203
Naguib Mahfouz, "Blessed Night" (1991) . . . . . . . . . . . . . . . . . . . . . . . 212

*Further Reading* . . . . . . . . . . . . . . . . . . . . . . . . . . . . . . . . . . . . . . . . . . 221

# Preface

This book began its journey in a classroom. Several years ago, students in one of my courses in English and Comparative Literature commented on the prevalence of intoxication, whether as casual background detail or major theme, in texts from different periods and countries. Class discussions of this subject led me to offer occasional courses on the literary depiction of intoxicants, especially alcohol, and to write a book on the topic (*Spirits of America: Intoxication in Nineteenth-Century American Literature*, 1997). After further research and conversations with colleagues working in this area, I realized that a collection of outstanding literary texts dealing with drinking, and organized along the lines of the present volume, would be useful to at least three groups of readers: literary scholars studying the depiction of drinking; social scientists investigating the socio-cultural aspects of alcohol use; and serious general readers wishing to learn more about drink's reflection in literature. The book I envisioned, and that now has taken shape as the present work, centers on some of the most prevalent themes both in literary portrayals of drinking and in the field of alcohol studies: these themes are drinking's causes, its effects, and its relations to the family, to gender, and to the public house or tavern. In addition, the work presents a concluding section that steps back from such specific areas to situate the topic within the broader, more intangible context of drinking's spiritual dimensions; these dimensions are sometimes forgotten in the understandable focus on alcohol as a social or medical issue, but in truth they are a deep-seated factor in the consumption of what we call "spirits."

While other anthologies on drink or drugs have appeared from time to time, important differences mark this collection from earlier ones. Most previous anthologies about alcohol in literature were not designed for serious study. *The Fireside Book of Wine* (1977), edited by Alexis Bespaloff, and *Inspired by Drink* (1988), edited by John and Joan Digby, while delightful, are clearly intended for casual perusal by casual readers, with the latter volume including tea and cocoa (!) under the rubric of drinking. *The New Compleat Imbiber* (1986), edited by Cyril Ray, includes passages from such luminaries as Samuel Johnson, Alphonse Daudet, Kingsley Amis, and Iris Murdoch, among others, but the selections are geared toward gastronomy and connoisseurship, not toward alcohol's complexity as a literary theme. Peter Haining's *Great Irish Drinking Stories* (2002) contains many fine selections with informative, entertaining headnotes, but its overall approach is one of cultural appreciation for what the dust jacket calls "the appetite for life you'll find in any Irish pub." One valuable but now out-of-print small anthology is *The Invisible Enemy: Alcoholism and the Modern Short Story* (1989), the subtitle of which might more accurately refer to the American modern short story. The literary quality of the contents is excellent, with selections on the "family," "children," "progression," "delusions," and "trying to stop," but the book has only a slight introduction of less than two pages, with no commentary or annotations to any of the fifteen stories selected.

Far more scholarly in approach is an anthology edited by John W. Crowley, who has also published extensively on the literary representation of drink. Entitled *Drunkard's Progress: Narratives of Addiction, Despair, and Recovery* (1999), the book takes as its purview not works of imaginative literature, but rather nineteenth-century accounts of alcoholism that are linked to the Washingtonian temperance movement, and that foreshadow today's "twelve-step" narratives of recovery from alcoholism. It is part of Crowley's purpose to give such texts more serious attention and recognition than the condescending dismissals they have usually received; thus the aims and contents of his book are obviously very different from mine. More recently, Rebecca Shannonhouse has edited *Under the Influence: The Literature of Addiction* (2003), a volume that brings alcohol and drugs together under the rubric of addiction, including sexual addiction, and that presents non-literary historical materials as well as more traditional literary texts. There is value in this approach, but my anthology offers a different kind of value in focusing on drinking rather than addiction, on a single type of intoxicant—in this case, alcohol—rather than on many different types, and on artistically compelling examples of fiction, poetry, the essay, and drama.

As the introduction explains in more detail, *In Vino Veritas* draws on works from different genres, periods, and languages. In so doing, the book facilitates comparisons and contrasts in the depiction of an almost universal human practice which nevertheless reveals divergent perceptions and assumptions both within and across cultures. Inevitably, the identification of meritorious material entails a subjective element which, I freely admit, has played a role in the selections here, as it must in any anthology. At the same time, my choices were not arbitrary. They have not been based on personal favorites among texts dealing with drink (some of those, in fact, do not even appear in the book), but on achieving a balance between contrast and complementarity in the texts selected; on the appropriateness of works for the chapter headings under which they appear; and on considerations of literary artistry. In this latter regard, some works are, to be sure, more impressive than others: Mark Twain is simply a better writer of fiction than Walt Whitman, great though Whitman is as a poet. But the presence of contrasting works from these two writers in one section of the book should itself spark reflection on the different ways that authors of genius have approached drinking, drinkers, and those who are affected by them. Such patterns of similarity and difference—in tone, attitude, style, and idea—inform each section and, thus, the book as a whole.

Regarding the work that follows, most selections in each section are arranged in chronological order, except for a few instances where two works from different periods share some features that made it appropriate to put them together under one headnote. As for references, the introduction uses conventional endnotes. For ease of reading, however, subsequent chapters use symbols in the headnotes and literary selections to refer readers to explanatory comments following the text.

Through the main introduction to the volume, the headnotes to individual selections, and where necessary through explanatory annotations, the text provides a theoretical framework for its multi-faceted, problematic topic, while also supplying useful background information and context for each author and work. In this way *In Vino Veritas* will, I hope, enable readers to explore the issues it addresses more deeply and variously on their own.

# Introduction

Literature has long explored the sometimes comic, sometimes tragic, but always potent role played by alcohol in human behavior, perception, and consciousness. Greek tragedy and comedy were long believed to stem from festivals celebrating Dionysos, the god of wine; the Roman poet Horace famously observed that no poems worthy of immortality could be written by water-drinkers; a common motif in classical Chinese poetry links poetry and poets alike with wine—indeed, the pages of world literature from classical times through postmodernism overflow with depictions of drink and drinkers.[1] Drawing on so rich a tradition, this anthology aims to provide a systematically arranged, annotated collection of outstanding literary works dealing with drink. As such, the book testifies to the diversity and longevity of literature's depiction of drinking. But so vast a topic poses an organizational challenge: how to arrange the material in a manner that will combine coherence, usefulness, and interest? The answer lies in an organizational principle that joins inclusiveness to a sound conceptual rationale. One such principle, which I employ here, grounds literary selections from different times and places in terms of several fundamental, recurring themes in sociocultural studies of drinking. Organized into sections reflecting these themes, the anthology seeks various readerships—social scientists examining cultural attitudes toward alcohol; the growing number of literary scholars concerned with the ways that writers of different periods and cultures have dealt with drink; students in literature or social science courses where the anthology could serve as a text; and general readers interested in literature's treatment of a controversial, pervasive aspect of human experience.

Throughout the deliberately broad temporal and geographic fabric of this collection, there run two chief unifying strands: a concern with the multiple symbolic and cultural dimensions of drink, and attention to certain enduring issues in alcohol studies which, as mentioned above, serve as the section headings for this book. These issues are causes of drinking; effects of drinking; drinking and family life; drinking and gender; the tavern or public drinking establishment; and the spiritual dimension of drinking.

Readers will, however, discover varying degrees of porousness between sections, since a text dealing with, say, family relations may well involve gender, or the causes of drinking, or drinking's spiritual dimensions. The headings are not meant to constitute rigid, mutually exclusive categories; rather, they reflect areas of emphasis that have traditionally provided some of the most useful frameworks within which research and treatment specialists have investigated, defined, and debated the many meanings of alcohol use and abuse. These areas have also provided major contexts for the literary representation of drinking in many different times and places.

Approaching literature's depiction of alcohol through these contexts, this volume encourages readers to think about drinking as a practice that is deeply cultural as well as biochemical. Far from being reducible to a fixed set of physical reactions, both alcohol use and abuse operate in a relational system of culturally defined meanings and associations. "Drinking," writes the anthropologist Mary Douglas, "is essentially a social act, performed in a recognized social context."[2] The *who, what, when,* and *where* of drinking—as well as the *how much* and *why* of it—profoundly affect the perception of drinking as normal or pathological; so too do the value systems of those who observe and describe the drinking in question. To different perceivers, and sometimes even to the same perceiver, an alcoholic beverage can appear as commodity, ritual, medicine, poison, or symbol. A specific drinking substance may even be all of these things, or combine any of them with yet other roles or associations, other layers of significance. What the oenologist and journalist Steve Charters has recently written of wine—that a "substantial 'mythology' surrounds its production and consumption," and that a "range of meanings" is attached to wine and its use—could easily be applied to other alcoholic beverages; indeed, few commodities and activities surpass drink and drinking in terms of symbolic or cultural meaningfulness. As Harvard Medical School Professor George E. Vaillant observes in his study of the etiology of drinking problems, *The Natural History of Alcoholism Revisited,* although "relatively unimportant as a cause of alcoholism, cultural patterns of alcohol *use* are very important." Similarly, describing the multiple cultural meanings attached to alcohol, the sociologist Robin Room refers to "alcohol's pervasiveness not only as a material artifact, but also as an object and occasion for symbolism ... the use of alcohol—or abstention—becomes an icon or a prop or an excuse in intimate dramas within the family, in daily performances within an ethnicity, and on the wider stage of interethnic contacts and relations."[3] As Room's theatrical metaphors suggest, the symbolic, meaning-laden aspects of drinking (a practice too easily written off as either a "problem" or as a mundane, insignificant activity) lend themselves particularly well to literary expression, which, of course, thrives on the interplay of symbol, cultural meaning, and lived experience. The present volume brings together a number of esthetically powerful, ethically thought-provoking examples of that interplay, organized into sections based on the contexts for understanding drink that I have outlined above.

These contexts will, of course, never be exactly replicated in different societies or periods, nor is that my purpose in using them. Contemporary readers need hardly be reminded that our understanding of matters like family, gender, or even the neighborhood bar, are inevitably mediated by culture, history, and socio-economic circumstance. With regard to drink, the most influential statement of this principle comes in Craig MacAndrew's and David Edgerton's once revolutionary, now classic study, *Drunken Comportment*. Examining stereotypes associated with Native American drinking patterns, MacAndrew and Edgerton convincingly demonstrate the ways that "drunken comportment" depends on a combination of learned patterns of drinking expectations about drink's effects. While genetics doubtless plays a major yet still not fully understood role in alcoholism, such questions as how people behave while drunk, and whether they are "alcoholic" or not, owe much to the behavior of those from whom drinkers have learned how to drink. As MacAndrew and Edgerton put it, "from one coast to the other, the evidence points to the fact that when the North American Indians' initial expectation with alcohol was untutored by expectations to the contrary, the result was neither the development of an all-consuming craving nor an epic of drunken mayhem and debauchery." Varying tribal traditions, as well as the drinking patterns of those whites who introduced Indians to drinking (e.g., the violent binge drinking that was common among mountain men on the one hand, or the moderate, decorous imbibing of Pennsylvania Quakers on the other), profoundly affected the ways that Native Americans responded to alcohol. Extrapolating from the Native American Indian experience, MacAndrew and Edgerton conclude that "persons learn about drunkenness what their societies impart to them, and comporting themselves in consonance with these understandings, they become living confirmations of their societies' teachings."[4]

Compelling as this conclusion is, it is also true that the use of common reference points, such as the section headings in this book, can help us understand cultural similarity and difference with regard to alcohol use. After all, drinking is a universal issue, even if some societies recognize it only by forbidding it; since, for example, families too are a universal issue, it is not surprising that drinking and the family are shown to intersect vividly in numerous literary works, several of which appear in the section on the family here. To look at such works within the framework of drinking and the family is to give comparative exploration a clarifying lens through which a mass of disparate details, loosely connected to the consumption of alcohol, comes into focus. To help sharpen that focus, this anthology provides a contextualizing commentary for each selection in the book. Intentionally brief and suggestive rather than definitive, the commentaries have three purposes: to draw readers' attention to aspects of the author's background or historical situation that may illuminate the treatment of drinking in any given text; to prompt readers to raise questions of their own for the purposes of comparative analysis; and to facilitate more intensive study of the broader national or cultural environment within which a particular literary depiction of drinking originally appeared. Through the commentaries, I wish to set the stage for a reader's independent investigation without preempting such activity or overly choreographing it. At a minimum, the commentaries should enable readers to hear more clearly the powerful cries of affinity or opposition that different works of literature can make to one another.

In addressing the organization of this book, I have already implicitly touched on the benefits that such an organization can provide. More explicitly, I believe that this book, with its conceptual structure and comparative, broad-based selection of texts, can be valuable in a number of ways. Because of its focus on a diverse range of esthetically compelling works, the book can promote and facilitate the serious analysis of drink as a literary subject, in and of itself; the history of such analysis is still very young. The book can also stimulate cross-fertilization of literary and social science perspectives, and discussion among disciplines in the humanities and social sciences, by connecting literary works to the social history of alcohol. In using widespread and basic issues in alcohol studies as rubrics for each section, this work also provides a coherent framework for comparative discussions of different cultures' literary representations of drink. Finally, through the commentaries introducing each selection, and the annotations to the selections, the book situates each text in a network of assumptions and references, so as to facilitate understanding both of the individual text and its relation to a broader socio-cultural spectrum of alcohol-related issues.

The anthology's topic itself is, of course, problematic—and therein lies a large part of its significance and interest. Few other areas of widespread human activity reveal so many different aspects, invite so many different perspectives, and assume so many different meanings. And few terms fluctuate as much in their connotations as the word "drinking." After all, what, when we speak of drinking, are we talking about? Problem drinking, normal drinking, alcoholism, addiction, drug dependence—these few phrases are but the tip of an iceberg of debate about the associations and implications behind the terminology applied to various aspects of alcohol consumption. In his study of the shifting rhetoric of addiction and drinking, William White notes that "words selected to define alcohol and other drug problems reflect personal, social, political, economic, professional, and clinical interests"; addressing a similar problem, Dwight B. Heath, whose long anthropological career has focused almost as much on debates about the meanings of drink as they have on actual drinking practices, once described a meeting where "delegates to the World Health Organization came to the realization that a shared concern about alcoholism did not mean the same thing to colleagues from various nations."[5] Indeed, not just between nations, but within a national culture or an ethnicity, there exist numerous variations on and exceptions to the norms of the culture at large, whether in the case of a culture's various subgroups, or of individuals whose psychological and biological histories lead to experiences with alcohol different from those of the culture as a whole.

The suggestive title of sociologist Joseph Gusfield's book, *Contested Meanings: The Construction of Alcohol Problems*, bears out the notion of drinking as an activity whose meanings show an unusual degree of variation, even of contradiction. Such variation or contradiction depends on the circumstances in which the drinking occurs, and the vantage point of those who observe and describe the drinking. Emphasizing alcohol's status as a "cultural object," Gusfield reminds us that the significance of drinking spans a dramatically wide range of possibilities that involve different socio-cultural definitions, expectations, and assumptions about drinking behavior. Although traditional studies of American drinking "are dominated by the framework of pathology, of drinking as a social problem"—indeed, largely because of this fact—it is important to remember that the same act of drinking can become deviant, acceptable, or even laudable in different countries, in different subgroups within a nation, even in different contexts or social situations within a subgroup. In this regard, Gusfield notes the conflicting attitudes toward temperance in two groups of American Christians—Catholics and Protestants—throughout much of the nineteenth century.[6] Such differences extend even to "objective," scientific analyses of alcohol use. After all, different disciplines tend to approach drinking from distinct angles of vision, and with distinct concerns or driving questions. Anthropologists, for instance, tend to focus mainly on alcohol's cultural significance apart from "problems"; by contrast, physicians and sociologists have tended to emphasize the pathological in their own research on drink. For this reason, it is wise to remember the following observation by Mark H. Moore and Dean R. Gerstein: "a simple equivalence of drinking with problems, and more drinking with more serious problems, while often true, can be somewhat misleading."[7] Compounding this complexity of meanings regarding drink is the range of associations that individual beverages can have in different communities of drinking—or even within the same community. Gin, champagne, tequila, bourbon, sherry—each of these drinks possesses a long and varied history of its own, as well as a shared history with other drinks as members of the larger group of alcoholic beverages. One can get equally drunk on any of these beverages, but each carries its own baggage of cultural associations and overtones.

Perhaps the most famous instance of the significant distinctiveness among beverage choices appears in a famous pair of engravings produced by that highly literary visual artist, William Hogarth—*Gin Lane* and *Beer Street*. Printed in London in 1742, Hogarth's interrelated images link the seemingly personal, idiosyncratic preference of gin or beer to a web of economic, moral, and social consequences. Although not a teetotaler himself, Hogarth was appalled by the epidemic of gin-related drunkenness, poverty, and mayhem infecting eighteenth-century England. In *Gin Lane*, Hogarth depicts an entire society disintegrating as the result of gin drinking, with its attendant poverty, disease, violence, and economic exploitation of the poor. The statue of King George in the background of the scene—presiding, as it were, over the decay of all areas of English life—emphasizes Hogarth's view of the gin disaster's national scope. In contrast, *Beer Street* not only celebrates the more nutritious, cheaper, and, by volume consumed, less intoxicating beverage of beer; the design also associates beer with health (the plump figures scattered throughout the picture, as opposed to the emaciated characters in *Gin Lane*), with animal spirits and sensual energy (the cheerfully lustful young couple in the foreground of the picture), and with prosperity (the thriving business establishments, the evidence of new construction projects, the enormous slabs of meat and bread wielded by the fat, pipe-smoking butcher.) Even if not always as dramatically presented as in Hogarth, the issue of beverage choice remains a charged one in many situations and cultures, with class, age, gender, ethnicity, even political affiliation affecting beverage choice and, what is equally significant, affecting the perceived *meanings* of such choice.

As the foregoing makes clear, the "unstable, chameleon-like quality" of alcoholism applies to drinking in general.[8] The topic involves a daunting multiplicity of different, at times conflicting notions of what even constitutes drinking, to say nothing of alcohol abuse or addiction. This very complexity offers great opportunities for literary investigation: as Walt Whitman wrote, "The subject [of drink] has so many sides—noble, devilish."[9] These many sides are part of what makes drink a rich subject for literary depiction. And literature itself, with its capacity for feeding off of the problematic and ambiguous, is a highly apt means of articulating the diversity of experiences and discourses that we find when we look at the various phenomena covered by the general term "drinking."

At the same time, literature's capacity for graphic rendering of the physical gives unforgettable expression to the tangible dimensions of drinking experience. I have already emphasized the ways that drink is powerfully mediated by culture. However, as demonstrated by alcohol's well-documented effects on brain and body, this culturally mediated phenomenon is also inescapably enmeshed with material reality. By virtue of its elastic, inclusive nature, literature can capture both the soul and the guts, as it were, of the drinking experience, conveying evanescent nuances of spiritual feeling as vividly as it does the inevitable flesh-and-blood processes of the body. Both the spiritual and physical aspects of alcohol use, particularly as captured in literature, have received cogent expression from Thomas B. Gilmore, Jr. While science can illuminate much about the physical processes of drinking and alcoholism, Gilmore points out that science is simply "not equipped to undertake" an analysis of drink in its spiritual dimension. As Gilmore observes, "'Spiritual' should certainly not be reduced in meaning to 'religious'; any good definition of the term would be capacious, including many elements of the irrational and the emotional. In realizing that literature is better than science at conveying what drunkenness or alcoholism feels like—its terror, its pitiableness, its degradation, its ludicrousness, occasionally even its glory—we are recognizing its ability to capture spiritual qualities." Gilmore's book is equally memorable in expressing the ineluctable physicality of alcoholism (and by extension, of drinking): assailing an oversimplified discussion of "will power" by a biographer of the alcoholic writer, Brendan Behan, Gilmore presents the following perspective on will power, expressed by some members of Alcoholics Anonymous: "If you think that will power can overcome alcoholism, try using it the next time you have diarrhea."[10]

But while literature can powerfully render both the physical and spiritual realities of alcohol use, some readers may challenge this book's selection of texts drawn from established, traditional literary genres: the poem, essay, or short story, the dramatic scene or novelistic passage. After all, in a canon-expanding/canon-busting age, why not extend the book's reach to other culturally significant, verbal renderings of drink: folk tales; popular songs; temperance tracts; newspapers, broadsides, advertisements, and various published ephemera? Because, though informed by anthropological and other social science perspectives, this is not a work of anthropology, popular culture, social history, or psychology. Its purpose is literary, and its focus reflects that purpose. Moreover, it is not meant to be exhaustive—nor could, in fact, any single volume of written materials about drink be exhaustive or even thoroughly representative. The range of experiences and perspectives and depictions of drink is simply too vast for any single volume to pretend to such thoroughness. I hope, in fact, that the following will incite yet others to explore further the presentations of drinking in different forms, and the interconnections that can emerge from comparative studies of these forms or areas of expression. Keeping the focus above all on literature in this volume does not preclude the extension of literature in other studies to include the "non-literary" or "sub-literary," or even to redefine the "literary." It is an ironic historical fact that, less than a century ago, in 1926, the literary study of intoxication was considered sufficiently unseemly that the eminent literary scholar, Emile Légouis, apologized for daring even to broach the topic of drink in the plays of Shakespeare. Since then, literary studies of drink have proliferated, but the field is still relatively young, offering readers and scholars many areas to explore both within the bounds of traditional literary texts and in the encounter of such texts with popular culture.[11]

Ultimately, what is most important for this book's approach is its guidance by what Stephen Greenblatt calls "literary power." Famous for extending the study of literature to include what earlier critics used to call "extrinsic" or "extra-literary" materials, the "New Historicist" Greenblatt has recently addressed the problem of neglecting or even fearing a focus on the literary: "It seems a bit absurd," Greenblatt writes, "to bear witness to the intensity of *Hamlet*; but my profession has become so oddly diffident and even phobic about literary power; so suspicious and tense, that it risks losing sight of—or at least failing to articulate—the whole reason anyone bothers with the enterprise in the first place."[12] If not always on the same plane of "intensity" as *Hamlet* (though Shakespeare is represented here), the literary texts in this volume—whether by Shakespeare himself (passages from *Othello* and *Macbeth*), or by Pablo Neruda, Leo Tolstoy, or Frances Ellen Watkins Harper, to name only a few authors—exist on a continuum with that intensity of form, emotion, and ideas that makes for an exciting, moving, and engaging work of literature.

The above discussion focuses on the possibility that this anthology may be too narrowly literary for some readers. But if it is too narrow for some, it may be too broad for others. After all, given the role of culture in drinking behavior, a point emphasized elsewhere in this introduction, some might ask why the book does not concentrate on one period, or on one national literature, or better yet, perhaps, on a single facet of a period and/or place within a national literature—the literary depiction of women drinking in *fin de siècle* Paris, or tavern scenes in antebellum American fiction. Would not such an approach more truly reflect the influence of culture on drinking? Do you not elide cultural difference by lumping together works from different nations, periods, and ethnic or racial identities? My answer is that compartmentalization has its virtues, but only to compartmentalize is just as myopic as it is never to define or set a boundary, be it one of cultural context or historical moment. To cut across periods and cultures is not necessarily to deny difference. In the present volume, the purpose of my broad-ranging comparative procedures is to affirm the pervasiveness of certain kinds of human experience, to bring into focus the global scope of the stage on which our own local dramas unfold, and to foreground patterns of both difference and similarity by presenting clashing and complementary perspectives on drink. The international, inter-temporal arrangement of this volume serves to connect the parish to the world—not to reduce the world to the parish.

In essence, I argue that placing cultural similarity "under erasure" is merely the flip side of placing cultural difference under erasure. By ignoring parallels between different societies, we become helplessly inscribed within a discourse of difference which can, ironically, lead to labeling anyone outside a narrowly defined group as inescapably "other." It is for this reason, in part, that anthropologists and other social scientists, even if focusing on a particular culture or ethnicity, often place the results of their disparate research projects side by side to allow for deeper cultural understanding of alcohol through the juxtaposition of various drinking communities. A fine instance of such an approach is *Constructive Drinking*, Mary Douglas's collection of essays by different hands, which includes studies of many diverse topics, e.g., Kava drinking ceremonies, symbolic action in Alcoholics Anonymous meetings, wine's role in the Tuscan countryside, and drinking in relation to political attitudes among Newfoundland longshoremen. Similarly, another important volume of research on alcohol, *Drink: Behavior and Belief in Modern History*, edited by Robin Room and Susanna Barrows, juxtaposes essays that deal with drink in various cultural, economic, political, and national settings, since the ways that drinking practices and beliefs both resemble and differ from one another is a key question in understanding the values and practices associated with alcohol use.

In relation to this kind of comparative approach, the example of gender's role in drinking is illuminating. As the Wilsnack alcohol research team has pointed out, societies "show different levels of concern about women's drinking behavior at different periods in their history." But at the same time, "in all countries and historical periods for which there are general population survey data, the two strongest predictors of drinking behavior are gender and age."[13] Moreover, female drinking has generally entailed far more rigid strictures than male drinking. Despite increasing openness in the United States about female drunkenness, only thirty years ago Marian Sandmaier could entitle her book on American female drinking problems *The Invisible Alcoholics*, thereby reflecting the long-standing stigmatization of, and secrecy surrounding, female drinkers in American society. Similar stigmatization of female drinkers has persisted even more strongly in places as distant and different as contemporary Japan, Ecuador, Lesotho, and Nigeria. In Nigeria, for instance, the double standard for male and female drinkers is all too reminiscent of attitudes that have only recently faded away, and that in some cases still persist in western nations. Describing Nigerian women's drinking, B.A. Ikuesan points out that "in Nigerian society ... alcoholic intoxication is pardoned only as a masculine feature. The woman is idealised and her role in the total social scheme is circumscribed, with alcohol being no part of the picture."[14] Thus, while remaining aware of different national, religious, and social circumstances, we can still strive to understand how women in such varied circumstances can be similarly—albeit not identically—constrained and even persecuted through their societies' institutionalized notions of gender, drink, and appropriate behavior. To pretend that such patterns of similarity do not exist, or to insist that they always be ignored because they occur in different racial and national settings, is to blinker our vision and needlessly limit our capacity for comparative reflection, and for exploring the use of alcohol both within and across cultures.

In addition to juxtapositions of culture, juxtapositions of period may also enhance our understanding of the complexities in literature's depiction of drink. A vivid demonstration of this point appears in a comparison of two quite different works, the diary of that worldly eighteenth-century English gentleman, Samuel Pepys, and the late nineteenth-century sentimental novel, *Rose in Bloom* (1876), written by none other than that unimpeachably proper American female author, celebrated as the "Children's Friend": Louisa May Alcott. Yet the texts by these very different writers both reveal a similar fascinating twist on the intersections of social class and gender with regard to drinking practices. In his entry for March 26, 1667, Pepys laments the fact that dining out in ladies' company invariably requires him to drink more than he wishes, because of the custom of drinking ladies' "healths"—a custom observed mostly in upper-class circles. Pepys' diary inverts the more usual pattern of social behavior, whereby women drink because of pressure from men (e.g., the infamous "Candy is dandy, but liquor is quicker" syndrome). Markedly different in tone, in national setting, and in period, the Alcott novel repeats the Pepysian motif of a man drinking against his will because of expectations surrounding a "gentleman's" role in relation to women; in one scene, Alcott describes Herbert, a young alcoholic who, struggling to remain sober, falls off the wagon at a wedding party, because the bride thoughtlessly demands that Herbert, as her guest, drink a health in her honor. Setting these two texts side by side reveals the persistence and deleterious power of behavioral conventions involving gender—texts in which, ironically, such conventions inadvertently constrain men's freedom *not* to drink in the presence of women.[15]

A more complex example of the illuminating interplay of texts from different periods concerns the evolution of what is commonly referred to as the disease concept of alcoholism, with the disease passing through ever worsening phases. The history of the progressive disease model of alcoholic addiction goes as far back as the third quarter of the eighteenth century, "but not further," in the words of Harry Gene Levine; the concept's first full articulation appeared, according to Levine, in Dr. Benjamin Rush's 1784 pamphlet, *An Inquiry into the Effects of Ardent Spirits*. (Rush's often-reprinted publication may have influenced Edgar Allan Poe in his own description of alcoholism as an inexorable, progressively destructive disease in his famous short story of 1843, "The Black Cat.") Rush's document was key in the development of the disease concept of progressive addiction. But the concept itself actually appears nearly a century earlier than Rush's text, in a poignant literary passage from Daniel Defoe's novel, *Colonel Jack*, published in 1697, and reprinted in the chapter on alcohol's causes below. A striking commonality, then, appears in such disparate sources as Defoe's late seventeenth-century English didactic novel; Rush's medico-moral *Inquiry*, popular on both sides of the Atlantic; Poe's American antebellum tale of horror; modern scientific accounts of the disease concept of alcoholism, such as those of the mid-twentieth century alcohol researcher, E.M. Jellinek; and modern, grittily realistic literary treatments of alcoholism, such as Charles Jackson's novel, *The Lost Weekend* (1944), or J.P. Miller's television script, *Days of Wine and Roses* (1958). Clearly, works of literature and of social and medical history can have much to say to each other across distances of time, as well as distances of geography or culture.[16]

The thrust of the examples above should be clear: it is in a spirit of welcoming analysis of difference as well as similarity, and of the layers of intertwined difference and similarity that literature often reveals, that the present book's selections were made. Indeed, the range of these selections makes all the more sense in an era of increasing multicultural awareness and of literary globalization. As Giles Gunn observes in a special issue of *PMLA* devoted to "Globalizing Literary Studies," recent developments in literary criticism have had the effect of "loosening national as well as temporal paradigms that once organized literary studies"; in the same issue, Paul Jay warns against the "homogenizing effects of cultural globalization," while also calling for literary scholarship to move away from "a traditional division of discrete national literatures into ossified literary-historical periods."[17] In the present volume, my goal as editor is to steer clear of a bland cultural homogenization on the one hand, and of a stubborn denial of intercultural connections and parallels on the other. Finally, just as more narrowly defined approaches have their value, so too the more capacious approach of this anthology accords with its multi-faceted topic; in truth, neither this book, nor the many more circumscribed (or more expansive) ones that could be designed, could encompass the subject of drinking in literature.

For all of this volume's breadth, readers will notice its tendency to draw on British and American literature of the past two centuries. The reasons for this are as follows: the historical prevalence of alcohol in Europe relative to other parts of the world; my own scholarly background in European and especially British and American literature; the intended audience of the book as primarily American and British readers of literature; and the voluminous amount of Anglo-American literary material on alcohol, something that is not surprising when we consider the intensity of feeling about drink and drink-related issues (such as temperance) in England and America during the past two centuries. At the same time, although English-language texts predominate here, the book also contains selections from the literatures of China, Russia, France, Latin America, and Egypt.

As far as the book's temporal choices are concerned, it is worth noting that most of the world's literatures deal more extensively with drink from the eighteenth century on. To be sure, literature's links to drink are ancient, and some earlier texts are represented here, but both as trope and theme, drinking increases in the literature of the past two to three hundred years. The early nineteenth century, with its burgeoning interest in and description of alcohol and drugs, has been aptly termed an "age of intoxication," a time when both alcohol and drugs became widely associated in the public mind with writers and when an increasing number of literary texts reflected the use of intoxicants in society.[18] This trend is also partly related to the development of realistic prose treatments of social problems in the novel and short story genres throughout the nineteenth century. And, of course, the twentieth century has witnessed yet further and deeper linkages between literature and drink, what with the ever-increasing openness about describing drink and drug use, the controversies surrounding Prohibition in America, the Lost Generation's romanticizing of alcohol, the continuing stereotype of the drunken or "high" writer being perpetuated on both sides of the Atlantic (e.g., F. Scott Fitzgerald, Malcolm Lowry, Dylan Thomas, Jean Rhys, writers of the Beat Generation), and the proliferation of an international "drug culture" throughout the 1960s and beyond.

A few more words are in order about the selections for this book. Literature does not always fall into conveniently symmetrical, proportional categories, whether in terms of quality, subject matter, or feasibility for compilations such as this one. In selecting texts for the book, my procedure has never been to impose a grid as to chronology or authorial selection (e.g., 15 percent classical, 25 percent Renaissance and Medieval, 20 percent contemporary, or 35 percent non–English-speaking authors, of whom at least 20 percent but no more than 40 percent should be women of color writing before 1960, etc.). I wanted to include writers of various periods, genres, and national and racial backgrounds, but my main criteria have been literary excellence and a variety of perspectives on drink. This is why such factors as gender, nationality, and ethnicity are not perfectly balanced in the book's selections. That the editor's subjectivity enters into such an enterprise is neither avoidable nor, in my view, undesirable. What I hope is that the subjective choices here, informed by the considerations I have outlined above, will resonate with readers interested in the depiction of drinking in different places, eras, and circumstances.

It is now time to address the rubrics within which I have situated the book's selections. Although each section's relevance to drinking is self-evident, some additional commentary can help to flesh out the links between the section rubrics and the representation of drinking, both in general, and in the specific texts gathered here.

"Why do you drink?" Big Daddy's question to his son, Brick, in Tennessee Williams' *Cat on a Hot Tin Roof* repeats the most pervasive question in all of alcohol studies. Contributing to, but never fully providing an answer to this question are the medical, psychological, religious, and socio-economic approaches to the reasons that people drink, and that some people drink to excess. Brick's answer to his father is that he drinks to escape the "mendacity" of life. But any one person's answer to this question is just that—a single answer that may be true in specific instances, or even be broadly accurate, but that cannot possibly apply to all situations and individuals. Differing, even conflicting interpretations of why people drink range across and within cultures, e.g., Donald Horton's argument that all drinking essentially stems from the desire to reduce anxiety, or David McClelland's view that drinking (especially by men) is a means of attaining feelings of power. Other studies argue that within a particular culture the reasons people drink take on significance specific to that culture (hence, for example, Richard Stivers distinguishes between Irish drinking and Irish-American drinking, the former reflecting the desire to assert manliness and independence, the latter reflecting a desire to assert Irish cultural identity).[19] The varied motivations for drinking, the different degrees to which drinkers are aware of these motivations and even the etiology of alcohol addiction inform the selections in the first section here, which deals with the persistent question of why people drink, and with the multi-faceted, often elusive answers to this question.

The topic of the second section, the effects of alcohol, often intersects with causes of drinking. Indeed, at times, whether drink is itself cause or effect becomes the issue; when, for example, is heavy drinking a result of poverty, when is it a cause of it, and when is the causal relationship between the two impossible to define? But whatever the cause of drinking, the physical, psychological, and economic effects of drink—the events and situations that drink itself causes to take place—receive considerable attention in literature. It is, of course, tempting to concentrate on the more horrific effects of alcohol, as several of the texts here vividly do. But instances of more benign or at least partly humorous effects of drink (e.g., in Burns, Shakespeare and Dickens), appear here along with bleaker treatments of the subject.

Section III, on drink and the family, explores a topic old both in literature and in alcohol studies, but steadily receiving even more attention in both areas. Overlapping with causes and effects, the debate about nature and nurture in relation to drinking inevitably involves attention to the family's role in people's drinking, as well as to the effects of a drinker's behavior on the family. Since both culture and genetics—key issues in contemporary study of alcohol use—connect back to family, the family's relevance to drinking is obvious. But less obvious is the way that the topic of alcohol and the family is important, even in works about which, it would seem, almost everything to be said has been said. A case in point is *The Adventures of Huckleberry Finn*, which saw more than a century of critical discussion before Timothy Rivinus and Brian Ford produced a provocative article interpreting this novel—one of the most analyzed of American literary masterpieces—as the tale of the child of an alcoholic. Once stated, the theme seems undeniably relevant to the novel, but it had not received more than passing reference prior to Rivinus' and Ford's detailed discussion.[20] This section examines an important dimension of drinking in literature, and contains potent depictions of the ways that drinking inevitably reflects and affects a drinker's relations with the family.

Section IV focuses on gender and alcohol, a topic that has preoccupied writers for centuries, but that has gained wide attention from alcohol researchers only in the past three decades. Until recently, most studies of alcohol derived their generalizations about alcohol consumption from research on men—the male drinker was the standard of measurement and study. Now biological and social factors affecting both men and women in relation to drink have begun to receive analysis that takes gender into careful account as a shaper of reactions and attitudes to drink. But gender concerns have long been important in literature and in cultural expressions of male and female roles. In some situations—early in the history of the United States, for example—women and men drank together, and condemnation of women's inebriety was only slightly stronger than that of men. In most other times and places—for most of United States history, in ancient Greece and Rome, and in fact in most parts of the world throughout history—women's drinking has been far more strictly controlled and judged than men's drinking. Literature has reflected these historical patterns, as well as showing that drink is a subject that intersects with gender, whether male or female, in complicated ways. A woman's ostracism and defiance through alcohol ("Janet's Repentance"), a youth's initiation into drinking as a symbol of masculine identity (*John Barleycorn*), a woman's growing alcoholism in an Irish social context where drunkenness is, ironically, "a good man's failing" (*The Lonely Passion of Judith Hearne*)—these are among the areas of alcohol's relation to gender explored in this section.

"The Saloon Must Go"—the famous slogan of the Anti-Saloon League of the late nineteenth and early twentieth centuries—speaks to the inherent power, symbolic and literal, of the tavern. A public institution devoted to the ingestion of alcohol, the tavern has played many roles in history and literature alike: center of communal gathering; rival of home and church; male sanctuary from wife and children; corrupter of youth; site of sexual adventure; shelter for the poverty-stricken; revolutionary breeding-ground; and political club, to name but some of these roles. Not surprisingly, the tavern serves as a significant setting in many works of drama, poetry, and fiction. In this, the book's fifth section, the selections illustrate the tavern's diverse associations and functions, with headnotes to the selections that draw on the social history of the public drinking space.

The book's sixth and final section reflects what anthropologist Mary Douglas has called the "ancient relation between religion and alcohol."[21] In this part of the book, religion as such is not the issue, but is part of a larger set of concerns, namely, the spiritual dimension of drink—of spirits. Numerous discussions of drinking have recognized the presence of dim but nonetheless powerful links between the mundane consumption of liquor and more intangible desires, concerns, and needs. In Section VI, selections from authors as different as William James, Li Bo, Emily Dickinson, Simon Ortiz, Naguib Mahfouz, and Pablo Neruda probe the spiritual or mystical aspects of such topics as drinking, alcoholism, and recovery from alcoholic addiction. In turning to spirituality and drink, the concluding section greatly extends the ramifications that the common occurrence of drinking can have; in so doing, it also helps to place the topic of drink in the broader, more philosophical perspective that it deserves and that literature so richly and so variously provides.

## Notes

1. On the supposed links between Dionysos and the theater, see the entries on "Comedy," "Dionysos," and "Tragedy" in Lilian Feder, *The Handbook of Classical Literature* (New

York: Da Capo Press, 1998). Horace's comments appear in Book 1, number 19 of his *Epistles* (lines 2–3).

2. Mary Douglas, "Introduction," in Douglas, ed., *Constructive Drinking: Perspectives on Drink from Anthropology* (Cambridge: Cambridge University Press, 1987), p. 4.

3. Steve Charters, *Wine and Society: The Cultural and Social Context of a Drink* (London: Butterworth-Heinemann, 2006), p. 6; George E. Vaillant, *The Natural History of Alcoholism Revisited* (Cambridge: Harvard University Press, 1995), p. 6; Robin Room, "Foreword," in Linda A. Bennett and Genevieve M. Ames, eds., *The American Experience with Alcohol: Contrasting Cultural Perspectives* (New York and London: Plenum, 1985), p. xvi.

4. Craig MacAndrew and Robert B. Edgerton, *Drunken Comportment: A Social Explanation* (Chicago: Aldine, 1969), pp. 114 and 172. The enduring legacy of MacAndrew's and Edgerton's perspectives on drinking behavior and social context is attested to by Malcolm Gladwell's recent article, "Annals of Anthropology: 'Drinking Games,'" *The New Yorker*, February 15, 2010, pp. 70–76.

5. William L. White, "The Lessons of Language: Historical Perspectives on the Rhetoric of Addiction," in Sarah W. Tracy and Caroline Jean Acker, eds., *Altering American Consciousness: The History of Alcohol and Drug Use in the United States, 1800–2000* (Amherst: University of Massachusetts Press, 2004), p. 43. Dwight B. Heath, "Sociocultural Perspectives on Addiction," in Edward Gottheil, Keith A. Druley, Thomas E. Skoloda, and Howard M. Waxman, eds., *Etiologic Aspects of Alcohol and Drug Use* (Springfield, Ill: Charles C. Thomas, 1983), p. 224.

6. Joseph A. Gusfield, *Contested Meanings: The Construction of Alcohol Problems* (Madison: University of Wisconsin Press, 1996), p. 31, and *passim*.

7. Mark H. Moore and Dean R. Gerstein, "The Nature of Alcohol Problems," in Moore and Gerstein, eds., *Alcohol and Public Policy: Beyond the Shadow of Prohibition* (Washington, D.C.: National Academy Press, 1981), p. 19.

8. Vaillant, *The Natural History of Alcoholism*, p. 1.

9. Quoted in David S. Reynolds, *Beneath the American Renaissance: The Subversive Imagination in the Age of Emerson and Melville* (New York: Knopf, 1988), p. 65. A fuller citation of Whitman's comment and its source, appears in the headnote to the Whitman selection in Chapter Three, below.

10. For the comments on literary and scientific approaches to alcohol, see Thomas B. Gilmore, *Equivocal Spirits: Alcoholism and Drinking in Twentieth-Century Literature* (Chapel Hill: University of North Carolina Press, 1987), p. 11; for the comments on will power and alcoholism, see Gilmore, p. 6.

11. Emile Légouis, "The Bacchic Element in Shakespeare's Plays," *Proceedings of the British Academy* 12 (1926), 115–32.

12. Stephen Greenblatt, *Hamlet in Purgatory* (Princeton: Princeton University Press, 2001), p. 4.

13. Sharon Wilsnack and Richard Wilsnack are quoted in Moira Plant's comprehensive study, *Women and Alcohol: Contemporary and Historical Perspectives* (London and New York: 1997), p. 13.

14. Ikuesan's study is quoted in Plant, *Women and Alcohol*, p. 13. Information on other texts cited in this paragraph are as follows: for Mary Douglas, see n. 2, above. See also Susanna Barrows and Robin Room, eds., *Drink: Behavior and Belief in Modern Society* (Berkeley: University of California Press, 1991); Marian Sandmaier, *The Invisible Alcoholics: Women and Alcohol Abuse in America* (New York: McGraw-Hill, 1980).

15. Alcott's *Rose in Bloom* was originally published in 1882; for Pepys' entry on drinking toasts to women, see the March 26, 1667, entry on the Project Gutenberg e-text of the diaries, at http://www.gutenberg.org/dirs/4/1/7/4174/4174.txt.

16. See Levine, "The Discovery of Addiction: Changing Conceptions of Habitual Drunkenness in America," *Journal of Studies on Alcohol* 39 (1978), pp. 143–74; on the earlier

date of Defoe's account of the progress of alcoholism, see Nicholas Warner, "The Drunken Wife in Defoe's *Colonel Jack*: An Early Description of Alcohol Addiction," *Dionysos* 1 (1989), pp. 3–9, and the headnote to the Defoe passage in Chapter Two.

17. See Giles Gunn, "Introduction: Globalizing Literary Studies," *PMLA* 116 (January, 2001), p. 16, and Paul Jay, "Beyond Discipline? Globalization and the Future of English," *PMLA* 116 (January, 2001), pp. 40 and 43. A similar argument for the values of multi-temporal and multi-national approaches, while remaining cognizant of the importance of specific cultural contexts, receives forceful expression in David Damrosch, *What is World Literature?* (Princeton: Princeton University Press, 2003), especially pp. 284 ff.

18. John Frederick Logan, "The Age of Intoxication," *Yale French Studies* 50 (1974), pp. 81–94; following in Logan's footsteps but zeroing in on English literature in the Romantic period is Anya Taylor's excellent *Bacchus in Romantic England: Writers and Drink, 1780–1830* (New York: St. Martin's Press, 1999).

19. See Donald Horton, "The Function of Alcohol in Primitive Societies: A Cross-Cultural Study," *Quarterly Journal of Studies on Alcohol* 4 (1943), pp. 199–320; David McClelland, *The Drinking Man* (New York: Free Press, 1972); and Richard Stivers, *A Hair of the Dog: Irish Drinking and American Stereotype* (University Park: Pennsylvania State University Press, 1976).

20. Rivinus, Timothy M. and Brian W. Ford, "Children of Alcoholics in Literature: Portraits of the Struggle (Part One)," *Dionysos* 1 (1989), pp. 13–23. Though not scholarly in purpose, a useful earlier anthology drew attention to alcoholism's relation to the family through its inclusion of three modern American short stories on this topic; see Miriam Dow and Jennifer Regan, eds., *The Invisible Enemy: Alcoholism and the Modern Short Story* (St. Paul: Graywolf Press, 1989). The vast, complex familial dimensions of alcohol use and abuse have received extensive study in the social sciences; the study of literature's depiction of these dimensions has begun, but much remains to be done in this regard.

21. Douglas, "Introduction," p. 11; similar points are raised more extensively with regard to one particular beverage in Patrick E. McGovern's impressive discussion of the physical and cultural history of wine, *Ancient Wine: The Search for the Origins of Viniculture* (Princeton: Princeton University Press, 2007). Although the complex relations between religious belief and actual patterns of drinking and abstinence have yet to be fully explored, more and more scholars are working on this problem; see, for example, Thomas J. Johnson, Virgil L. Sheets, Jean L. Kristeller, "Identifying Mediators of the Relationship between Religiousness/Spirituality and Alcohol Use," *Journal of Studies on Alcohol and Drugs* 69 (2008), pp. 160–170, and Marc Galanter and Lee Anne Kaskutas, eds., *Research on Alcoholics Anonymous and Spirituality in Addiction Recovery* (New York: Springer, 2008).

# I. Causes of Drinking

## Li Bo, "Drinking Song" (8th century)

The poet Li Bo or Li Bai, long known in the west as Li Po, lived from 701–762, thriving during the second century of the artistically rich Tang Dynasty (618–906.) He has long been recognized as one of the greatest, if not the greatest, of all Chinese poets. To English-speaking readers he has become familiar through Ezra Pound's loose adaptations of his verse (e.g., Pound's "The River Merchant's Wife"). A prolific creator of poems emphasizing a visionary communion with the natural world, but tinged with melancholy and a wry celebration of drink, Li Bo himself is said to have drowned one night "while bibulously reciting verses to the moon,"* thus forever entwining his reputation with wine and drunkenness. Many of his poems celebrate drink, freely admitting its suppression of reason and alertness, but welcoming this very quality as a motive for drinking—for Li Bo, drinking is a palliative for the sadness of life. Precisely because of this, however, wine is inexorably linked to that sadness; even many of Li Bo's most celebratory poems on drinking are tinged with an aching sense of loss. Like much of Li Bo's work, the poem below depicts wine in the context of the fleeting beauties of life—the waters of the Yellow River flow inexorably into the ocean, and hair that is like shining black thread in the morning changes by night to "snow"; indeed, the poet asserts that to forget the sorrows of time and mortality, it is worth exchanging "dappled flower horses" and precious fur coats for the solace and pleasure of "delectable wine." The translation (1921) comes from the collaboration of sinologist Florence Ayscough and the poet Amy Lowell who, like her contemporary and fellow American poet, Ezra Pound, was drawn to the highly imagistic nature of classical Chinese poetry.†

*Lillian Herlands Hornstein, et al., eds., The Reader's Companion to World Literature *(New York: Penguin, 1984), p. 298.*
 †*Useful sources for western students of Chinese poetry include the following: Wai-Lim Yip, ed.,* Chinese Poetry: An Anthology of Major Modes and Genres *(Durham: Duke University Press, 1997) and* Diffusion of Distances: Dialogues Between Chinese and Western Poetics *(Berkeley: University of California Press, 1993); Ezra Pound,*

Cathay *(Princeton: Princeton University Press, 1969); the notes and translations in Stephen Owen, ed. and trans.,* An Anthology of Chinese Literature: Beginnings to 1911 *(New York: Norton, 1996).* The Anchor Book of Chinese Poetry, *edited by Tony Barnstone and Chou Ping (New York: Random House, 2005), contains an excellent discussion of the principles of Chinese poetry, as well as informative headnotes to the Tang period and to the poetic achievement of Li Bo. On the richness of wine imagery's significance in classical Chinese poetry, see James R. Hightower, "Tao Ch'ien's 'Drinking Wine' Poems," in Chow Tse-tsung, ed.,* Wen-lin: Studies in the Chinese Humanities *(Madison: University of Wisconsin Press, 1968), pp. 3–44.*

Do you not see the waters of the Yellow River coming down from Heaven?
They rush with incredible speed to the sea, and they never turn and come back again.
Do you not see, in the clear mirror of the Guest hall, the miserable white hair on my head?
At dawn it is like shining thread, but at sunset it is snow.
In this life, to be perfectly happy, one must drain one's pleasures;
The golden wine-cup must not stand empty opposite the moon.
Heaven put us here, we must use what we have.
Scatter a thousand ounces of silver and you are but where you were.
Boil the sheep,
Kill the ox,
Be merry.
We should drink three hundred cups at once.
Mr. Wise Gentleman Ts'en,
And you, Mr. Scholar Tan Ch'iu,
Drink, you must not stop.
I will sing one of my poems for you,
Please lean over and listen:

"Bells! Drums! Delicacies
Worth their weight in jade—
These things
Are of the slightest value.
I only want to be drunk
For ages and never wake.
The sages and worthies of old times
Have left not a sound,
Only those who drank
Have achieved lasting fame.
The King of Ch'ên, long ago, caroused
In the Hall of Peaceful Content.

They drank wine paid
At a full ten thousand a gallon;
They surpassed themselves in mirth,
And the telling of obscene stories.
How can a host say
He has very little money.
It is absolutely imperative
That he buy wine for his friends.
Horses of five colours, dappled flower horses,
Fur coats costing
A thousand ounces of silver—
He sends his son to exchange
All these for delectable wine,
So that you and I together
May drown our ancient grief."

## *Ralph Waldo Emerson, from "The Poet" (1844)*

*One of Emerson's most celebrated essays, "The Poet" became a key text in American Romantic literary theory, covering a wide range of issues, including poetic creativity, language, and the relation of poetry to truth and beauty. In the excerpt reprinted here, Emerson (1803–1882) describes the widespread human yearning for intoxication, lists a remarkable variety of intoxicating sources, and focuses on the particular attractions of intoxicants for the "intellectual man," especially the poet. The passage is notable in distinguishing between mere physical intoxicants—what Emerson calls "devil's wine"—and the loftier, more imaginative intoxicant provided by art and spiritual exhilaration, or "God's wine." All too often, in our longing for "God's wine" we succumb to the baser pleasures of "devil's wine," a point Emerson also makes in his poem "Bacchus." A similar distinction between a higher, spiritual intoxication and a lower, material one appears in a notebook entry by Samuel Taylor Coleridge, in which he writes: "Man before the Fall possessed of the Heavenly Bacchus ... his fall—forsaken by the savage state—and dreadful consequences of the interspersed vacancies left in his mind by the absence of Dionysos—the Bastard Bacchus comes to his Relief."\**

*Both Coleridge and Emerson echo a distinction between material and spiritual intoxication that was already apparent in ancient times, e.g., in the Biblical injunction, "Be drunk, but not with wine; stagger, but not with strong drink" (Isaiah 29:9). In a sense, then, Emerson's text, while addressing the causes of drinking (among other forms of intoxicating experience), connects with the spiritual dimensions of intoxication covered in the seventh chapter of this volume.*

*\*Samuel Taylor Coleridge,* The Notebooks of Samuel Taylor Coleridge, *ed. Kathleen Coburn (Princeton: Princeton University Press, 1973), Vol. 3, notebook entry 3263.*

[The] insight, which expresses itself by what is called Imagination, is a very high sort of seeing, which does not come by study, but by the intellect being where and what it sees, by sharing the path, or circuit of things through forms, and so making them translucid to others. The path of things is silent. Will they suffer a speaker to go with them? A spy they will not suffer; a lover, a poet, is the transcendency of their own nature,—him they will suffer. The condition of true naming, on the poet's part, is his resigning himself to the divine *aura* which breathes through forms, and accompanying that.

It is a secret which every intellectual man quickly learns, that, beyond the energy of his possessed and conscious intellect, he is capable of a new energy (as of an intellect doubled on itself), by abandonment to the nature of things; that, beside his privacy of power as an individual man, there is a great public power, on which he can draw, by unlocking, at all risks, his human doors, and suffering the ethereal tides to roll and circulate through him: then he is caught up into the life of the Universe, his speech is thunder, his thought is law, and his words are universally intelligible as the plants and animals. The poet knows that he speaks adequately, then, only when he speaks somewhat wildly, or, "with the flower of the mind;" not with the intellect, used as an organ, but with the intellect released from all service, and suffered to take its direction from its celestial life; or, as the ancients were wont to express themselves, not with intellect alone, but with the intellect inebriated by nectar. As the traveler who has lost his way, throws his reins on his horse's neck, and trusts to the instinct of the animal to find his road, so must we do with the divine animal who carries us through this world. For if in any manner we can stimulate this instinct, new passages are opened for us into nature, the mind flows into and through things hardest and highest, and the metamorphosis is possible.

This is the reason why bards love wine, mead, narcotics, coffee, tea, opium, the fumes of sandal-wood and tobacco, or whatever other species of animal exhilaration. All men avail themselves of such means as they can, to add this extraordinary power to their normal powers; and to this end they prize conversation, music, pictures, sculpture, dancing, theatres, traveling, war, mobs, fires, gaming, politics, or love, or science, or animal intoxication, which are several coarser or finer *quasi*-mechanical substitutes for the true nectar, which is the ravishment of the intellect by coming nearer to the fact. These are auxiliaries to the centrifugal tendency of a man, to his passage out into free space, and they help him to escape the custody of that body in which he is pent up, and of that jail-yard of individual relations in which he is enclosed. Hence a great number of such as were professionally expressors of Beauty, as painters, poets, musicians, and actors, have been more than others wont to lead a life of pleasure and indulgence; all but the few who received the true nectar; and, as it was a spurious mode of attaining freedom, as it was an emancipation not into the heavens, but into the freedom of baser places, they were punished for that advantage they won, by a dissipation and deterioration. But never can any advantage be taken of nature by a trick. The spirit of the world, the great calm presence of the creator, comes not forth to the sorceries of opium or of wine. The sublime vision comes to the pure and simple soul in a clean and chaste body. That is not an inspiration which we owe to narcotics, but some counterfeit excitement and fury. Milton says, that the lyric poet may drink wine and live generously, but the epic poet, he who shall sing of the gods, and their descent unto men, must drink water out of a wooden bowl.* For poetry is not 'Devil's wine,' but God's wine. It is with this as it is with toys. We fill the hands and nurseries of our children with all manner of dolls, drums, and horses, withdrawing their eyes from the plain face and sufficing objects of nature, the sun, and moon, the animals, the water, and stones, which should be their toys. So the poet's habit of living should be set on a key so low and plain, that the common influences should delight him. His cheerfulness should be the gift of the sunlight; the air should suffice for his inspiration, and he should be tipsy with water. That spirit which suffices quiet hearts, which seems to come forth to such from every dry knoll of sere grass, from every pine-stump, and half-imbedded stone, on which the dull March sun shines, comes forth to the poor and hungry, and such as are of simple taste. If thou fill thy brain with Boston and New York, with fashion and covetousness, and wilt stimulate thy jaded senses with wine and French coffee, thou shalt find no radiance of wisdom in the lonely waste of the pinewoods.

*Milton makes this observation in his sixth Elegy, originally composed in Latin.

# *Nathaniel Hawthorne, from* The Blithedale Romance *(1852)*

*Most famous for his tale of adultery in Puritan New England,* The Scarlet Letter, *Nathaniel Hawthorne (1804–1864) dealt extensively with drinking throughout his fiction. The present excerpt is the twenty-first chapter of* The Blithedale Romance, *a novel based on Hawthorne's own experience with the idealistic New England community known as Brook Farm. The novel itself is told from the perspective of one of its characters, Miles Coverdale. Although it is risky to attribute Coverdale's views to Hawthorne, the temptation of such an attribution is strong at various points in the text where Coverdale expresses ideas that receive no contradiction or undercutting; such is the case with the passage here, in which Coverdale visits a saloon searching for the character known as old Moodie. Here Coverdale—and through him, perhaps, Hawthorne—seeks to explain the universal human attraction to intoxicants in terms of "a naughty instinct" that turns to wine, or even "stronger liquor" in an effort to soften the harshness of reality. (This attitude recalls that of Li Bo, though Hawthorne's emphasis is less on drink as an antidote to sorrow than as an avenue to good cheer.) Explicitly addressing the causes of drinking, Coverdale claims that the "true purpose" of drinking is "renewed youth and vigor," as well as a "brisk, cheerful sense of things present and to come."*

*An intriguing aspect of the passage is its ambivalence toward the temperance movement so dominant in Hawthorne's time. For instance, at the end of the paragraph explaining drinking's "true purpose," the narrator includes himself in the group he calls "we temperance people"; however, in the section on the "naughty instinct" for drink, the text criticizes "temperance-men" and the "negative" rather than "positive" efforts of reformers.\* In calling on temperance supporters to provide some substitute for the joys of drink, instead of merely condemning alcohol and those who use it, the passage recalls Hawthorne's memoir of his London experiences,* Our Old Home, *where he sympathetically describes the numerous drunkards of London as having no other palliatives in their lives but gin. In a similar vein, Richard Henry Dana, in his popular* Two Years Before the Mast *(originally published in 1840), complained that the U.S. Navy, under the influence of the temperance movement, would withhold grog from a sailor without giving him the substitute of, say, coffee or hot chocolate. "When the rum is taken from him," writes an indignant Dana, "he ought to have something in its place" (*Two Years Before the Mast, *New York: Macmillan, 1926, p. 352). All in all, while aware of the dangers of heavy drinking, and sympathetic to some of the temperance movement's views, Hawthorne clearly sees the issues of drinking, drunkenness, and abstinence as too complicated to admit of a simple solution or program.*

Thus excluded from everybody's confidence, and attaining no further, by my most earnest study, than to an uncertain sense of something hidden from me, it would appear reasonable that I should have flung off all these alien perplexities. Obviously, my best course was to betake myself to new scenes. Here I was only an intruder. Elsewhere there might be circumstances in which I could establish a personal interest, and people who would respond, with a portion of their sympathies, for so much as I should bestow of mine.

Nevertheless, there occurred to me one other thing to be done. Remembering old Moodie, and his relationship with Priscilla, I determined to seek an interview, for the purpose of ascertaining whether the knot of affairs was as inextricable on that side as I found it on all others. Being tolerably well acquainted with the old man's haunts, I went, the next day, to the saloon of a certain establishment about which he often lurked. It was a reputable place enough, affording good entertainment in the way of meat, drink, and fumigation; and there, in my young and idle days and nights, when I was neither nice nor wise, I had often amused myself with watching the staid humors and sober jollities of the thirsty souls around me.

At my first entrance, old Moodie was not there. The more patiently to await him, I lighted a cigar, and establishing myself in a corner, took a quiet, and, by sympathy, a boozy kind of pleasure in the customary life that was going forward. *The saloon was fitted up with a good deal of taste. There were pictures on the walls, and among them an oil-painting of a beef-steak, with such an admirable show of juicy tenderness, that the beholder sighed to think it merely visionary, and incapable of ever being put upon a gridiron. Another work of high art was the life-like representation of a noble sirloin; another, the hind-quarters of a deer, retaining the hoofs and tawny fur; another, the head and shoulders of a salmon; and, still more exquisitely finished, a brace of canvas-back ducks, in which the mottled feathers were depicted with the accuracy of a daguerreotype. Some very hungry painter, I suppose, had wrought these subjects of still-life, heightening his imagination with his appetite, and earning, it is to be hoped, the privilege of a daily dinner off whichever of his pictorial viands he liked best. Then, there was a fine old cheese, in which you could almost discern the mites; and some sardines, on a small plate, very richly done, and looking as if oozy with the oil in which they had been smothered. All these things were so perfectly imitated, that you seemed to have the genuine article before you, and yet with an indescribable, ideal charm; it took away the grossness from what was fleshiest and fattest, and thus helped the life of man, even in its earthliest relations, to appear rich and noble, as well as warm, cheerful, and substantial. There were pictures, too, of gallant revelers,—those of the old time,—Flemish, apparently,— with doublets and slashed sleeves,—drinking their wine out of fantastic, long-stemmed glasses; quaffing joyously, quaffing forever, with inaudible laughter and song, while the Champagne bubbled immortally against their moustaches, or the purple tide of Burgundy ran inexhaustibly down their throats.

But, in an obscure corner of the saloon, there was a little picture—excellently done, moreover—of a ragged, bloated, New England toper, stretched out on a bench, in the heavy, apoplectic sleep of drunkenness. The death-in-life was too well portrayed. You smelt the fumy liquor that had brought on this syncope. Your only comfort lay in the forced reflection, that, real as he looked, the poor caitiff was but imaginary,—a bit of painted canvass, whom no delirium tremens, nor so much as a retributive headache, awaited, on the morrow.

By this time, it being past eleven o'clock, the two barkeepers of the saloon were in pretty constant activity. One of these young men had a rare faculty in the concoction of gin-cocktails. It was a spectacle to behold, how, with a tumbler in each hand, he tossed the contents from one to the other. Never conveying it awry, nor spilling the least drop, he compelled the frothy liquor, as it seemed to me, to spout forth from one glass and descend into the other, in a great parabolic curve, as well defined and calculable as a planet's orbit. He had a good forehead, with a particularly large development just above the eyebrows; fine intellectual gifts, no doubt, which he had educated to this profitable end; being famous for nothing but gin-cocktails, and commanding a fair salary by his one accomplishment. These cocktails, and other artificial combinations of liquor (of which there were at least a score, though mostly, I suspect, fantastic in their differences), were much in favor with the younger class of customers, who, at furthest, had only reached the second stage of potatory life. The stanch old soakers, on the other hand,—men men who, if put on tap, would have yielded a red alcoholic liquor by way of blood,—usually usually confined themselves to plain brandy-and-water, gin, or West India rum; and, oftentimes, they prefaced their dram with some medicinal remark as to the wholesomeness and stomachic qualities of that particular drink. Two or three appeared to have bottles of their own behind the counter; and, winking one red eye to the barkeeper, he forthwith produced these choicest and peculiar cordials, which it was a matter of great interest and favor, among their acquaintances, to obtain a sip of.

Agreeably to the Yankee habit, under whatever circumstances, the deportment of all these good fellows, old or young, was decorous and thoroughly correct. They grew only the more sober in their cups; there was no confused babble nor boisterous laughter. They sucked in the joyous fire of the decanters and kept it smouldering in their inmost recesses, with a bliss known only to the heart which it warmed and comforted. Their eyes twinkled a little, to be sure; they hemmed vigorously after each glass, and laid a hand upon the pit of the stomach, as if the pleasant titillation there was what constituted the tangible part of their enjoyment. In that spot, unquestionably, and not in the brain, was the acme of the whole affair. But the true purpose of their drinking—and one that will induce men to drink, or do something equivalent, as long as this weary world shall endure—was the renewed youth and vigor, the brisk, cheerful sense of things present and to come, with which, for about a quarter of an hour, the dram permeated their systems. And when such quarters of an hour can be obtained in some mode less baneful to the great sum of a man's life,—but nevertheless, with a little spice of impropriety, to give it a wild flavor,—we temperance people may ring out our bells for victory!

The prettiest object in the saloon was a tiny fountain, which threw up its feathery jet through the counter, and sparkled down again into an oval basin, or lakelet, containing several gold-fishes. There was a bed of bright sand at the bottom, strewn with coral and rock-work; and the fishes went gleaming about, now turning up the sheen of a golden side, and now vanishing into the shadows of the water, like the fanciful thoughts that coquet with a poet in his dream. Never before, I imagine, did a company of water-drinkers remain so entirely uncontaminated by the bad example around them; nor could I help wondering that it had not occurred to any freakish inebriate to empty a glass of liquor into their lakelet. What a delightful idea! Who would not be a fish, if he could inhale jollity with the essential element of his existence!

I had begun to despair of meeting old Moodie, when, all at once, I recognized his hand and arm protruding from behind a screen that was set up for the accommodation of bashful topers. As a matter of course, he had one of Priscilla's little purses, and was quietly insinuating it under the notice of a person who stood near. This was always old Moodie's way. You hardly ever saw him advancing towards you, but became aware of his proximity without being able to guess how he had come thither. He glided about like a spirit, assuming visibility close to your elbow, offering his petty trifles of merchandise, remaining long enough for you to purchase, if so disposed, and then taking himself off, between two breaths, while you happened to be thinking of something else.

By a sort of sympathetic impulse that often controlled me in those more impressible days of my life, I was induced to approach this old man in a mode as undemonstrative as his own. Thus, when, according to his custom, he was probably just about to vanish, he found me at his elbow.

"Ah!" said he, with more emphasis than was usual with him. "It is Mr. Coverdale!"

"Yes, Mr. Moodie, your old acquaintance," answered I. "It is some time now since we ate our luncheon together at Blithedale, and a good deal longer since our little talk together at the street-corner."

"That was a good while ago," said the old man.

And he seemed inclined to say not a word more. His existence looked so colorless and torpid,—so very faintly shadowed on the canvas of reality,—that I was half afraid lest he should altogether disappear, even while my eyes were fixed full upon his figure. He was certainly the wretchedest old ghost in the world, with his crazy hat, the dingy handkerchief about his throat, his suit of threadbare gray, and especially that patch over his right eye, behind which he always seemed to be hiding himself. There was one method, however, of bringing him out into somewhat stronger relief. A glass of brandy would effect it. Perhaps the gentler influence of a bottle of claret might do the same. Nor could I think it a matter for the recording angel to write down against me, if—with my painful consciousness of the frost in this old man's blood, and the positive ice that had congealed about his heart—I should thaw him out, were it only for an hour, with the summer warmth of a little wine. What else could possibly be done for him? How else could he be imbued with energy enough to hope for a happier state hereafter? How else be inspired to say his prayers? For there are states of our spiritual system when the throb of the soul's life is too faint and weak to render us capable of religious aspiration.

"Mr. Moodie," said I, "shall we lunch together? And would you like to drink a glass of wine?"

His one eye gleamed. He bowed; and it impressed me that he grew to be more of a man at once, either in anticipation of the wine, or as a grateful response to my good fellowship in offering it.

"With pleasure," he replied.

The barkeeper, at my request, showed us into a private room, and soon afterwards set some fried oysters and a bottle of claret on the table; and I saw the old man glance curiously at the label of the bottle, as if to learn the brand.

"It should be good wine," I remarked, "if it have any right to its label."

"You cannot suppose, sir," said Moodie, with a sigh, "that a poor old fellow like me knows any difference in wines."

And yet, in his way of handling the glass, in his preliminary snuff at the aroma, in his first cautious sip of the wine, and the gustatory skill with which he gave his palate the full advantage of it, it was impossible not to recognize the connoisseur.

"I fancy, Mr. Moodie," said I, "you are a much better judge of wines than I have yet learned to be. Tell me fairly,—did you never drink it where the grape grows?"

"How should that have been, Mr. Coverdale?" answered old Moodie shyly; but then he took courage, as it were, and uttered a feeble little laugh. "The flavor of this wine," added he, "and its perfume still more than its taste, makes me remember that I was once a young man."

"I wish, Mr. Moodie," suggested I,—not that I greatly cared about it, however, but was only anxious to draw him into some talk about Priscilla and Zenobia,—"I wish, while we sit over our wine, you would favor me with a few of those youthful reminiscences."

"Ah," said he, shaking his head, "they might interest you more than you suppose. But I had better be silent, Mr. Coverdale. If this good wine,—though claret, I suppose, is not apt to play such a trick,—but if it should make my tongue run too freely, I could never look you in the face again."

"You never did look me in the face, Mr. Moodie," I replied, "until this very moment."

"Ah!" sighed old Moodie.

It was wonderful, however, what an effect the mild grape-juice wrought upon him. It was not in the wine, but in the associations which it seemed to bring up. Instead of the mean, slouching, furtive, painfully depressed air of an old city vagabond, more like a gray kennel-rat than any other living thing, he began to take the aspect of a decayed gentleman. Even his garments—especially after I had myself quaffed a glass or two—looked less shabby than when we first sat down. There was, by and by, a certain exuberance and elaborateness of gesture and manner, oddly in contrast with all that I had hitherto seen of him. Anon, with hardly any impulse from me, old Moodie began to talk. His communications referred exclusively to a long-past and more fortunate period of his life, with only a few unavoidable allusions to the circumstances that had reduced him to his present state. But, having once got the clue, my subsequent researches acquainted me with the main facts of the following narrative; although, in writing it out, my pen has perhaps allowed itself a trifle of romantic and legendary license, worthier of a small poet than of a grave biographer.

*At this point in Hawthorne's manuscript, the passage quoted below appears, crossed out by an unknown hand. Although the passage was not included in the first editions of the novel, most modern texts print it on the assumption that it expresses Hawthorne's own original intentions, and that its omission reflected the pro-temperance views and influence of Hawthorne's wife, Sophia. (See Nicholas Warner, Spirits of America: Intoxication in Nineteenth-Century American Literature [Norman: University of Oklahoma Press, 1997], p. 133.)*

Human nature, in my opinion, has a naughty instinct that approves of wine, at least, if not of stronger liquor. The temperance-men may preach till doom's day; and still this cold and barren world will look warmer, kindlier, mellower, through the medium of a toper's glass; nor can they, with all their efforts, really spill his draught upon the floor, until some hitherto unthought-of discovery shall supply him with a truer element of joy. The general atmosphere of life must first be rendered so inspiriting that he will not need his delirious solace. The custom of tippling has its defensible side, as well as any other question. But these good people snatch at the old, time-honored demijohn, and offer nothing—either sensual or moral—nothing whatever to supply its place; and human life, as it goes with a multitude of men, will not endure so great a vacuum as would be left by the withdrawal of that big-bellied convexity. The space, which it now occupies, must somehow or other be filled up. As for the rich, it would be little matter if a blight fell upon their vineyards; but the poor man—whose only glimpse of a better state is through the muddy medium of his liquor—what is to be done for him? The reformers should make their efforts positive, instead of negative; they must do away with evil by substituting good.

## *Leo Tolstoy, "Why Then Do Men Stupefy Themselves?" (1890)*

*Tolstoy's vast range of social and moral concerns included problem drinking, something he was already writing about in his twenties: several early diary entries express Tolstoy's regrets over his own drinking and wild behavior while drunk. During the last three decades of his long life, Tolstoy (1828–1910) became increasingly involved in various reform movements—struggling against his own considerable appetites, Tolstoy became a vegetarian, a pacifist, avoided alcohol and tobacco and even joined a temperance society. It was because of this temperance membership, according to his wife Sophia's diary, that at Tolstoy's 70th birthday party, the traditional Russian drinking of toasts to the birthday celebrant's health was not permitted.\**

*The present essay locates the causes of drinking in a larger context of the desire for some form of intoxication to stupefy the moral conscience. This explanation sharply contrasts with Hawthorne's notions of conviviality, with Emerson's emphasis on drink as romantic inspiration or as a reflection of humanity's yearning transcendent experience, and with Li Bo's lyrical tribute to drink as an antidote to the inevitable disappointments and sorrows of our time-bound, mortal existence. For Tolstoy, drinking is a sign of humanity's refusal to face moral realities, and enables moral self-deception: through drinking, human beings lie to themselves, seeking to numb the very jabs of conscience that they should, in fact, earnestly seek to feel so as to improve their conduct and their relation to the world.*

*The essay was originally published as Tolstoy's preface to Dr. P.S. Alekseyev's 1890 study,* Drunkenness, *and is translated here by Alekseyev's brother-in-law, the American Tolstoyan disciple Aylmer Maude. Together with his wife, Louise Maude, Aylmer Maude translated several of Tolstoy works, including* War and Peace, *and is the author of a famous biography of the Russian writer, based in part on Maude's own personal acquaintance with Tolstoy and his family.*

*Henri Troyat, Tolstoy (New York: Doubleday, 1967), pp. 551–52.

## I.

What is the explanation of the fact that people use things that stupefy them: vódka, wine, beer, hashish, opium, tobacco, and other things less common: ether, morphia, fly-agaric, etc.? Why did the practice begin? Why has it spread so rapidly, and why is it still spreading among all sorts of people, savage and civilized? How is it that where there is no vodka, wine or beer, we find opium, hashish, fly-agaric, and the like, and that tobacco is used everywhere?

Why do people wish to stupefy themselves?

Ask anyone why he began drinking wine and why he now drinks it. He will reply, "Oh, I like it, and everybody drinks," and he may add, "it cheers me up." Some—those who have never once taken the trouble to consider whether they do well or ill to drink wine—may add that wine is good for the health and adds to one's strength; that is to say, will make a statement long since proved baseless.

Ask a smoker why he began to use tobacco and why he now smokes, and he also will reply: "To while away the time; everybody smokes."

Similar answers would probably be given by those who use opium, hashish, morphia, or fly-agaric.

"To while away time, to cheer oneself up; everybody does it." But it might be excusable to twiddle one's thumbs, to whistle, to hum tunes, to play a fife or to do something of that sort "to while away the time," "to cheer oneself up," or "because everybody does it"—that is to say, it might be excusable to do something for which one need not waste Nature's wealth, nor spend what has cost great labor to produce, nor do what brings evident harm to one's self and to others. But to produce tobacco, wine, hashish, and opium, the labor of millions of men is spent, and millions and millions of acres of the best land (often amid a population that is short of land) are employed to grow potatoes, hemp, poppies, vines, and tobacco. Moreover, the use of these evidently harmful things produces terrible evils known and admitted by everyone, and destroys more people than all wars and contagious diseases added together. And people know this, so that it cannot be that they use these things "to while away time," "to be cheerful," or because "everybody does it."

There must be some other reason. Continually and everywhere one meets people who love their children and are ready to make all kinds of sacrifices for them, but who yet spend on vodka, wine and beer, or on opium, hashish, and even on tobacco, as much as would quite suffice to feed their hungry and poverty-stricken children, or at least as much as would suffice to save them from misery. Evidently, if a man who has to choose between the want and sufferings of a family he loves, on the one hand, and abstinence from stupefying things on the other, chooses the former—he must be induced thereto by something more potent than the consideration that "everybody does it," or that it is pleasant. Evidently it is done not "to while away time," nor merely "to be cheerful," but he is actuated by some more powerful cause.

This cause—as far as I have detected it by reading about this subject and by observing other people, and particularly by observing my own case when I used to drink wine and smoke tobacco—this cause, I think, may be explained as follows:

When observing his own life, a man may often notice in himself two different beings: the one is blind and physical, the other sees and is spiritual. The blind animal being eats, drinks, rests, sleeps, propagates, and moves, like a wound-up machine. The seeing, spiritual being that is bound up with the animal does nothing of itself, but only appraises the activity of the animal being; coinciding with it when approving its activity, and diverging from it when disapproving.

This observing being may be compared to the arrow of a compass, pointing with one end to the north and with the other to the south, but screened along its whole length by something not noticeable so long as it and the arrow both point the same way; but which becomes obvious as soon as they point different ways.

In the same manner the seeing, spiritual being, whose manifestation we commonly call conscience, always points with one end towards right and with the other towards wrong, and we do not notice it while we follow the course it shows: the course from wrong to right. But one need only do something contrary to the indication of conscience to become aware of this spiritual being, which then shows how the animal activity has diverged from the direction indicated by conscience. And as a navigator, conscious that he is on the wrong track, cannot continue to work the oars, engine, or sails, till he has adjusted his course to the indications of the compass, or has obliterated his consciousness of this divergence—each man who has felt the duality of his animal activity and his conscience can continue his activity only by adjusting that activity to the demands of conscience, or by hiding from himself the indications conscience gives him of the wrongness of his animal life.

All human life, we may say, consists solely of these two activities:

(1) bringing one's activities into harmony with conscience, or (2) hiding from one's self the indications of conscience in order to be able to continue to live as before.

Some do the first, others the second. To attain the first there is but one means: moral enlightenment—the increase of light in one's self and attention to what it shows; for the second—to hide from one's self the indications of conscience—there are two means: one external and the other internal. The external means consists in occupations that divert one's attention from the indications given by conscience; the internal method consists in darkening conscience itself.

As a man has two ways of avoiding seeing an object that is before him: either by diverting his sight to other more striking objects, or by obstructing the sight of his own eyes—just so a man can hide from himself the indications of conscience in two ways: either by the external method of diverting his attention to various occupations, cares, amusements, or games; or by the internal method of obstructing the organ of attention itself. For people of dull, limited moral feeling, the external diversions are often quite sufficient to enable them not to perceive the indications conscience gives of the wrongness of their lives. But for morally sensitive people those means are often insufficient.

The external means do not quite divert attention from the consciousness of discord between one's life and the demands of conscience. This consciousness hampers one's life: and people, in order to be able to go on living as before, have recourse to the reliable, internal method, which is that of darkening conscience itself by poisoning the brain with stupefying substances.

One is not living as conscience demands, yet lacks the strength to reshape one's life in accord with its demands. The diversions which might distract attention from the consciousness of this discord are insufficient, or have become stale, and so—in order to be able to live on, disregarding the indications conscience gives of the wrongness of their life—people (by poisoning it temporarily) stop the activity of the organ [the brain] through which conscience manifests itself, as a man by covering his eyes hides from himself what he does not wish to see.

## II.

Not in the taste, nor in any pleasure, recreation, or mirth they afford, lies the cause of the world-wide consumption of hashish, opium, wine, and tobacco, but simply in man's need to hide from himself the demands of conscience.

I was going along the street one day, and passing some cabmen who were talking, I heard one of them say: "Of course when one's sober, one's ashamed to do it!"

When one's sober one is ashamed of what seems all right when one is drunk. In these words we have the essential underlying cause, prompting men to resort to stupefiers. People resort to them, either to escape feeling ashamed after having done something contrary to their consciences, or to bring themselves, beforehand, into a state in which they can commit actions contrary to conscience, but to which their animal nature prompts them.

A man when sober is ashamed to go after a prostitute, ashamed to steal, ashamed to kill. Of none of these things is a drunken man ashamed, and therefore if a man wishes to do something his conscience condemns—he stupefies himself.

I remember being struck by the evidence of a man cook who was tried for murdering a relation of mine, an old lady in whose service he lived. He related that when he had sent away his paramour, the servant-girl, and the time had come to act, he wished to go into the bedroom with a knife, but felt that while sober he could not commit the deed he had planned ... "when one's sober one's ashamed." He turned back, drank two tumblers of vódka he had prepared beforehand, and only then felt himself ready, and committed the crime.

Nine-tenths of the crimes are committed in that way: "Drink to keep up your courage."

Half the women who fall do so under the influence of wine. Nearly all visits to disorderly houses are paid by men who are intoxicated. People know this capacity of wine to stifle the voice of conscience, and intentionally use it for that purpose.

Not only do people stupefy themselves to stifle their own consciences, but (knowing how wine acts) when they wish to make others commit actions contrary to conscience, they intentionally stupefy them—that is, they arrange to stupefy people in order to deprive them of conscience. In war, soldiers are usually intoxicated before a hand-to-hand fight. All the French soldiers in the assaults on Sevastopol were drunk.

When a fortified place has been captured but the soldiers do not sack it and slay the defenseless old men and children, orders are often given to make them drunk and then they do what is expected of them.\*

Every one knows people who have taken to drink in consequence of some wrong-doing that has tormented their conscience. Anyone can notice that those who lead immoral lives are more attracted than others by stupefying substances. Bands of robbers or thieves, and prostitutes, cannot live without intoxicants.

Every one knows and admits that the use of stupefying substances is a consequence of the pangs of conscience, and that in certain immoral ways of life stupefying substances are employed to stifle conscience. Every one knows and admits also that the use of stupefiers does stifle conscience: that a drunken man is capable of deeds of which when sober he would not think for a moment.

Every one agrees to this, but, strange to say, when the use of stupefiers does not result in such deeds as thefts, murders, violations, and so forth—when the use of stupefiers does not result in such deeds as thefts, murders, violations and so forth—when stupefiers are taken not after some terrible crimes, but by men following professions which we do not consider criminal, and when the substances are consumed not in large quantities at once but continually in moderate doses—then (for some reason) it is assumed that stupefying substances have no tendency to stifle conscience.

Thus, it is supposed that a well-to-do Russian's glass of vódka before each meal and tumbler of wine with the meal; or a Frenchman's absinthe; or an Englishman's port wine and porter; or a German's lager-beer; or a well-to-do Chinaman's moderate dose of opium; and the smoking of tobacco with them—is done only for pleasure, and has no effect whatever on these people's consciences.

It is supposed that if after this customary stupefaction no crime is committed: nor theft, nor murder, but only customary bad and stupid actions—then these actions have occurred of themselves and are not evoked by the stupefaction. It is supposed that if these people have not committed offences against the criminal law they have no need to stifle the voice of conscience, and that the life led by people who habitually stupefy themselves is quite a good life, and would be precisely the same if they did not stupefy themselves. It is supposed that the constant use of stupefiers does not in the least darken their consciences.

Though everybody knows by experience that one's frame of mind is altered by the use of wine or tobacco, that one is not ashamed of things which but for the stimulant he would be ashamed of, that after each twinge of conscience, however slight, he is inclined to have recourse to some stupefier, and that under the influence of stupefiers it is difficult to reflect on his life and position, and that the constant and regular use of stupefiers produces the same physiological effect as its occasional immoderate use does—yet in spite of all this it seems to men who drink and smoke moderately that they use stupefiers not at all to stifle conscience, but only for the flavor or for pleasure.

But one need only think of the matter seriously and impartially—not trying to excuse one's self—to understand, first, that if the use of stupefiers in large occasional doses stifles man's conscience, their regular use must have a like effect (always first intensifying and then dulling the activity of the brain) whether they are taken in large or small doses. Secondly, that all stupefiers have the quality of stifling conscience, and have this always—both when under their influence murders, robberies, and violations are committed, and when under their influence words are spoken which would not have been spoken, or things are thought and felt which would not have been thought and felt but for them; and, thirdly, that if the use of stupefiers is needed to pacify and stifle the consciences of thieves, robbers, and prostitutes, it is also wanted by people engaged in occupations condemned by their own consciences, even though these occupations may by other people be considered proper and honorable.

In a word, it is impossible to avoid understanding that that the use of stupefiers, in large or small amounts, occasionally or regularly, in the higher or lower circles of society, is evoked by one and the same cause, the need to stifle the voice of conscience in order not to be aware of the discord existing between one's way of life and the demands of one's conscience.

*(Omitted here is section III of Tolstoy's essay, which deals with smoking rather than drinking.)*

## IV.

But can such a small—such a trifling—alteration as the slight intoxication produced by the moderate use of wine or tobacco produce important consequences?

"If a man smokes opium or hashish, or intoxicates himself with wine till he falls down and loses his senses, of course the consequences may be very serious; but it surely cannot have any serious consequences if a man merely comes slightly under the influence of hops or tobacco," is what is usually said. It seems to people that a slight stupefaction, a little darkening of the judgment, cannot have any important influence. But to think so is like supposing that it may harm a watch to be struck against a stone, but that a little dirt introduced into it cannot be harmful.

Remember, however, that the chief work actuating man's whole life is not done by his hands, his feet, or his back, but by his consciousness. Before a man can do anything with his feet or hands, a certain alteration has first to take place in his consciousness. And this alteration defines all the subsequent movements of the man. Yet these alterations are always minute and almost imperceptible.

Brulloff† one day corrected a pupil's study. The pupil, having glanced at the altered drawing, exclaimed: "Why, you only touched it a tiny bit, but it is quite another thing." Brullof replied: "Art begins where the tiny bit begins."

That saying is strikingly true not only of art but of all life. One may say that true life begins where the tiny bit begins—where what seem to us minute and infinitely small alterations take place. True life is not lived where great external changes take place—where people move about, clash, fight, and slay one another—it is lived only where these tiny, tiny, infinitesimally small changes occur.

Raskólnikof‡ did not live his true life when he murdered the old woman or her sister. When murdering the old woman herself, and still more when murdering her sister, he did not live his true life, but acted like a machine, doing what he could not help doing—discharging the cartridge with which he had long been loaded. One old woman was killed, another stood before him, the axe was in his hand.

Raskólnikof lived his true life, not when he met the old woman's sister, but at the time when he had not yet killed any old woman, nor entered a stranger's lodging with intent to kill, nor held the axe in his hand, nor had the loop in his overcoat by which the axe hung—at the time when he was lying on the sofa in his room, deliberating not at all about the old woman, nor even as to whether it is, or is not, permissible at the will of one man to wipe from the face of the earth another, unnecessary and harmful, man, but whether he ought to live in Petersburg or not, whether he ought to accept money from his mother or not, and on other questions not at all relating to the old woman.

And then—in that region quite independent of animal activities—the question whether he would or would not kill the old woman was decided.

That question was decided—not when, having killed one old woman, he stood before another, axe in hand—but when he was doing nothing and was only thinking, when only his consciousness was active: and in that consciousness tiny, tiny alterations were taking place. It is at such times that one needs the greatest clearness to decide correctly the questions that have arisen, and it is just then that one glass of beer, or one cigarette, may prevent the solution of the question, may postpone the decision, stifle the voice of conscience, prompt a decision of the question in favor of one's lower, animal nature—as was the case with Raskólnikof.

Tiny, tiny alterations—but on them depend the most immense, the most terrible consequences. Many material changes may result from what happens when a man has taken a decision and begun to act: houses, riches, and people's bodies may perish, but nothing more important can happen than what was hidden in the man's consciousness. The limits of what can happen are set by consciousness.

But from most minute alterations occurring in the domain of consciousness, boundless results of unimaginable importance may follow.

Do not let it be supposed that what I am saying has anything to do with the question of free will or determinism. Discussion on that question is superfluous for my purpose, or for any other for that matter. Without deciding the question whether a man can, or cannot, act as he wishes (a question, in my opinion, not correctly stated), I am merely saying that since human activity is conditioned by infinitesimal alterations in consciousness, it follows (no matter whether we admit, or do not admit, the existence of free will) that we must pay particular attention to the condition in which these minute alterations take place, just as one must be specially attentive to the condition of scales on which other things are to be weighed. We must, as far as it depends on us, try to put ourselves and others in conditions which will not disturb the clearness and delicacy of thought necessary for the correct working of conscience, and must not act in the contrary manner; trying to hinder and confuse the work of conscience by the use of stupefying substances.

For man is a spiritual as well as an animal being. Man may be moved by things that influence his spiritual nature, or by things that influence his animal nature, as a clock may be moved by its hands or by its main wheel. And just as it is best to regulate the movement of a clock by means of its inner mechanism, so a man—one's self or another—is best regulated by means of his consciousness. And as with a clock one has to take special care of that part by means of which one can best move the inner mechanism, so with a man, one must attend most of all to the cleanness and clearness of consciousness; consciousness being the thing that best moves the whole man.

To doubt this is impossible; everyone knows it. But a need to deceive one's self arises. People are not as anxious that consciousness should work correctly as they are that it should seem to them that what they are doing is right, and they deliberately make use of substances that disturb the proper working of their consciousness.

## V.

People drink and smoke, not casually, not from dullness, not to cheer themselves up, not because it is pleasant, but in order to drown the voice of conscience in themselves. And if that is so, how terrible must be the consequences! Indeed, think what a building would be like erected by people who did not use a straight plumb-rule to get the walls perpendicular, nor right-angled squares to get the corners correct, but used a soft rule which would bend to suit all irregularities in the walls, and a square that expanded to fit any angle, acute or obtuse.

Yet, thanks to self-stupefaction, that is just what is being done in life. Life does not accord with conscience, so conscience is made to bend to life.

This is done in the life of individuals, and it is done in the life of humanity as a whole, which consists of the lives of individuals.

To grasp the full significance of such stupefying of one's consciousness, let each one carefully recall the spiritual conditions he has passed through at each period of his life. Every one will find that at each period of his life certain moral questions confronted him, which he ought to solve, and on the solution of which the whole welfare of his life depended. For the solution of these questions great concentration of attention was needful. Such concentration of attention is a labor. In every labor, especially at the beginning, there is a time when the work seems difficult and painful, and when human weakness prompts a desire to abandon it. Physical work seems painful at first; mental work seems yet more painful. As Lessing says: people are inclined to cease to think at the point at which thought begins to be difficult; but it is just there, I would add, that thinking begins to be fruitful. A man feels that to decide the questions confronting him needs labor — often painful labor — and he wishes to evade this. If he had no means of stupefying his faculties he could not expel from his consciousness the questions that confront him, and the necessity of solving them would be forced upon him.

But man finds that there exists a means to drive off these questions whenever they present themselves — and he uses it. As soon as the questions awaiting solution begin to torment him, he has recourse to these means, and avoids the disquietude evoked by the troublesome questions. Consciousness ceases to demand their solution, and the unsolved questions remain unsolved till his next period of enlightenment. But when that period comes, the same thing is repeated, and the man goes on for months, years, or even for his whole life, standing before those same moral questions and not moving a step towards their solution. Yet it is in the solution of moral questions that life's whole movement consists.

What occurs is as if a man who needs to see to the bottom of some muddy water to obtain a precious pearl, but who dislikes entering the water, should stir it up each time it begins to settle and become clear. Many a man continues to stupefy himself all his life long, and remains immovable at the same, once-accepted, obscure, self-contradictory view of life — pressing, as each period of enlightenment approaches, ever at one and the same wall against which he pressed ten or twenty years ago, and which he cannot break through because he intentionally blunts that sharp point of thought which alone could pierce it.

Let each man remember himself as he has been during the years of his drinking or smoking, and let him test the matter in his experience of other people, and everyone will see a definite constant line dividing those who are addicted to stupefiers from those who are free from them. The more a man stupefies himself the more he is morally immovable.

## VI.

Terrible, as they are described to us, are the consequences of opium and hashish on individuals; terrible, as we know them, are the consequences of alcohol to flagrant drunkards; but incomparably more terrible to our whole society are the consequences of what is considered the harmless, moderate use of spirits, wine, beer, and tobacco, to which the majority of men, and especially our so-called cultured classes, are addicted.

The consequences must naturally be terrible, admitting the fact, which must be admitted—that the guiding activities of society: political, official, scientific, literary, and artistic—are carried on for the most part, by people in an abnormal state: by people who are drunk.

It is generally supposed that a man who, like most people of our well-to-do-classes, takes alcoholic drink almost every time he eats, is in a perfectly normal and sober condition next day, during working hours. But this is quite an error. A man who drank a bottle of wine, a glass of spirits, or two glasses of ale, yesterday, is now in the usual state of drowsiness or depression which follows excitement, and is therefore in a condition of mental prostration, which is increased by smoking. For a man who habitually smokes and drinks in moderation, to bring his brain into a normal condition would require at least a week or more of abstinence from wine and tobacco. But that hardly ever occurs.**

So that most of what goes on among us, whether done by people who rule and teach others, or by those who are ruled and taught, is done when the doers are not sober.

And let not this be taken as a joke or an exaggeration; the confusion, and above all, the imbecility, of our lives, arises chiefly from the constant state of intoxication in which most people live. Could people who are not drunk possibly do all that is being done around us—from building the Eiffel Tower to accepting military service?

Without any need whatever, a company is formed, capital collected, men labor, make calculations, and draw plans; millions of working days and thousands of tons of iron are spent to build a tower; and millions of people consider it their duty to climb up it, stop awhile on it, and then climb down again; and the building and visiting of this tower evoke no other reflection than a wish and intention to build other towers, in other places, still bigger. Could sober people act like that? Or take another case. All the European peoples have for dozens of years past been busy devising the very best ways of killing people, and teaching as many young men as possible, as soon as they reach manhood, how to murder. Everyone knows that there can be no invasion by barbarians, but that these preparations made by the different civilized and Christian nations are directed against one another; all know that this is burdensome, painful, inconvenient, ruinous, immoral, impious, and irrational—but all continue to prepare for mutual murder.

Some devise political combinations to decide who, with what allies, is to kill whom; others direct those who are being taught to murder; and others, again, yield—against their will, against their conscience, against their reason—to these preparations for murder.

Could sober people do these things? Only drunkards who never reach a state of sobriety could do them, and live on in the horrible state of discord between life and conscience in which, not only in this, but in all other respects, the people of our society are now living.

Never before, I suppose, have people lived with the demands of their conscience so evidently in contradiction to their actions.

Humanity today has, as it were, stuck fast. It is as though some external cause hindered it from occupying a position naturally in accord with its perceptions. And the cause—if not the only one, then certainly the greatest—is this physical condition of stupefaction, to which, by wine and tobacco, to which the great majority of people in our society reduce themselves.

Emancipation from this terrible evil will be an epoch in the life of humanity; and that epoch seems to be at hand. The evil is recognized. An alteration has already taken place in our perception concerning the use of stupefying substances. People have understood the terrible harm of these things, and are beginning to point them out, and this almost unnoticed alteration in perception will inevitably bring about the emancipation of men from the use of stupefying things—will enable them to open their eyes to the demands of their consciences, and they will begin to order their lives in accord with their perceptions.

And this seems to be already beginning. But, as always, it is beginning among the upper classes only after all the lower classes have already been infected.

*See the allusion to Skobelef's conduct at Geok-Tepe in a preface by Tolstoy, given in Grant Richards' sixpenny edition of Sevastopol and other Stories (Maude's note).

†K.P. Brullof, a celebrated Russian painter (1799–1852) (Maude's note).

‡The hero of Dostoyevsky's novel, Crime and Punishment (Maude's note).

\*\*But how is it that people who do not drink or smoke are often morally on an incomparably lower plane than others who drink and smoke? And why do people who drink and smoke often manifest the highest qualities both mentally and morally?

The answer is, first, that we do not know the height that those who drink and smoke would have attained had they not drunk and smoked. And, secondly, from the fact that morally gifted people achieve great things in spite of the deteriorating effect of stupefying substances, we can but conclude that they would have produced yet greater things had they not stupefied themselves. It is very probable, as a friend remarked to me, that Kant's works would not have been written in such a curious and bad style had he not smoked so much. Lastly, the lower a man's mental and moral plane the less does he feel the discord between his conscience and his life, and therefore the less does he feel a craving to stupefy himself; and on the other hand a parallel reason explains why the most sensitive natures—those which immediately and morbidly feel the discord between life and conscience—so often indulge in narcotics and perish by them. (Tolstoy's note)

## *Tennessee Williams, from* Cat on a Hot Tin Roof *(1955)*

*One of America's most influential, distinguished, and poetic playwrights, Tennessee Williams (1911–1983) dealt extensively with alcohol and other drugs in his work.* A Streetcar Named Desire, Sweet Bird of Youth, The Night of the Iguana *and, of course,* Cat on a Hot Tin Roof *all reflect Williams' interest in the use of intoxicants and in the varieties of motivations for, and responses to, such use. Although rich, famous, and honored, Williams was himself chemically dependent on a variety of drugs and alcohol at the time of this death. After a period of living on little more than coffee, wine, and Seconal, the playwright was found dead with a barbiturate bottle overcap stuck in his throat in his New York apartment.*

*In the scene included here from act two of* Cat on a Hot Tin Roof, *the young alcoholic, Brick, confronted by his domineering, wealthy father, Big Daddy, struggles to explain the reasons for his drinking. For Brick, the attractions of drink are multiple: it becomes a means of guilty self-destruction over Brick's sexually ambiguous relationship with a dead friend, Skipper; it is also a way of denying his confused sexual identity; finally, it represents Brick's effort to escape the lies and deception—what Brick calls the "mendacity"—of the world around him. (Some clarification of names referred to in the excerpt: Gooper and Mae are Brick's brother and sister-in-law, respectively; Big Mama is his mother; and Margaret (Maggie), the "cat" of the play's title, is his beautiful but frustrated wife, who suffers from her unrequited yearning for her husband.) The scene takes place during the celebration of Big Daddy's birthday party, just after Big Daddy has been deliberately misinformed that his health condition is less serious than he had feared. Watching his son drink and move about nervously, Big Daddy speaks first.*

BIG DADDY: ... What makes you so restless? Have you got ants in your britches?
BRICK: Yes, sir...
BIG DADDY: Why?
BRICK: Something—hasn't happened yet.
BIG DADDY: Yeah? What is that!
Brick (*sadly*): —the click...
BIG DADDY: Did you say "click"?
BRICK: Yes, click.
BIG DADDY: What click?
BRICK: A click that I get in my head that makes me feel peaceful.
BIG DADDY: I sure in hell don't know what you're talking about, but it disturbs me.
BRICK: It's just a mechanical thing.
BIG DADDY: What is a mechanical thing?
BRICK: This click that I get in my head that makes me peaceful. I got to drink till I get it. It's just a mechanical thing, something like a—like a—like a—
BIG DADDY: Like a—
BRICK: Switch clicking off in my head, turning the hot light off and the cool night on and—

(*He looks up, smiling sadly.*)

—all of a sudden there's—peace!
BIG DADDY: (*whistles long and soft with astonishment; he goes back to Brick and clasps his son's two shoulder*): Jesus! I didn't know it had gotten that bad with you. Why, boy, you're—alcoholic!
BRICK: That's the truth, Big Daddy, I'm alcoholic.
BIG DADDY: This shows how I—let things go!
BRICK: I have to hear that little click in my head that makes me peaceful. Usually I hear it sooner than this, sometimes as early as—noon, but— —Today it's—dilatory...
—I just haven't got the right level of alcohol in my bloodstream yet!

(*This last statement is made with energy as he freshens his drink.*)

BIG DADDY: Uh—huh. Expecting death made me blind. I didn't have no idea that a son of mine was turning into a drunkard under my nose.
Brick (*gently*): Well, now you do, Big Daddy, the news has penetrated.
BIG DADDY: UH-huh, yes, now I do, the news has—penetrated...
BRICK: And so if you'll excuse me—
BIG DADDY: No, I won't excuse you.
BRICK:—I'd better sit by myself till I hear that click in my head, it's just a

mechanical thing but it don't happen except when I'm alone or talking to no one...

BIG DADDY: You got a long, long time to sit still, boy, and talk to no one, but now you're talkin' to me. At least I'm talking to you. And you set there and listen until I tell you the conversation is over!

BRICK: But this talk is like all the others we've ever had together in our lives! It's nowhere, nowhere!—it's—it's *painful*, Big Daddy...

BIG DADDY: All right, then let it be painful, but don't you move from that chair!—I'm going to remove that crutch...

(*He seizes the crutch and tosses it across room.*)

BRICK: I can hop on one foot, and if I fall, I can crawl!

BIG DADDY: If you ain't careful you're gonna crawl off this plantation and then, by Jesus, you'll have to hustle your drinks along Skid Row!

BRICK: That'll come, Big Daddy.

BIG DADDY: Naw, it won't. You're my son and I'm going to straighten you out; now that *I'm* straightened out, I'm going to straighten out you!

BRICK: Yeah?

BIG DADDY: Today the report come in from Ochsner clinic. Y'know what they told me?

(*His face glows with triumph.*)

The only thing that they could detect with all the instruments of science in that great hospital is a little spastic condition of the colon! And nerves torn to pieces by all that worry about it.

(*A little girl bursts into room with a sparkler clutched in each fist, hops and shrieks like a monkey gone mad and rushes back out again as Big Daddy strikes at her.*

(*Silence. The two men stare at each other. A woman laughs gaily outside.*)

I want you to know I breathed a sigh of relief almost as powerful as the Vicksburg tornado!

BRICK: You weren't ready to go?

BIG DADDY: GO WHERE?—crap...

—When you are gone from here, boy, you are long gone and no where! The human machine is not so different from the animal machine or the fish machine or the bird machine or the reptile machine or the insect machine! IT's just a whole God damn lot more complicated and consequently more trouble to keep together. Yep. I thought I had it. The earth shook under my foot, the sky come down like the black lid of a kettle and I couldn't breath!—Today!!—that lid was lifted, I drew my first free breath in—how many years?—*God!*—three...

(*There is laughter outside, running footsteps, the soft, plushy sound and light of exploding rockets.*)

(*Brick stares at him soberly for a long moment; then makes a sort of startled sound in his nostrils and springs up on one foot and hops across the room to grab his crutch, swinging on the furniture for support. He gets the crutch and flees as if in horror for the gallery. His father seizes him by the sleeve of his white silk pajamas.*)

Stay here, you son of a bitch!—till I say go!
BRICK: I can't.
BIG DADDY: You sure in hell will, God damn it.
BRICK: No, I can't. We talk, you talk, in—circles! We get no where, no where! It's always the same, you say you want to talk to me and don't have a ruttin' thing to say to me!
BIG DADDY: Nothin' to say to when I'm tellin' you I'm going to live when I thought I was dying?!
BRICK: Oh—*that!*—Is that what you have to say to me?
BIG DADDY: Why, you son of a bitch! Ain't that, ain't that—*important?!*
BRICK: Well, you said that, that's said, and now I—
BIG DADDY: Now you set back down.
BRICK: You're all balled up, you—
BIG DADDY: I ain't balled up!
BRICK: You are, you're all balled up!
BIG DADDY: Don't tell me what I am, you drunken whelp! I'm going to tear this coat sleeve off if you don't set down!
BRICK: Big Daddy—
BIG DADDY: Do what I tell you! I'm the boss here, now! I want you to know I'm back in the driver's seat now!

(*Editor's note: Omitted here is a brief interruption of the conversation by Brick's mother, Big Mama*)

Brick (*softly, sadly*): Christ...
BIG DADDY: (*fiercely*): Yeah! Christ!—is right...

(*Big Daddy jerks his crutch from under Brick so he steps with the injured ankle. He utters a hissing cry of anguish, clutches a chair and pulls it over on top of him on the floor.*)

Son of a—tub of—hog fat...
BRICK: Big Daddy! Give me my crutch.

(*Big Daddy throws the crutch out of reach.*)

Give me that crutch, Big Daddy.
BIG DADDY: Why do you drink?

BRICK: Don't know, give me my crutch!
BIG DADDY: You better think why you drink or give up drinking!
BRICK: Will you please give me my crutch so I can get up off this floor?
BIG DADDY: First you answer my question. Why do you drink? Why are you throwing your life away, boy, like somethin' disgusting you picked up on the street?
Brick (*getting onto his knees*): Big Daddy, I'm in pain, I stepped on that foot.
BIG DADDY: Good! I'm glad you're not too dumb with the liquor in you to feel some pain!
BRICK: You—spilled—my drink...
BIG DADDY: I'll make a bargain with you. You tell me why you drink and I'll hand you one. I'll pour you the liquor myself and hand it to you.
BRICK: Why do I drink?
BIG DADDY: Yea! Why?
BRICK: Give me a drink and I'll tell you.
BIG DADDY: Tell me first!
BRICK: I'll tell you in one word.
BIG DADDY: What word?
BRICK: DISGUST!

(*The clock chimes softly, sweetly, Big Daddy gives it a short, outraged glance.*)

Now how about that drink?
BIG DADDY: What are you disgusted with? You got to tell me that, first. Otherwise being disgusted don't make no sense!
BRICK: Give me my crutch.
BIG DADDY: You heard me, you got to tell me what I asked you first.
BRICK: I told you, I said to kill my disgust!
BIG DADDY: DISGUST WITH WHAT!
BRICK: You strike a hard bargain.
BIG DADDY: What are you disgusted with?—an' I'll pass you the liquor.
BRICK: I can hop on one foot, and if I fall, I can crawl.
BIG DADDY: You want liquor that bad?
Brick (*dragging himself up, clinging to bedstead*): Yeah, I want it that bad.
BIG DADDY: If I give you a drink, will you tell me what it is you're disgusted with, Brick?
BRICK: Yes, sir, I will try to.

(*The old man ours him a drink and solemnly passes it to him.*)
(*There is silence as Brick drinks.*)

Have you ever heard the word "mendacity"?

BIG DADDY: Sure. Mendacity is one of them five dollar words that cheap politicians throw back and forth at each other.
BRICK: You know what it means?
BIG DADDY: Don't it mean lying and liars?
BRICK: Yes, sir, lying and liars.
BIG DADDY: Has someone been lying to you?
Children (*chanting in chorus offstage*):
> We want Big Dad-dee!
> We want Big Dad-dee!

(*Gooper appears in the gallery door.*)

Gooper: Big Daddy, the kiddies are shouting for you out there.
Big Daddy (*fiercely*): Keep out, Gooper!
Gooper: 'Scuse *me*!

(*Big Daddy slams the doors after Gooper.*)

BIG DADDY: Who's been lying to you, has Margaret been lying to you, has your wife been lying to you about something, Brick?
BRICK: Not her. That wouldn't matter.
BIG DADDY: Then who's been lying to you, and what about?
BRICK: No one single person and no one lie...
BIG DADDY: Then what, what then, for Christ's sake?
BRICK: —The whole, the whole—thing...
BIG DADDY: Why are you rubbing your head? You got a headache?
BRICK: No, I'm tryin' to—
BIG DADDY: —Concentrate, but you can't because your brain's all soaked with liquor, is that the trouble? Wet brain!

(*He snatches the glass from Brick's hand.*)

What do you know about this mendacity thing? Hell! I could write a book on it! Don't you know that? I could write a book on it and still not cover the subject? Well, I could, I could write a goddam book on it and still not cover the subject anywhere near enough!!—Think of all the lies I got to put up with!—Pretenses! Ain't that mendacity? Having to pretend stuff you don't think or feel or have any idea of? Having for instance to act like I care for Big Mama!—I haven't been able to stand the sight, sound, or smell of that woman for forty years now!—even when I *laid* her!—regular as a piston...

Pretend to love that son of a bitch of a Gooper and his wife Mae and those five same screechers out there like parrots in a jungle? Jesus! Can't stand to look at 'em!

Church!—it bores the Bejesus out of me but I go!—I go an' sit there and listen to the fool preacher!

Clubs!—Elks! Masons! Rotary!—*crap!*

(*A spasm of pain makes him clutch his belly. He sinks into a chair and his voice is softer and hoarse.*)

*You* I *do* like for some reason, did always have some kind of real feeling for—affection—respect—yes, always...

You and being a success as a planter is all I ever had any devotion to in my whole life!—and that's the truth.

I don't know why, but it is!

*I've* lived with mendacity!—Why can't *you* live with it? Hell, you *got* to live with it, there's nothing *else* to *live* with except mendacity, is there?

BRICK: Yes, sir. Yes, sir, there is something else that you can live with!

BIG DADDY: What?

Brick (*lifting his glass*): This!—Liquor...

BIG DADDY: That's not living, that's dodging away from life.

BRICK: I want to dodge away from it.

BIG DADDY: Then why don't you kill yourself, man?

BRICK: I like to drink...

BIG DADDY: Oh, God, I can't talk to you...

BRICK: I'm sorry, Big Daddy.

BIG DADDY: Not as sorry as I am. I'll tell you something. A little while back when I thought my number was up—

(*This speech should have torrential pace and fury.*)

—before I found out it was just this—spastic—colon. I thought about. Should I or should I not, if the jig was up, give you this place when I go—since I hate Gooper an' Mae an' know that they hate me, and since all five same monkeys are little Maes an' Goopers.—And I thought, No!—than I thought, Yes!—I couldn't make up my mind. I hate Gooper and his five same monkeys and that bitch Mae! Why should I turn over twenty-eight thousand acres of the richest land this side of the valley Nile to not my kind?—But why in hell, on the other hand, Brick—should I subsidize a goddam fool on the bottle?—Liked or not liked, well maybe even—*loved!*—Why should I do that?—Subsidize worthless behavior? Rot? Corruption?

Brick (*smiling*): I understand.

BIG DADDY: Well, if you do, you're smarter than I am, God damn it, because I don't understand. And this I will tell you frankly. I didn't make up my mind at all on that question and still to this day I ain't made out no will!—Well, now I don't *have* to. The pressure is gone. I can just wait and see if you pull yourself together or if you don't.

BRICK: That's right, Big Daddy.

BIG DADDY: You sound like you thought I was kidding.
Brick (*rising*): No, sir, I know you're not kidding.
BIG DADDY: But you don't care—?
Brick (*hobbling toward the gallery door*): No, sir, I don't care...
Now how about taking a look at your birthday fireworks and getting some of that cool breeze off the river.

(*He stands in the gallery doorway as the night sky turns pink and green and gold with successive flashes of light.*)

BIG DADDY: *WAIT!*—Brick...

(*His voice drops. Suddenly there is something shy, almost tender, in his restraining gesture.*)

Don't let's—leave it like this, like them other talks we've had, we've always—talked around things, we've—just talked around things for some rotten reason, I don't know what, it's always like something was left not spoken something avoided because neither of us was honest enough with the—other...
BRICK: I never lied to you, Big Daddy.
BIG DADDY: Did I every to *you*?
BRICK: No, sir...
BIG DADDY: Then there is at least two people that never lied to each other.
BRICK: But we've never *talked* to each other.
BIG DADDY: We can *now*.
BRICK: Big Daddy, there don't seem to be anything much to say.
BIG DADDY: You say that you drink to kill your disgust with lying.
BRICK: You said to give you a reason.
BIG DADDY: Is liquor the only thing that'll kill this disgust?
BRICK: Now. Yes.
BIG DADDY: But not once, huh?
BRICK: Not when I was still young an' believing. A drinking man's someone who wants to forget he isn't still young an' believing.
BIG DADDY: Believing what?
BRICK: Believing...
BIG DADDY: Believing *what*?
Brick (*stubbornly evasive*): Believing.

# II. Effects of Drinking

## *William Shakespeare, from* Macbeth *(1605), and* Othello *(1604)*

*Although Shakespeare created literature's arguably most famous drunkard, Sir John Falstaff, in general his plays treat drink only in passing. Alcohol may be a key component in the make-up of Falstaff (e.g., in* Henry IV *Parts 1 and 2, and* The Merry Wives of Windsor*), and of Sir Toby Belch (in* Twelfth Night*), but Shakespeare tends not to focus on drink in relation to character, or as a theme in and of itself. But notable exceptions to this pattern appear in the two selections presented here. The first passage, from* Macbeth, *concisely, hilariously, and unforgettably anatomizes drink's effects with regard to sex. In a style reminiscent of the comic gravediggers in* Hamlet, *the drunken porter in* Macbeth *expounds on drink as a "great provoker" and an "equivocator" in its sexual effects. The second, far more sinister and lengthy passage, from* Othello, *shows drink as a tool of manipulation, as a source of poor judgment and impulsiveness, as an incitement to violence, and ultimately as a threat to the drinker's employment and reputation. The scene centers on the first step in Iago's infamous scheme of retaliation on Othello for passing him up for promotion in favor of Cassio. By getting Cassio drunk, Iago correctly counts on fomenting a drunken brawl whereby Cassio will lose favor with Othello; Iago then urges the despondent Cassio to ask Othello's wife, Desdemona, to intercede with Othello on Cassio's behalf, which intercession Iago will in turn use to inflame Othello's jealous suspicion of the guiltless Desdemona. While not the main concern of the scene, drink and attitudes toward it permeate the entire passage, and are crucial both to the plot and to the psychological interactions among the characters.*

*The passages below are based on the early quartos and the first folio of Shakespeare's plays.*

From *Macbeth*, Act II, scene III

Enter a Porter. *Knocking within.*

PORTER: Here's a knocking indeed! If a man were porter of hell-gate,
Gate, he should have old turning the key. [*Knocking.*]
Knock, knock, knock! Who's there, i' the name of Beelzebub?
Here's a farmer, that hang'd himself on the expectation of plenty.
Come in time; have napkins enow about you; here you'll sweat for't.
[*Knocking.*] Knock, knock! Who's there, in the other
devil's name? Faith, here's an equivocator, that could swear
in both the scales against either scale; who committed treason
enough for God's sake, yet could not equivocate to heaven. O,
come in, equivocator. [*Knocking.*] Knock, knock, knock!
Who's there? Faith, here's an English tailor come hither, for
stealing out of a French hose. Come in, tailor; here you may
roast your goose. [*Knocking.*] Knock, knock! Never at
quiet! What are you? But this place is too cold for hell.
I'll devil-porter it no further. I had thought to have let in some
of all professions that go the primrose way to the everlasting
bonfire. [*Knocking.*] Anon, anon! I pray you, remember
the porter.

*(Opens the gate.)*

*Enter Macduff and Lennox.*

MACDUFF: Was it so late, friend, ere you went to bed, That you do lie so late?

PORTER: Faith, sir, we were carousing till the second cock; and drink, sir, is a great provoker of three things.

MACDUFF: What three things does drink especially provoke?

PORTER: Marry, sir, nose-painting, sleep, and urine. Lechery, sir, it provokes, and unprovokes: it provokes the desire, but it takes away the performance; therefore, much drink may be said to be an equivocator with lechery: it makes him, and it mars him; it sets him on, and it takes him off; it persuades him and disheartens him; makes him stand to, and not stand to; in conclusion, equivocates him in a sleep, and, giving him the lie, leaves him.

MACDUFF: I believe drink gave thee the lie last night.

PORTER: That it did, sir, i' the very throat on me. But I requited him for his lie; and, I think, being too strong for him, though he took up my legs sometime, yet I made a shift to cast him.

### From *Othello*, Act II, scene III

IAGO: ... Come, lieutenant, I have a stoup of wine; and here without are a brace of Cyprus gallants that would fain have a measure to the health of black Othello.

CASSIO: Not to-night, good Iago. I have very poor and unhappy brains for drinking; I could well wish courtesy would invent some other custom of entertainment.

IAGO: O, they are our friends. But one cup; I'll drink for you.

CASSIO: I have drunk but one cup to-night, and that was craftily qualified too, and behold, what innovation it makes here. I am unfortunate in the infirmity, and dare not task my weakness with any more.

IAGO: What, man! 'tis a night of revels. The gallants desire it.

CASSIO: Where are they?

IAGO: Here at the door; I pray you, call them in.

CASSIO: I'll do't; but it dislikes me.

*[Exit.]*

IAGO: If I can fasten but one cup upon him,
With that which he hath drunk to-night already,
He'll be as full of quarrel and offence
As my young mistress' dog. Now, my sick fool Roderigo,
Whom love hath turn'd almost the wrong side out,
To Desdemona hath to-night carous'd
Potations pottle-deep; and he's to watch.
Three lads of Cyprus, noble swelling spirits
That hold their honours in a wary distance,
The very elements of this warlike isle,
Have I to-night fluster'd with flowing cups,
And they watch too. Now, 'mongst this flock of drunkards
Am I to put our Cassio in some action
That may offend the isle. But here they come.

*Re-enter Cassio; with him Montano and Gentlemen
[Servants follow with wine].*

If consequence do but approve my dream,
My boat sails freely, both with wind and stream.

CASSIO: 'Fore God, they have given me a rouse already.

MONTANO: Good faith, a little one; not past a pint, as I am a soldier.

IAGO: Some wine, ho!

*[Sings.]*

"And let me the canakin* clink, clink;

    And let me the canakin clink.
    A soldier's a man;
    O, man's life's but a span;
    Why, then, let a soldier drink."
Some wine, boys!
CASSIO: 'Fore God, an excellent song.
IAGO: I learn'd it in England, where, indeed, they are most potent in potting: your Dane, your German, and your swag-belli'd Hollander—Drink, ho!—are nothing to your English.
CASSIO: Is your Englishman so expert in his drinking?
IAGO: Why, he drinks you, with facility, your Dane dead drunk; he sweats not to overthrow your Almain;† he gives your Hollander a vomit ere the next pottle can be fill'd.
CASSIO: To the health of our general!
MONTANO: I am for it, lieutenant; and I'll do you justice.
IAGO: O sweet England!

    "King Stephen was and a worthy peer,
    His breeches cost him but a crown;
    He held them sixpence all too dear,
    With that he call'd the tailor down;

    He was a wightffi of high renown,
    And thou art but of low degree:
    'Tis pride that pulls the country down;
    Then take thy auld cloak about thee."

Some wine, ho!
CASSIO: Why, this is a more exquisite song than the other.
IAGO: Will you hear't again?
CASSIO: No; for I hold him to be unworthy of his place that does those things. Well, God's above all; and there be souls must be saved, and there be souls must not be saved.
IAGO: It's true, good lieutenant.
CASSIO: For mine own part,—no offence to the general, nor any man of quality,—I hope to be saved.
IAGO: And so do I too, lieutenant.
CASSIO: Ay, but, by your leave, not before me; the lieutenant is to be saved before the ancient. Let's have no more of this; let's to our affairs.—God forgive us our sins!—Gentlemen, let's look to our business. Do not think, gentlemen, I am drunk. This is my ancient; this is my right hand, and this is my left. I am not drunk now; I can stand well enough, and I speak well enough.

GENTLEMEN: Excellent well.
CASSIO: Why, very well then; you must not think then that I am drunk.
  [*Exit.*]
MONTANO: To the platform, masters; come, let's set the watch.
IAGO: You see this fellow that is gone before:
  He is a soldier fit to stand by Caesar
  And give direction; and do but see his vice.
  'Tis to his virtue a just equinox,
  The one as long as the other; 'tis pity of him.
  I fear the trust Othello puts him in,
  On some odd time of his infirmity,
  Will shake this island.
MONTANO: But is he often thus?
IAGO: 'Tis evermore his prologue to his sleep.
  He'll watch the horologe† a double set,
  If drink rock not his cradle.
MONTANO: It were well
  The general were put in mind of it.
  Perhaps he sees it not; or his good nature
  Prizes the virtue that appears in Cassio,
  And looks not on his evils. Is not this true?
  *Enter Roderigo*
IAGO: [*Aside to him.*] How now, Roderigo!
  I pray you, after the lieutenant; go.
  [*Exit Roderigo.*]
MONTANO: And 'tis great pity that the noble Moor
  Should hazard such a place as his own second
  With one of an ingraft infirmity.
  It were an honest action to say
  So to the Moor.
IAGO: Not I, for this fair island.
  I do love Cassio well; and would do much
  To cure him of this evil.—But, hark! what noise?
  [*Cry within:* "Help! help!"]
  *Re-enter Cassio, pursuing Roderigo.*
CASSIO: 'Zounds, you rogue! you rascal!
MONTANO: What's the matter, lieutenant?
CASSIO: A knave teach me my duty! I'll beat the knave into a twiggen bottle.††

RODERIGO: Beat me!
CASSIO: Dost thou prate, rogue? [*Striking Roderigo.*]
MONTANO: Nay, good lieutenant; [*Staying him.*]
   I pray you, sir, hold your hand.
CASSIO: Let me go, sir,
   Or I'll knock you o'er the mazzard.
MONTANO: Come, come, you're drunk.
CASSIO: Drunk!

   [*They fight.*]

IAGO: [*Aside to Roderigo.*] Away, I say; go out, and cry a mutiny.

   [*Exit Roderigo.*]

   Nay, good lieutenant,—God's will, gentlemen;—
   Help, ho!—Lieutenant,—sir,—Montano,—sir;—
   Help, masters!—Here's a goodly watch indeed!

   [*Bell rings.*]

   Who's that which rings the bell?—Diablo, ho!
   The town will rise. God's will, lieutenant, hold!
   You will be sham'd forever.

   *Re-enter Othello and Attendants.*

OTHELLO: What is the matter here?
MONTANO: 'Zounds, I bleed still; I am hurt to the death. He dies!
OTHELLO: Hold, for your lives!
IAGO: Hold, ho! Lieutenant,—sir,—Montano,—gentlemen,—
   Have you forgot all sense of place and duty?
   Hold! the general speaks to you; hold, for shame!
OTHELLO: Why, how now, ho! from whence ariseth this?
   Are we turn'd Turks, and to ourselves do that
   Which Heaven hath forbid the Ottomites?‡‡
   For Christian shame, put by this barbarous brawl.
   He that stirs next to carve for his own rage
   Holds his soul light; he dies upon his motion.
   Silence that dreadful bell; it frights the isle
   From her propriety. What is the matter, masters?—
   Honest Iago, that looks dead with grieving,
   Speak, who began this? On thy love, I charge thee.
IAGO: I do not know. Friends all but now, even now,
   In quarter, and in terms like bride and groom
   Devesting them for bed; and then, but now—
   As if some planet had unwitted men—

    Swords out, and tilting one at other's breast,
    In opposition bloody. I cannot speak
    Any beginning to this peevish odds;
    And would in action glorious I had lost
    Those legs that brought me to a part of it!
OTHELLO: How comes it, Michael, you are thus forgot?
CASSIO: I pray you, pardon me; I cannot speak.
OTHELLO: Worthy Montano, you were wont be civil;
    The gravity and stillness of your youth
    The world hath noted, and your name is great
    In mouths of wisest censure. What's the matter,
    That you unlace your reputation thus,
    And spend your rich opinion for the name
    Of a night-brawler? Give me answer to it.
MONTANO: Worthy Othello, I am hurt to danger.
    Your officer, Iago, can inform you—
    While I spare speech, which something now offends me—
    Of all that I do know: nor know I aught
    By me that's said or done amiss this night,
    Unless self-charity be sometimes a vice,
    And to defend ourselves it be a sin
    When violence assails us.
OTHELLO: Now, by heaven,
    My blood begins my safer guides to rule;
    And passion, having my best judgement collied,
    Assays to lead the way. If I once stir,
    Or do but lift this arm, the best of you
    Shall sink in my rebuke. Give me to know
    How this foul rout began, who set it on;
    And he that is approv'd in this offence,
    Though he had twinn'd with me, both at a birth,
    Shall lose me. What! in a town of war,
    Yet wild, the people's hearts brimful of fear,
    To manage private and domestic quarrel,
    In night, and on the court and guard of safety!
    'Tis monstrous. Iago, who began't?
MONTANO: If partially affin'd, or leagu'd in office,
    Thou dost deliver more or less than truth,
    Thou art no soldier.
IAGO: Touch me not so near:
    I had rather have this tongue cut from my mouth

Than it should do offence to Michael Cassio;
Yet, I persuade myself, to speak the truth
Shall nothing wrong him. Thus it is, general:
Montano and myself being in speech,
There comes a fellow crying out for help;
And Cassio following him with determin'd sword,
To execute upon him. Sir, this gentleman
Steps in to Cassio and entreats his pause;
Myself the crying fellow did pursue,
Lest by his clamour—as it so fell out—
The town might fall in fright. He, swift of foot,
Outran my purpose; and I return'd the rather
For that I heard the clink and fall of swords,
And Cassio high in oath; which till to-night
I ne'er might say before. When I came back—
For this was brief—I found them close together,
At blow and thrust; even as again they were
When you yourself did part them.
More of this matter cannot I report.
But men are men; the best sometimes forget.
Though Cassio did some little wrong to him,
As men in rage strike those that wish them best,
Yet surely Cassio, I believe, receiv'd
From him that fled some strange indignity
Which patience could not pass.

OTHELLO: I know, Iago,
Thy honesty and love doth mince this matter,
Making it light to Cassio. Cassio, I love thee;
But never more be officer of mine.

*Re-enter Desdemona, attended.*

Look, if my gentle love be not rais'd up!
I'll make thee an example.

DESDEMONA: What's the matter, dear?

OTHELLO: All's well now, sweeting; come away to bed.
Sir, for your hurts, myself will be your surgeon.—
Lead him off. [*To Montano, who is led off.*]
Iago, look with care about the town,
And silence those whom this vile brawl distracted.
Come, Desdemona; 'tis the soldiers' life
To have their balmy slumbers wak'd with strife.

[*Exeunt all but Iago and Cassio.*]

IAGO: What, are you hurt, lieutenant?

CASSIO: Ay, past all surgery.

IAGO: Marry, God forbid!

CASSIO: Reputation, reputation, reputation! O, I have lost my reputation! I have lost the immortal part of myself, and what remains is bestial. My reputation, Iago, my reputation!

IAGO: As I am an honest man, I thought you had received some bodily wound; there is more sense in that than in reputation. Reputation is an idle and most false imposition; oft got without Merit, and lost without deserving. You have lost no reputation at all, unless you repute yourself such a loser. What, man! there are ways to recover the general again. You are but now cast in his mood, a punishment more in policy than in malice; even so as one would beat his offenceless dog to affright an imperious lion. Sue to him again, and he's yours.

CASSIO: I will rather sue to be despis'd than to deceive so good a commander with so slight, so drunken, and so indiscreet an officer. Drunk? and speak parrot? and squabble? swagger? swear? and discourse fustian with one's own shadow?—O thou invisible spirit of wine, if thou hast no name to be known by, let us call thee devil!

IAGO: What was he that you follow'd with your sword? What had he done to you?

CASSIO: I know not.

IAGO: Is't possible?

CASSIO: I remember a mass of things, but nothing distinctly; a quarrel, but nothing wherefore. O God, that men should put an enemy in their mouths to steal away their brains! that we should, with joy, pleasance, revel, and applause, transform ourselves into beasts!

IAGO: Why, but you are now well enough: how came you thus recovered?

CASSIO: It hath pleas'd the devil drunkenness to give place to the devil wrath: one unperfectness shows me another, to make me frankly despise myself.

IAGO: Come, you are too severe a moraler. As the time, the place, and the condition of this country stands, I could heartily wish this had not befallen; but since it is as it is, mend it for your own good.

CASSIO: I will ask him for my place again; he shall tell me I am a drunkard! Had I as many mouths as Hydra, such an answer would stop them all. To be now a sensible man, by and by a fool, and presently a beast! O strange! Every inordinate cup is unbless'd, and the ingredient is a devil.

IAGO: Come, come, good wine is a good familiar creature, if it be well us'd: exclaim no more against it. And, good lieutenant, I think you think I love you.
CASSIO: I have well approved it, sir. I drunk!
IAGO: You, or any man living, may be drunk at a time, man. I'll tell you what you shall do. Our general's wife is now the general;—I may say so in this respect, for that he hath devoted and given up himself to the contemplation, mark, and denotement of her parts and graces;—confess yourself freely to her; importune her help to put you in your place again. She is of so free, so kind, so apt, so blessed a disposition, she holds it a vice in her goodness not to do more than she is requested. This broken joint between you and her husband entreat her to splinter; and, my fortunes against any lay worth naming, this crack of your love shall grow stronger than it was before.
CASSIO: You advise me well.
IAGO: I protest, in the sincerity of love and honest kindness.
CASSIO: I think it freely; and betimes in the morning I will beseech the virtuous Desdemona to undertake for me. I am desperate of my fortunes if they check me here.
IAGO: You are in the right. Good-night, lieutenant; I must to the watch.
CASSIO: Good-night, honest Iago.

*canakin clink: the clink of a small drinking can or cup; the later clink of swords in the passage plays on the notion of the clinking of drinking cups leading to the violent clinking of weapons.
†Almain: German
‡wight: archaic word for a creature or person
**horologe: clock
††twiggen bottle: a bottle encased in wicker or twigs
‡‡Ottomites: Ottomans (in the sense of Turks)

## *Robert Burns, "John Barleycorn" (1782)*

One of the most beloved of Scottish writers, Robert Burns (1759–1796) produced a large body of work dealing with nature, love, social commentary, and scenes that have become virtually synonymous with Scotland. In addition, many of his poems deal in some way, whether explicitly or implicitly with drinking, drunkenness, and specific beverages, especially whiskey. Considering this poetic output, and his own reputation as a prodigious drinker, it is appropriate that the archetypal song of bibulous celebration on New Year's Eve is Burns's "Auld Lang

*Syne.*" Showing the power of drink to delude the drinker in "Tam O'Shanter," Burns also celebrated drink's power to bring joy and comfort and fortitude in such poems as "Scotch Drink" and the selection reprinted below, "John Barleycorn." Originally published by Burns in 1782, "John Barleycorn," like many of Burns's other poems, derives from an even older folk song tradition that Burns transferred to the medium of written poetry—as was the case with "Auld Lang Syne." The personification of whiskey and beer as John Barleycorn long antedates Burns, and its origins are as disputed and mysterious as the liquid forms of John Barleycorn are numerous and varied. In the present poem, the resilient spirit of John Barleycorn survives all attempts to destroy it, leading the poet to pay tribute to the emboldening and heartening qualities he sees in the "blood"—i.e., the drink—of John Barleycorn.*

## "John Barleycorn"

There was three kings into the east,
Three kings both great and high,
And they hae sworn a solemn oath
John Barleycorn should die.

They took a plough and plough'd him down,
Put clods upon his head,
And they hae sworn a solemn oath
John Barleycorn was dead.

But the cheerful Spring came kindly on,
And show'rs began to fall;
John Barleycorn got up again,
And sore surpris'd them all.

The sultry suns of Summer came,
And he grew thick and strong;
His head weel arm'd wi' pointed spears,
That no one should him wrong.

The sober Autumn enter'd mild,
When he grew wan and pale;
His bending joints and drooping head
Show'd he began to fail.

His colour sicken'd more and more,
He faded into age;
And then his enemies began
To show their deadly rage.

They've taen a weapon, long and sharp,
And cut him by the knee;

Then tied him fast upon a cart,
Like a rogue for forgerie.

They laid him down upon his back,
And cudgell'd him full sore;
They hung him up before the storm,
And turn'd him o'er and o'er.

They laid him out upon the floor,
To work him further woe;
And still, as signs of life appear'd,
They toss'd him to and fro.

They wasted, o'er a scorching flame,
The marrow of his bones;
But a miller us'd him worst of all,
For he crush'd him between two stones.

And they hae taen his very heart's blood,
And drank it round and round;
And still the more and more they drank,
Their joy did more abound.

John Barleycorn was a hero bold,
Of noble enterprise;
For if you do but taste his blood,
'Twill make your courage rise.

'Twill make a man forget his woe;
'Twill heighten all his joy;
'Twill make the widow's heart to sing,
Tho' the tear were in her eye.

Then let us toast John Barleycorn,
Each man a glass in hand;
And may his great posterity
Ne'er fail in old Scotland!

# *Thomas Dekker and John Ford, "Cast Away Care" (1656)*

*A fitting companion to the Burns poem is Thomas Dekker's and John Ford's song, "Cast Away Care," from Act Four of the play that they both contributed to,*

## II. Effects of Drinking

The Sun's Darling *(1624). The text's origins as a song appear in the "etc" instruction for the chorus beginning with the words, "Merrily, merrily..." Some eight years younger than Shakespeare, Dekker (1572–1632) collaborated with a number of Renaissance playwrights, and though he garnered success on the stage in his lifetime, he is now among the less well-known writers of his period, studied largely as part of Renaissance literary history. John Ford (c. 1586–c.1640), like Dekker an active playwright of the period, is best known today for the dark play on incest entitled* 'Tis Pity She's a Whore. *Like Burns's poem, "Cast Away Care" presents courage and gladness as positive effects of drinking.*

### "CAST AWAY CARE"

Cast away care, he that loves sorrow,
    Lengthens not a day, nor can buy tomorrow:
Money is trash, and he that will spend it,
    let him drink merrily, Fortune will send it.
Merrily, Merrily, Merrily, *Oh ho.*
Play it off stiffly, we may not part so:
Merrily, &c.
Wine is a Charm, it heats the blood too;
    Cowards it will arm, if the wine be good, too;
    quickens the wit, and makes the back able;
    scorns to submit to the watch or Constable.
Merrily, &c.
Pots fly about, give us more Liquor;
Brothers of a rout, our brains will flow quicker;
    empty the Cask, score up, we care not,
    fill all the Pots again, drink on, and spare not,
Merrily, etc.

## *Daniel Defoe, from* Colonel Jack *(1722)*

*Best known for his classic novels,* Robinson Crusoe *and* Moll Flanders, *Daniel Defoe (1660–1731) was a prolific author of journalism and fiction, including the late novel,* Colonel Jack, *from which the passage below is taken. While drink appears regularly throughout Defoe's work,* Colonel Jack *stands out from Defoe's usual depictions of drink either as realistic social detail or as a vice of various dissolute characters;* Colonel Jack *presents a sympathetic portrayal of the* eponymous narrator's alcoholic wife, and emphasizes the influence that the encouragement of others can have on an individual's use of alcohol. Colonel Jack's wife, originally a light drinker, takes to more frequent potations as a remedy for a cold; furthermore, under the well-intentioned but misguided suggestions of a nurse, she increases drinking, as the text points out, "from a drop to a sup, from a sup to a dram, from a dram to a glass, and so on to two, till at last she took in short, to what we call drinking." The alcoholic addiction depicted here stems not from a conscious effort to attain drunkenness, or to alleviate depression, or to keep up with a group of drinking peers; rather, an insidious, almost invisible set of factors combine to lead, inexorably, to the condition that we currently label alcoholism.

Defoe's passage is also noteworthy in being the first literary representation of the notion of alcoholism as a progressive disease. While this concept of alcoholism is generally dated to the late eighteenth century, e.g., in Dr. Benjamin Rush's Inquiry into the Effects of Ardent Spirits *(1784)*, Defoe's novel unmistakably shows alcoholism as both a disease and as a progressive condition, coming upon his wife "gradually and insensibly."\* Considering the double standard for male and female drinking that has long been dominant in many cultures, including Defoe's own, the absence of any gender-specific condemnation of Colonel Jack's wife, and the sympathy and sorrow with which the text describes her descent into alcoholic addiction, are further distinguishing marks of this important example of the literary depiction of drink.

\*On the eighteenth-century origins of the disease concept of alcoholism, see Harry Gene Levine's still indispensable article, "The Discovery of Addiction: Changing Conceptions of Habitual Drunkenness in America," Journal of Studies on Alcohol 19 (1978), pp.143–174. Rush, a prominent Philadelphia physician, abolitionist, and signer of the Declaration of Independence, helped to popularize the notion of alcoholism as a disease with both physical and mental aspects in his Inquiry, which went through many subsequent printings after its initial publication in 1784. Eventually, however, the medical approach to alcoholism gave way to the increasingly moralistic approach of the most vocal partisans of the nineteenth-century temperance movement in both the U.S. and England. While the notion of alcoholism as a disease never disappeared, it was only through the work of E.M. Jellinek, e.g., his influential book, The Disease Concept of Alcoholism *(New Brunswick: Hillhouse Press, 1960)*, and other twentieth-century researchers that it gained the prominence that it holds today.

But I that was to be the most unhappy fellow alive in the article of matrimony, had at last a disappointment of the worst sort, even here; I had three fine children by her, and in her time of lying-in with the last, she got some cold, that she did not in a long time get off, and in short, she grew very sickly. In being so continually ill, and out of order, she very unhappily got a habit of drinking cordials and hot liquors. Drink, like the devil, when it gets hold of any one, though but a little, it goes on by little and little to their destruction; so in my wife, her stomach being weak and faint, she first took this cordial, then that, till in short she could not live without them, and from a drop to a sup, from a sup to a dram, from a dram to a glass, and so on to two, till at last she took in short, to what we call drinking.

As I likened drink to the devil, in its gradual possession of the habits and person, so it is yet more like the devil in its encroachment on us, where it gets hold of our senses; in short, my beautiful, good humoured modest, well-bred wife, grew a beast, a slave to strong liquor, and would be drunk at her own table, nay in her own closet by herself, till instead of a well made, fine shape, she was as fat as an hostess; her fine face bloated and blotched, had not so much as the ruins of the most beautiful person alive, nothing remained but a good eye, that indeed she held to the last. In short, she lost her beauty, her shape, her manners, and at last her virtue; and giving herself up to drinking, killed herself in about a year and half after she first began that cursed trade, in which time she twice was exposed in the most scandalous manner with a captain of a ship, who like a villain, took the advantage of her being in drink and not knowing what she did; but it had this unhappy effect, that instead of her being ashamed and repenting of it when she came to herself, it hardened her in the crime, and she grew as void of modesty at last as of sobriety.

O! the power of intemperance! and how it encroaches on the best dispositions in the world; how it comes upon us gradually and insensibly, and what dismal effects it works upon our morals, changing the most virtuous, regular, well-instructed, and well-inclined tempers into worse than brutal. That was a good story, whether real or invented, of the devil tempting a young man to murder his father; No, he said, that was unnatural. Why then, says the devil, go and lie with your mother. No, says he, that is abominable. Well then, says the devil, if you will do nothing else to oblige me, go and get drunk. Ay, ay, says the fellow, I will do that; so he went and made himself drunk as a swine, and when he was drunk he murdered his father, and lay with his mother.

Never was a woman more virtuous, modest, chaste, sober, she never so much as desired to drink anything strong; it was with the greatest entreaty that I could prevail with her to drink a glass or two of wine, and rarely, if ever, above one or two at a time; even in company she had no inclination to it. Not an immodest word ever came out of her mouth, nor would she suffer it in any one else in her hearing, without resentment and abhorrence; but upon that weakness and illness after her last lying-in as above, the nurse pressed her whenever she found herself faint and a sinking of her spirits, to take this cordial, and that dram, to keep up her spirits, till it became necessary even to keep her alive, and gradually increased to a habit, so that it was no longer her physic but her food. Her appetite sunk and went quite away, and she eat little or nothing, but came at last to such a dreadful height, that as I have said, she would be drunk in her own dressing-room by eleven o'clock in the morning, and, in short, at last was never sober.

*(The narrator goes on briefly to describe his wife's increasing illness and eventual death.)*

## *James Fenimore Cooper,* from The Pioneers *(1823)*

*Both Mark Twain and D.H. Lawrence got a good deal of mileage out of mocking James Fenimore Cooper's "literary offenses," as Twain called them, and it is easy enough to poke fun at Cooper's stiff circumlocutions, sentimentality, and often wooden dialogue.\* At the same time, Cooper has seized the imagination of readers both past and present through memorable characters, such as Chingachgook—"Last of the Mohicans"—and his companion, the white hunter Deerslayer (Natty Bumppo); through his ability to recreate the American colonial milieu; and through his affecting depictions of the tragic conflict between whites and Indians, vividly presented against the dramatic setting of a relatively untouched American wilderness. A prominent feature of American colonial life and of white relations to Indians is, of course, alcohol; not surprisingly, then, drink—its use, abuse, traditions, and varieties—is a theme appearing throughout Cooper's fiction. The present selection from one of Cooper's most successful novels,* The Pioneers, *is significant primarily not for illustrating intoxication's debilitating effects—though it certainly does that—but for uncovering the insidious process by which a seemingly benign, friendly social occasion can mask a slow, unintended but nonetheless deadly form of murder.*

*The scene takes place on Christmas Eve, 1793, and the setting is the Bold Dragoon Tavern in the central part of New York state. Here a small group of celebrants, including Natty Bumppo and his friend, Chingachgook, sit in the warm, smoky, fireplace-heated room. In this atmosphere of supposed conviviality and celebration, Chingachgook is steadily plied with liquor; given Chingachgook's obvious and well-known susceptibility to alcohol, the actions of the tavern's hostess and, especially, the bluff and drunken Richard, a prominent white man in the community, take on a sinister twist. The superficially egalitarian, misdirected generosity of Richard, as he cheerfully thrusts drink after drink upon the already stupefied Chingachgook, conduces merely to an even more inexorable entwining of the sodden Mohican in the coils of addiction. As Natty's comment in this revealing passage* about the way "savages" always drink suggests, Cooper has in mind not only a single person's unfortunate descent into alcoholism, but the broader sweep of alcohol through Native American peoples. The passage is thus reminiscent of Benjamin Franklin's earlier statement that, "indeed, if it be the design of Providence to extirpate these savages in order to make room for the cultivators of the earth, it seems not improbably that rum may be the appointed means."† This notion of alcohol as a scourge of an entire race, indeed, as a genocidal tool, appears in the famous speech of the Seneca chief Red Jacket, in which he declared, in 1805, "your forefathers crossed the great waters, and landed on this island. Their numbers were small; they found friends, and not enemies; they told us they had fled from their own country for fear of wicked men, and come here to enjoy their religion. They asked for a small seat; we took pity on them, granted their request, and they sat down amongst us; we gave them corn and meat; they gave us poison [i.e., liquor] in return."‡ (Chingachgook himself, in a later passage from The Pioneers, makes a similar point when he calls rum the "tomahawk" with which whites are destroying the Indian way of life.)

*For Twain's over-the-top critique of Cooper, see "The Literary Offenses of Fenimore Cooper" (originally published in 1895) at http://xroads.virginia.edu/~HYPER/HNS/Indians/offense.html. Lawrence's estimate of Cooper appears in his Studies in Classic American Literature (New York: Thomas Seltzer, 1923, and frequently reprinted since then).

†John Bigelow, ed., The Works of Benjamin Franklin (New York: G.P. Putnam's Sons, 1904), vol. 1, p. 244.

‡For Red Jacket's speech, see Alan R. Velie, ed., American Indian Literature (Norman: University of Oklahoma Press, 1979), p. 56.

> "There's quart-pot, pint-pot. Mit-pint,
> Gill-pot, half-gill. nipperkin.
> And the brown bowl- Here's a health to the barley mow,
> My brave boys, Here's a health to the barley mow."—Drinking Song.

Some little commotion was produced by the appearance of the new guests, during which the lawyer slunk from the room. Most of the men approached Marmaduke, and shook his offered hand, hoping "that the Judge was well," while Major Hartmann, having laid aside his hat and wig, and substituted for the latter a warm, peaked woollen nightcap, took his seat very quietly on one end of the settee, which was relinquished by its former occupants. His tobacco-box was next produced, and a clean pipe was handed him by the landlord. When he had succeeded in raising a smoke, the Major gave a long whiff, and, turning his head toward the bar, he said,—

"Petty, pring in ter toddy."

*(Omitted is a portion of the chapter containing a political conversation involving a French guest.)*

The Frenchman continued to move about the room with great alacrity for a few minutes, repeating his exclamations to himself; when overcome by the contrary nature of his emotions, he suddenly burst out of the house, and was seen wading through the snow toward his little shop, waving his arms on high, as if to pluck down honor from the moon.

His departure excited but little surprise, for the villagers were used to his manner; but Major Hartmann laughed outright, for the first during his visit, as he lifted the mug, and observed:

"Ter Frenchman is mat—put he is goot as for noting to trink: he is trunk mit joy."

"The French are good soldiers," said Captain Hollister; "they stood us in hand a good turn at Yorktown; nor do I think, although I am an ignorant man about the great movements of the army, that his excellency would have been able to march against Cornwallis without their reinforcements."

"Ye spake the trut', sargeant," interrupted his wife, "and I would iver have ye be doing the same. It's varry pratty men is the French; and jist when I stopt the cart, the time when ye was pushing on in front it was, to kape the rig'lers in, a rigiment of the jontlemen marched by, and so I dealt them out to their liking. Was it pay I got? Sure did I, and in good solid crowns; the divil a bit of continental could they muster among them all, for love nor money. Och! the Lord forgive me for swearing and sp'aking of such vanities; but this I will say for the French, that they paid in good silver; and one glass would go a great way wid 'em, for they gin'rally handed it back wid a drop in the cup; and that's a brisk trade, Jooge, where the pay is good, and the men not over-partic'lar."

"A thriving trade, Mrs. Hollister," said Marmaduke. "But what has become of Richard? he jumped up as soon as seated, and has been absent so long that I am really fearful he has frozen."

"No fear of that, Cousin 'Duke," cried the gentleman himself; "business will sometimes keep a man warm the coldest night that ever snapt in the mountains. Betty, your husband told me, as we came out of church, that your hogs were getting mangy, and so I have been out to take a look at them, and found it true. I stepped across, doctor, and got your boy to weigh me out a pound of salts, and have been mixing it with their swill. I'll bet a saddle of venison against a gray squirrel that they are better in a week. And now, Mrs. Hollister, I'm ready for a hissing mug of flip."

"Sure I know'd ye'd be wanting that same," said the landlady; "it's mixt and ready to the boiling. Sargeant, dear, be handing up the iron, will ye?—no, the one on the far fire; it's black, ye will see. Ah! you've the thing now; look if it's not as red as a cherry."

The beverage was heated, and Richard took that kind of draught which men are apt to indulge in who think that they have just executed a clever thing, especially when they like the liquor.

"O! you have a hand, Betty, that was formed to mix flip," cried Richard, when he paused for breath. "The very iron has a flavor in it. Here, John, drink, man, drink! I and you and Dr. Todd have done a good thing with the shoulder of that lad this very night. 'Duke, I made a song while you were gone-one day when I had nothing to do; so I'll sing you a verse or two, though I haven't really determined on the tune yet.

"What is life but a scene of care,
Where each one must toil in his way?
Then let us be jolly, and prove that we are
A set of good fellows, who seem very rare,
And can laugh and sing all the day.
Then let us be jolly,
And cast away folly,
For grief turns a black head to gray."

"There, 'Duke, what do you think of that? There is another verse of it, all but the last line. I haven't got a rhyme for the last line yet. Well, old John, what do you think of the music? as good as one of your war-songs, ha?"

"Good!" said Mohegan, who had been sharing deeply in the potations of the landlady, besides paying a proper respect to the passing mugs of the Major and Marmaduke.

"Pravo! pravo! Richart," cried the Major, whose black eyes were beginning to swim in moisture; "pravissimo it is a goot song; put Natty Pumppo has a petter. Letter-Stockint, vilt sing? say, olt poy, vilt sing ter song as apout ter woots?"

"No, no, Major," returned the hunter, with a melancholy shake of the head, "I have lived to see what I thought eyes could never behold in these hills, and I have no heart left for singing. If he that has a right to be master and ruler here is forced to squinch his thirst, when a-dry, with snow-water, it ill becomes them that have lived by his bounty to be making merry, as if there was nothing in the world but sunshine and summer."

When he had spoken, Leather-Stocking again dropped his head on his knees, and concealed his hard and wrinkled features with his hands. The change from the excessive cold without to the heat of the bar-room, coupled with the depth and frequency of Richard's draughts, had already leveled whatever inequality there might have existed between him and the other guests, on the score of spirits; and he now held out a pair of swimming mugs of foaming flip toward the hunter, as he cried:

"Merry! ay! Merry Christmas to you, old boy! Sunshine and summer! no! you are blind, Leather-Stocking, 'tis moonshine and winter; take these spectacles, and open your eyes,—

So let us be jolly,
And cast away folly,
For grief turns a black head to gray."

"Hear how old John turns his quavers. What damned dull music an Indian song is, after all, Major! I wonder if they ever sing by note."

While Richard was singing and talking, Mohegan was uttering dull, monotonous tones, keeping time by a gentle motion of his head and body. He made use of but few words, and such as he did utter were in his native language, and consequently only understood by himself and Natty. Without heeding Richard, he continued to sing a kind of wild, melancholy air, that rose, at times, in sudden and quite elevated notes, and then fell again into the low, quavering sounds that seemed to compose the character of his music.

The attention of the company was now much divided, the men in the rear having formed themselves into little groups, where they were discussing various matters; among the principal of which were the treatment of mangy hogs and Parson Grant's preaching; while Dr. Todd was endeavoring to explain to Marmaduke the nature of the hurt received by the young hunter. Mohegan continued to sing, while his countenance was becoming vacant, though, coupled with his thick, bushy hair, it was assuming an expression very much like brutal ferocity. His notes were gradually growing louder, and soon rose to a height that caused a general cessation in the discourse. The hunter now raised his head again, and addressed the old warrior warmly in the Delaware language, which, for the benefit of our readers, we shall render freely into English.

"Why do you sing of your battles, Chingachgook, and of the warriors you have slain, when the worst enemy of all is near you, and keeps the Young Eagle from his rights? I have fought in as many battles as any warrior in your tribe, but cannot boast of my deeds at such a time as this."

"Hawkeye," said the Indian, tottering with a doubtful step from his place, "I am the Great Snake of the Delawares; I can track the Mingos like an adder that is stealing on the whip-poor-will's eggs, and strike them like the rattlesnake, dead at a blow. The white man made the tomahawk of Chingachgook bright as the waters of Otsego, when the last sun is shining; but it is red with the blood of the Maquas."

"And why have you slain the Mingo warriors? Was it not to keep these hunting-grounds and lakes to your father's children? and were they not given in solemn council to the Fire-eater? and does not the blood of a warrior run in the veins of a young chief, who should speak aloud where his voice is now too low to be heard?"

The appeal of the hunter seemed in some measure to recall the confused faculties of the Indian, who turned his face toward the listeners and gazed intently on the Judge. He shook his head, throwing his hair back from his countenance, and exposed eyes that were glaring with an expression of wild resentment. But the man was not himself. His hand seemed to make a fruitless effort to release his tomahawk, which was confined by its handle to his belt, while his eyes gradually became vacant. Richard at that instant thrusting a mug before him, his features changed to the grin of idiocy, and seizing the vessel with both hands, he sank backward on the bench and drank until satiated, when he made an effort to lay aside the mug with the helplessness of total inebriety.

"Shed not blood!" exclaimed the hunter, as he watched the countenance of the Indian in its moment of ferocity, "but he is drunk and can do no harm. This is the way with all the savages; give them liquor, and they make dogs of themselves. Well, well, the time will come when right will be done; and we must have patience."

Natty still spoke in the Delaware language, and of course was not understood. He had hardly concluded before Richard cried,—

"Well, old John is soon sewed up. Give him a berth, captain, in the barn, and I will pay for it. I am rich to-night, ten times richer than 'Duke, with all his lands, amid military lots, and funded debts, and bonds, and mortgages.

"Come, let us be jolly,
And cast away folly,
For grief—

Drink, King Hiram—drink, Mr. Doo-nothing—drink, sir, I say. This is a Christmas Eve, which comes, you know, but once a year."

"He! he! he! the Squire is quite moosical to-night," said Hiram, whose visage began to give marvelous signs of relaxation. "I rather guess we shall make a church on't yet, squire?"

"A church, Mr. Doolittle! we will make a cathedral of it! bishops, priests, deacons, wardens, vestry, and choir; organ, organist, amid bellows! By the Lord Harry, as Benjamin says, we will clap a steeple on the other end of it, and make two churches of it. What say you, "Duke, will you pay? ha! my cousin Judge, wilt pay?"

"Thou makest such a noise, Dickon," returned Marmaduke, "it is impossible that I can hear what Dr. Todd is saying,—I think thou observedst, it is probable the wound will fester, so as to occasion danger to the limb in this cold weather?"

"Out of natur', sir, quite out of natur'," said Elnathan, attempting to expectorate, but succeeding only in throwing a light, frothy substance, like a flake of snow, into the fire, "quite out of natur' that a wound so well dressed, and with the ball in my pocket, should fester. I s'pose, as the Judge talks of taking the young man into his house, it will be most convenient if I make but one charge on't."

"I should think one would do," returned Marmaduke, with that arch smile that so often beamed on his face; leaving the beholder in doubt whether he most enjoyed the character of his companion or his own covert humor. The landlord had succeeded in placing the. Indian on some straw in one of his outbuildings, where, covered with his own blanket, John continued for the remainder of the night.

In the mean time, Major Hartmann began to grow noisy and jocular; glass succeeded glass, and mug after mug was introduced, until the carousal had run deep into the night, or rather morning; when the veteran German expressed an inclination to return to the Mansion-house. Most of the party had already retired, but Marmaduke knew the habits of his friend too well to suggest an earlier adjournment. So soon, however, as the proposal was made, the Judge eagerly availed himself of it, and the trio prepared to depart. Mrs. Hollister attended them to the door in person, cautioning her guests as to the safest manner of leaving her premises

"Lane on Mister Jones, Major," said she "he's young, and will be a support to ye. Well, it's a charming sight to see ye, anyway, at the Bould Dragoon; and sure it's no harm to be kaping a Christmas Eve wid a light heart, for it's no telling when we may have sorrow come upon us. So good-night, Jooge, and a Merry Christmas to ye all, tomorrow morning."

The gentlemen made their adieus as well as they could, and taking the middle of the road, which was a fine, wide, and well-beaten path, they did tolerably well until they reached the gate of the mansion-house: but on entering the Judge's domains they encountered some slight difficulties. We shall not stop to relate them, but will just mention that in the morning sundry diverging paths were to be seen in the snow; and that once during their progress to the door, Marmaduke, missing his companions, was enabled to trace them by one of these paths to a spot where he discovered them with nothing visible but their heads; Richard singing in a most vivacious strain,—

"Come, let us be jolly,
And cast away folly,
For grief turns a black head to gray."

## *Charles Dickens, from* David Copperfield *(1849–50)*

*Dickens's depictions of drink were far from monochromatic. In "Gin-Shops," reprinted in the "Tavern" section of this anthology, Dickens (1812–1870) delves*

*into the dark side of drink, condemning the viciously cyclical relation of drink and poverty in Victorian England. In contrast, Dickens's first novel,* The Pickwick Papers, *treats drink with sympathy and humor, emphasizing the frivolity, good nature, and essential innocence of its bumbling, often tipsy characters. The following passage, from "My First Dissipation," chapter 24 of one of Dickens' most celebrated works,* David Copperfield, *blends an amusing account of the ludicrous effects of drink with more sinister touches—the miserable hangover of the inexperienced David, and the deceptive nature of friendship fomented by liquor; after all, David's boon companion, Steerforth—who indeed "steers" David at this point in the story—turns out to be a false friend, selfish and treacherous. Moreover, while we laugh at David's deadpan description of drink's effects, e.g., his increasingly bombastic speechifying, slurred speech, sentimentality, and exaggerated clumsiness, we cannot help but note the spuriousness of "friendship" between David and his guests; we are also obliquely directed by Dickens himself to recall the fate of the previous occupant of David Copperfield's apartment: death from alcoholism.*

*In a famous essay, "Some Remarks on Humor," E.B. White noted the potential of comic writing to convey a substantial, even disturbingly substantial, point: "there is often a rather fine line between laughing and crying, and if a humorous piece of writing brings a person to the point where his emotional responses are untrustworthy and seem likely to break over into the opposite realm, it is because humor, like poetry, has an extra content. It plays close to the big hot fire which is Truth, and sometimes the reader feels the heat" (E.B. White,* Essays of E.B. White, *New York: Harper & Row, 1977, p. 244). Amusing as it is in language and in its literary rendering of drunken pratfalls, "My First Dissipation" uses its humor to suggest the ways that misuse of drink can in turn become part of a larger pattern of failing to recognize ourselves, and of mistaking counterfeit feelings and counterfeit people for the genuine article.*

*The passage below begins at that point in the chapter where David Copperfield, having arranged to host a dinner party, surveys the wine bottles that stand waiting for his guests. (The text's reference to David as "Trotwood" reflects the nickname given him by his aunt, Betsey Trotwood.)*

Being a little embarrassed at first, and feeling much too young to preside, I made Steerforth take the head of the table when dinner was announced, and seated myself opposite to him. Everything was very good; we did not spare the wine; and he exerted himself so brilliantly to make the thing pass off well, that there was no pause in our festivity. I was not quite such good company during dinner as I could have wished to be, for my chair was opposite the door, and my attention was distracted by observing that the handy young man went out of the room very often, and that his shadow always presented itself, immediately afterwards, on the wall of the entry, with a bottle at its mouth. The "young gal" likewise occasioned me some uneasiness; not so much by neglecting to wash the plates, as by breaking them. For being of an inquisitive disposition, and unable to confine herself (as her positive instructions were) to the pantry, she was constantly peering in at us, and constantly imagining herself detected; in which belief, she several times retired upon the plates (with which she had carefully paved the floor), and did a great deal of destruction.

These, however, were small drawbacks, and easily forgotten when the cloth was cleared, and the dessert put on the table; at which period of the entertainment the handy young man was discovered to be speechless. Giving him private directions to seek the society of Mrs. Crupp, and to remove the "young gal" to the basement also, I abandoned myself to enjoyment.

I began, by being singularly cheerful and light-hearted; all sorts of half-forgotten things to talk about, came rushing into my mind, and made me hold forth in a most unwonted manner. I laughed heartily at my own jokes, and everybody else's; called Steerforth to order for not passing the wine; made several engagements to go to Oxford; announced that I meant to have a dinner-party exactly like that, once a week, until further notice; and madly took so much snuff out of Grainger's box, that I was obliged to go into the pantry, and have a private fit of sneezing ten minutes long.

I went on, by passing the wine faster and faster yet, and continually starting up with a corkscrew to open more wine, long before any was needed. I proposed Steerforth's health. I said he was my dearest friend, the protector of my boyhood, and the companion of my prime. I said I was delighted to propose his health. I said I owed him more obligations than I could ever repay, and held him in a higher admiration than I could ever express. I finished by saying, "I'll give you Steerforth! God bless him! Hurrah!" We gave him three times three, and another, and a good one to finish with. I broke my glass in going round the table to shake hands with him, and I said (in two words) "Steerforth—you'retheguidingstarofmyexistence."

I went on, by finding suddenly that somebody was in the middle of a song. Markham was the singer, and he sang "When the heart of a man is depressed with care." He said, when he had sung it, he would give us "Woman!" I took objection to that, and I couldn't allow it. I said it was not a respectful way of proposing the toast, and I would never permit that toast to be drunk in my house otherwise than as "The Ladies!" I was very high with him, mainly I think because I saw Steerforth and Grainger laughing at me—or at him—or at both of us. He said a man was not to be dictated to. I said a man *was*. He said a man was not to be insulted, then. I said he was right there— never under my roof, where the Lares were sacred, and the laws of hospitality paramount. He said it was no derogation from a man's dignity to confess that I was a devilish good fellow. I instantly proposed his health.

Somebody was smoking. We were all smoking. *I* was smoking, and trying to suppress a rising tendency to shudder. Steerforth had made a speech about me, in the course of which I had been affected almost to tears. I returned thanks, and hoped the present company would dine with me tomorrow, and the day after—each day at five o'clock, that we might enjoy the pleasures of conversation and society through a long evening. I felt called upon to propose an individual. I would give them my aunt. Miss Betsey Trotwood, the best of her sex!

Somebody was leaning out of my bedroom window, refreshing his forehead against the cool stone of the parapet, and feeling the air upon his face. It was myself. I was addressing myself as "Copperfield," and saying, "Why did you try to smoke? You might have known you couldn't do it." Now, somebody was unsteadily contemplating his features in the looking-glass. That was I too. I was very pale in the looking-glass; my eyes had a vacant appearance; and my hair—only my hair, nothing else—looked drunk.

Somebody said to me, "Let us go to the theatre, Copperfield!" There was no bedroom before me, but again the jingling table covered with glasses; the lamp; Grainger on my right hand, Markham on my left, and Steerforth opposite—all sitting in a mist, and a long way off. The theatre! To be sure. The very thing. Come along! But they must excuse me if I saw everybody out first, and turned the lamp off—in case of fire.

Owing to some confusion in the dark, the door was gone. I was feeling for it in the window-curtains, when Steerforth, laughing, took me by the arm and led me out. We went down-stairs, one behind another. Near the bottom, somebody fell, and rolled down. Somebody else said it was Copperfield. I was angry at that false report, until, finding myself on my back in the passage, I began to think there might be some foundation for it.

A very foggy night, with great rings round the lamps in the streets! There was an indistinct talk of its being wet. *I* considered it frosty. Steerforth dusted me under a lamp-post, and put my hat into shape, which somebody produced from somewhere in a most extraordinary manner, for I hadn't had it on before. Steerforth then said, "You are all right, Copperfield, are you not?" and I told him, "Neverberrer."

A man, sitting in a pigeon-hole place, looked out of the fog, and took money from somebody, inquiring if I was one of the gentlemen paid for, and appearing rather doubtful (as I remember in the glimpse I had of him) whether to take the money for me or not. Shortly afterwards, we were very high up in a very hot theatre, looking down into a large pit, that seemed to me to smoke; the people with whom it was crammed were so indistinct. There was a great stage, too, looking very clean and smooth after the streets; and there were people upon it, talking about something or other, but not at all intelligibly. There was an abundance of bright lights, and there was music, and there were ladies down in the boxes, and I don't know what more. The whole building looked to me as if it were learning to swim; it conducted itself in such an unaccountable manner, when I tried to steady it.

On somebody's motion, we resolved to go down-stairs to the dress-boxes, where the ladies were. A gentleman lounging, full dressed, on a sofa, with an opera-glass in his hand, passed before my view, and also my own figure at full length in a glass. Then I was being ushered into one of these boxes, and found myself saying something as I sat down, and people about me crying "Silence!" to somebody, and ladies casting indignant glances at me, and—what! yes!—Agnes, sitting on the seat before me, in the same box, with a lady and gentleman beside her, whom I didn't know. I see her face now, better than I did then, I dare say, with its indelible look of regret and wonder turned upon me.

"Agnes!" I said, thickly, "Lorblessmer! Agnes!"

"Hush! Pray!" she answered, I could not conceive why. "You disturb the company. Look at the stage!"

I tried, on her injunction, to fix it, and to hear something of what was going on there, but quite in vain. I looked at her again by and by, and saw her shrink into her corner, and put her gloved hand to her forehead.

"Agnes!" I said. "I'mafraidyou'renorwell."

"Yes, yes. Do not mind me, Trotwood," she returned. "Listen! Are you going away soon?"

"Amigoarawaysoo?" I repeated.

"Yes."

I had a stupid intention of replying that I was going to wait, to hand her down-stairs. I suppose I expressed it, somehow; for after she had looked at me attentively for a little while, she appeared to understand, and replied in a low tone:

"I know you will do as I ask you, if I tell you I am very earnest in it. Go away now, Trotwood, for my sake, and ask your friends to take you home."

She had so far improved me, for the time, that though I was angry with her, I felt ashamed, and with a short "Goori!" (which I intended for "Good night!") got up and went away. They followed, and I stepped at once out of the box-door into my bedroom, where only Steerforth was with me, helping me to undress, and where I was by turns telling him that Agnes was my sister, and adjuring him to bring the corkscrew, that I might open another bottle of wine.

How somebody, lying in my bed, lay saying and doing all this over again, at cross purposes, in a feverish dream all night—the bed a rocking sea that was never still! How, as that somebody slowly settled down into myself, did I begin to parch, and feel as if my outer covering of skin were a hard board; my tongue the bottom of an empty kettle, furred with long service, and burning up over a slow fire; the palms of my hands, hot plates of metal which no ice could cool!

But the agony of mind, the remorse, and shame I felt, when I became conscious next day! My horror of having committed a thousand offences I had forgotten, and which nothing could ever expiate—my recollection of that indelible look which Agnes had given me—the torturing impossibility of communicating with her, not knowing, Beast that I was, how she came to be in London, or where she stayed—my disgust of the very sight of the room where the revel had been held—my racking head—the smell of smoke, the sight of glasses, the impossibility of going out, or even getting up! Oh, what a day it was!

Oh, what an evening, when I sat down by my fire to a basin of mutton broth, dimpled all over with fat, and thought I was going the way of my predecessor, and should succeed to his dismal story as well as to his chambers, and had half a mind to rush express to Dover and reveal all! What an evening, when Mrs. Crupp, coming in to take away the broth-basin, produced one kidney on a cheese-plate as the entire remains of yesterday's feast, and I was really inclined to fall upon her nankeen breast, and say, in heartfelt penitence, "Oh, Mrs. Crupp, Mrs. Crupp, never mind the broken meats! I am very miserable!"—only that I doubted, even at that pass, if Mrs. Crupp were quite the sort of woman to confide in!

## *Herman Melville, from* Moby-Dick *(1851)*

*The present excerpt—a single short chapter ("The Blacksmith," chapter CXII) from Melville's most famous novel—constitutes a temperance tale in miniature, following the standard American temperance template of a happy, fully employed family man whose fortunes disappear before alcohol's inexorable power. (This narrative structure appears not only in countless temperance texts, but in popular works of visual art as well, such as the didactic temperance prints of Currier and Ives.) In "The Blacksmith," Melville (1819–1891) specifically employs what David S. Reynolds calls the "dark temperance" mode, marked by sensationalistic detail and an emphasis on the horrors of drink, as opposed to the lighter temperance mode that stresses the benefits of sobriety.\* Drink occupied a good deal of Melville's atten-*

tion, both in his art and his life. *His famous literary friendship with Nathaniel Hawthorne, commemorated in Melville's lyrical letters to his fellow author, entailed considerable convivial drinking and reference to such drinking in Melville's letters; a charming example of this occurs where Melville assures Hawthorne that "I won't believe in a temperance heaven," and goes on to imagine the two writers clinking glasses in a mellow hereafter.† Similarly, drinking as a sign of relaxation and good fellowship permeates Melville's prose, e.g., in the South Seas novel* Omoo *and in the extravagantly imaginative, extravagantly long novel,* Mardi, *and in a number of his poems. Drink appears as well numerous times in* Moby-Dick, *as one might expect of a book set on an American whaling ship of the mid nineteenth century.*

*Throughout his work, Melville experiments with the various discourses of drinking and temperance that co-existed and, at times, clashed in the United States of his time—e.g., the discourse of gentlemanly connoisseurship found in* The Confidence Man, *of easy camaraderie on shipboard found in various sections of* Moby-Dick, *of the symbolic association of drink with a solemn bond between the drinkers, as in Captain Ahab's insistence that his harpooners drink with him in a kind of parodic inversion of holy communion, when, quaffing liquor out of the caps of their harpoons, they swear to kill the white whale. In the present selection, Melville presents drink as a source of familial disintegration and loss of employment, major concerns in temperance narratives of his time. The notion of drink as a burglar stealing into the blacksmith's home, found in this passage, parallels not only temperance writing* per se, *but mainstream American fiction's tendency to personify or trope drink in threatening terms; in James Fenimore Cooper's novel* The Oak-Openings, *for instance, drink appears as an "enemy" of the drinker, and in Hawthorne's short story, "Daniel Swan," drink is figuratively described as a lethal weapon—a pistol. At the conclusion of Melville's passage here, drink points the way toward death, with the ironic twist that, having nothing but death to look forward to, the blacksmith, Perth, "went a-whaling," ending up on Captain Ahab's ship of death,* The Pequod.

*\*In Reynolds' view, Melville both relies on and subverts the traditional "dark-reform" mode by using that mode as a way of expressing a deeper, more somber view of humanity in general, and as a source of the "mythic imagery" that is so important in Melville's work. The argument is developed at length in David S. Reynolds,* Beneath the American Renaissance: The Subversive Imagination in the Age of Emerson and Melville *(New York: Alfred A. Knopf, 1988).*

*†From a letter to Hawthorne in 1851; see Harrison Hayford et al., eds.,* The Writings of Herman Melville *(Evanston and Chicago: Northwestern University Press and Newberry Library, 1968–), vol. 14, p. 191.*

Availing himself of the mild, summer-cool weather that now reigned in these latitudes, and in preparation for the peculiarly active pursuits shortly to be anticipated, Perth, the begrimed, blistered old blacksmith, had not removed his portable forge to the hold again, after concluding his contributory work for Ahab's leg, but still retained it on deck, fast lashed to ringbolts by the foremast; being now almost incessantly invoked by the headsmen, and harpooners, and bowsmen to do some little job for them; altering, or repairing, or new shaping their various weapons and boat furniture. Often he would be surrounded by an eager circle, all waiting to be served; holding boat-spades, pike-heads, harpoons, and lances, and jealously watching his every sooty movement, as he toiled. Nevertheless, this old man's was a patient hammer wielded by a patient arm. No murmur, no impatience, no petulence did come from him. Silent, slow, and solemn; bowing over still further his chronically broken back, he toiled away, as if toil were life itself, and the heavy beating of his hammer the heavy beating of his heart. And so it was.—Most miserable!

A peculiar walk in this old man, a certain slight but painful appearing yawing in his gait, had at an early period of the voyage excited the curiosity of the mariners. And to the importunity of their persisted questionings he had finally given in; and so it came to pass that every one now knew the shameful story of his wretched fate.

Belated, and not innocently, one bitter winter's midnight, on the road running between two country towns, the blacksmith half-stupidly felt the deadly numbness stealing over him, and sought refuge in a leaning, dilapidated barn. The issue was, the loss of the extremities of both feet. Out of this revelation, part by part, at last came out the four acts of the gladness, and the one long, and as yet uncatastrophied fifth act of the grief of his life's drama.

He was an old man, who, at the age of nearly sixty, had postponedly encountered that thing in sorrow's technicals called ruin. He had been an artisan of famed excellence, and with plenty to do; owned a house and garden; embraced a youthful, daughter-like, loving wife, and three blithe, ruddy children; every Sunday went to a cheerful-looking church, planted in a grove. But one night, under cover of darkness, and further concealed in a most cunning disguisement, a desperate burglar slid into his happy home, and robbed them all of everything. And darker yet to tell, the blacksmith himself did ignorantly conduct this burglar into his family's heart. It was the Bottle Conjuror! Upon the opening of that fatal cork, forth flew the fiend, and shriveled up his home. Now, for prudent, most wise, and economic reasons, the blacksmith's shop was in the basement of his dwelling, but with a separate entrance to it; so that always had the young and loving healthy wife listened with no unhappy nervousness, but with vigorous pleasure, to the stout ringing of her young-armed old husband's hammer; whose reverberations, muffled by passing through the floors and walls, came up to her, not unsweetly, in her nursery; and so, to stout Labor's iron lullaby, the blacksmith's infants were rocked to slumber.

Oh, woe on woe! Oh, Death, why canst thou not sometimes be timely? Hadst thou taken this old blacksmith to thyself ere his full ruin came upon him, then had the young widow had a delicious grief, and her orphans a truly venerable, legendary sire to dream of in their after years; and all of them a care-killing competency. But Death plucked down some virtuous elder brother, on whose whistling daily toil solely hung the responsibilities of some other family, and left the worse than useless old man standing, till the hideous rot of life should make him easier to harvest.

Why tell the whole? The blows of the basement hammer every day grew more and more between; and each blow every day grew fainter than the last; the wife sat frozen at the window, with tearless eyes, glitteringly gazing into the weeping faces of her children; the bellows fell; the forge choked up with cinders; the house was sold; the mother dived down into the long church-yard grass; her children twice followed her thither; and the houseless, familyless old man staggered off a vagabond in crape; his every woe unreverenced; his grey head a scorn to flaxen curls!

Death seems the only desirable sequel for a career like this; but Death is only a launching into the region of the strange Untried; it is but the first salutation to the possibilities of the immense Remote, the Wild, the Watery, the Unshored; therefore, to the death-longing eyes of such men, who still have left in them some interior compunctions against suicide, does the all-contributed and all-receptive ocean alluringly spread forth his whole plain of unimaginable, taking terrors, and wonderful, new-life adventures; and from the hearts of infinite Pacifics, the thousand mermaids sing to them—"Come hither, broken-hearted; here is another life without the guilt of intermediate death; here are wonders supernatural, without dying for them. Come hither! bury thyself in a life which, to your now equally abhorred and abhorring, landed world, is more oblivious than death. Come hither! put up *thy* gravestone, too, within the churchyard, and come hither, till we marry thee!"

Hearkening to these voices, East and West, by early sun-rise, and by fall of eve, the blacksmith's soul responded, Aye, I come! And so Perth went a-whaling.

## *Mark Twain, "Edward Mills and George Benton" (1880)*

*A staple of Mark Twain's writing is his treatment of alcohol in numerous anecdotes, stories, and novels. And a favorite target of Twain's satire was the ever-*

*growing temperance movement. Born in 1835, Twain grew to manhood in a period when temperance, particularly in its strictly abstinent version, gained power in the United States, as evidenced in the Maine Laws of the 1850s, the establishment of the Women's Christian Temperance Union in 1873, and of the Anti-Saloon League in 1893. When he died in 1910, Twain missed by only a decade the enactment of Prohibition—a legal and cultural institution that would, doubtless, have provoked yet more ink to flow from his sardonic pen. In the short story reprinted here, Twain turns temperance activities to comic effect as he describes, with mock solemnity, the selfish manipulativeness of one of his do-gooder characters, and satirizes the blend of sanctimoniousness and naiveté on the part of social reformers in general. The tale also burlesques the dire effects of drink portrayed in the temperance literature so popular in Twain's day, and inverts the kind of didacticism familiar in, for example, William Hogarth's series of engravings,* Industry and Idleness, *which relied on the contrast between virtuous and profligate individuals.\* Twain's story, moreover, hilariously shows the supposed victim of drink using his misdeeds to exploit the very society that condemns his inebriety.*

\**For an informative account of the temperance theme's prevalence in nineteenth-century American writing, see John W. Frick and Don B. Wilmeth,* Theatre, Culture and Temperance Reform in Nineteenth-Century America *(Cambridge: Cambridge University Press, 2003), p. 18.*

These two were distantly related to each other—seventh cousins, or something of that sort. While still babies they became orphans, and were adopted by the Brants, a childless couple, who quickly grew very fond of them. The Brants were always saying: "Be pure, honest, sober, industrious, and considerate of others, and success in life is assured." The children heard this repeated some thousands of times before they understood it; they could repeat it themselves long before they could say the Lord's Prayer; it was painted over the nursery door, and was about the first thing they learned to read. It was destined to be the unswerving rule of Edward Mills's life. Sometimes the Brants changed the wording a little, and said: "Be pure, honest, sober, industrious, considerate, and you will never lack friends."

Baby Mills was a comfort to everybody about him. When he wanted candy and could not have it, he listened to reason, and contented himself without it. When Baby Benton wanted candy, he cried for it until he got it. Baby Mills took care of his toys; Baby Benton always destroyed his in a very brief time, and then made himself to insistently disagreeable that, in order to have peace in the house, little Edward was persuaded to yield up his play-things to him.

When the children were a little older, Georgie became a heavy expense in one respect: he took no care of his clothes; consequently, he shone frequently in new ones, with was not the case with Eddie. The boys grew apace. Eddie was an increasing comfort, Georgie an increasing solicitude. It was always sufficient to say, in answer to Eddie's petitions, "I would rather you would not do it"—meaning swimming, skating, picnicking, berrying, circusing, and all sorts of things which boys delight in. But no answer was sufficient for Georgie; he had to be humored in his desires, or he would carry them with a high hand. Naturally, no boy got more swimming skating, berrying, and so forth than he; no body ever had a better time. The good Brants did not allow the boys to play out after nine in summer evenings; they were sent to bed at that hour; Eddie honorably remained, but Georgie usually slipped out of the window toward ten, and enjoyed himself until midnight. It seemed impossible to break Georgie of this bad habit, but the Brants managed it at last by hiring him, with apples and marbles, to stay in. The good Brants gave all their time and attention to vain endeavors to regulate Georgie; they said, with grateful tears in their eyes, that Eddie needed no efforts of theirs, he was so good, so considerate, and in all ways so perfect.

By and by the boys were big enough to work, so they were apprenticed to a trade: Edward went voluntarily; George was coaxed and bribed. Edward worked hard and faithfully, and ceased to be an expense to the good Brants; they praised him, so did his master; but George ran away, and it cost Mr. Brant both money and trouble to hunt him up and get him back. By and by he ran away again—more money and more trouble. He ran away a third time—and stole a few things to carry with him. Trouble and expense for Mr. Brant once more; and, besides, it was with the greatest difficulty that he succeeded in persuading the master to let the youth go unprosecuted for the theft.

Edward worked steadily along, and in time became a full partner in his master's business. George did not improve; he kept the loving hearts of his aged benefactors full of trouble, and their hands full of inventive activities to protect him from ruin. Edward, as a boy, had interested himself in Sunday-schools, debating societies, penny missionary affairs, anti-tobacco organizations, anti-profanity associations, and all such things; as a man, he was a quiet but steady and reliable helper in the church, the temperance societies, and in all movements looking to the aiding and uplifting of men. This excited no remark, attracted no attention—for it was his "natural bent."

Finally, the old people died. The will testified their loving pride in Edward, and left their little property to George—because he "needed it"; whereas, "owing to a bountiful Providence," such was not the case with Edward. The property was left to George conditionally: he must buy out Edward's partner with it; else it must go to a benevolent organization called the Prisoner's Friend Society. The old people left a letter, in which they begged their dear son Edward to take their place and watch over George, and help and shield him as they had done.

Edward dutifully acquiesced, and George became his partner in the business. He was not a valuable partner: he had been meddling with drink before; he soon developed into a constant tippler now, and his flesh and eyes showed the fact unpleasantly. Edward had been courting a sweet and kindly spirited girl for some time. They loved each other dearly, and—But about this period George began to haunt her tearfully and imploringly, and at last she went crying to Edward, and said her high and holy duty was plain before her—she must not let her own selfish desires interfere with it: she must marry "poor George" and "reform him." It would break her heart, she knew it would, and so on; but duty was duty. So she married George, and Edward's heart came very near breaking, as well as her own. However, Edward recovered, and married another girl—a very excellent one she was, too.

Children came to both families. Mary did her honest best to reform her husband, but the contract was too large. George went on drinking, and by and by he fell to misusing her and the little ones sadly. A great many good people strove with George—they were always at it, in fact—but he calmly took such efforts as his due and their duty, and did not mend his ways. He added a vice, presently—that of secret gambling. He got deeply in debt; he borrowed money on the firm's credit, as quietly as he could, and carried this system so far and so successfully that one morning the sheriff took possession of the establishment, and the two cousins found themselves penniless.

Times were hard, now, and they grew worse. Edward moved his family into a garret, and walked the streets day and night, seeking work. He begged for it, but in was really not to be had. He was astonished to see how soon his face became unwelcome; he was astonished and hurt to see how quickly the ancient interest which people had had in him faded out and disappeared. Still, he must get work; so he swallowed his chagrin, and toiled on in search of it. At last he got a job of carrying bricks up a ladder in a hod, and was a grateful man in consequence; but after that nobody knew him or cared anything about him. He was not able to keep up his dues in the various moral organizations to which he belonged, and had to endure the sharp pain of seeing himself brought under the disgrace of suspension.

But the faster Edward died out of public knowledge and interest, the faster George rose in them. He was found lying, ragged and drunk, in the gutter one morning. A member of the Ladies' Temperance Refuge fished him out, took him in hand, got up a subscription for him, kept him sober a whole week, then got a situation for him. An account of it was published.

General attention was thus drawn to the poor fellow, and a great many people came forward and help ed him toward reform with their countenance and encouragement. He did not drink a drop for two months, and meantime was the pet of the good. Then he fell—in the gutter; and there was general sorrow and lamentation. But the noble sisterhood rescued him again. They cleaned him up, they fed him, they listened to the mournful music of his repentances, they got him his situation again. An account of this, also, was published, and the town was drowned in happy tears over the re-restoration of the poor beast and struggling victim of the fatal bowl. A grand temperance revival was got up, and after some rousing speeches had been made the chairman said, impressively: "We are not about to call for signers; and I think there is a spectacle in store for you which not many in this house will be able to view with dry eyes." There was an eloquent pause, and then George Benton, escorted by a red-sashed detachment of the Ladies of the Refuge, stepped forward upon the platform and signed the pledge. The air was rent with applause, and everybody cried for joy. Everybody wrung the hand of the new convert when the meeting was over; his salary was enlarged next day; he was the talk of the town, and its hero. An account of it was published.

George Benton fell, regularly, every three months, but was faithfully rescued and wrought with, every time, and good situations were found for him. Finally, he was taken around the country lecturing, as a reformed drunkard, and he had great houses and did an immense amount of good.

He was so popular at home, and so trusted—during his sober intervals—that he was enabled to use the name of a principal citizen, and get a large sum of money at the bank. A mighty pressure was brought to bear to save him from the consequences of his forgery, and it was partially successful—he was "sent up" for only two years. When, at the end of a year, the tireless efforts of the benevolent were crowned with success, and he emerged from the penitentiary with a pardon in his pocket, the Prisoner's Friend Society met him at the door with a situation and a comfortable salary, and all the other benevolent people came forward and gave him advice, encouragement and help. Edward Mills had once applied to the Prisoner's Friend Society for a situation, when in dire need, but the question, "Have you been a prisoner?" made brief work of his case.

While all these things were going on, Edward Mills had been quietly making head against adversity. He was still poor, but was in receipt of a steady and sufficient salary, as the respected and trusted cashier of a bank. George Benton never came near him, and was never heard to inquire about him. George got to indulging in long absences from the town; there were ill reports about him, but nothing definite.

One winter's night some masked burglars forced their way into the bank, and found Edward Mills there alone. They commanded him to reveal the "combination," so that they could get into the safe. He refused. They threatened his life. He said his employers trusted him, and he could not be traitor to that trust. He could die, if he must, but while he lived he would be faithful; he would not yield up the "combination." The burglars killed him.

The detectives hunted down the criminals; the chief one proved to be George Benton. A wide sympathy was felt for the widow and orphans of the dead man, and all the newspapers in the land begged that all the banks in the land would testify their appreciation of the fidelity and heroism of the murdered cashier by coming forward with a generous contribution of money in aid of his family, now bereft of support. The result was a mass of solid cash amounting to upward of five hundred dollars—an average of nearly three-eights of a cent for each bank in the Union. The cashier's own bank testified its gratitude by endeavoring to show (but humiliatingly failed in it) that the peerless servant's accounts were not square, and that he himself had knocked his brains out with a bludgeon to escape detection and punishment.

George Benton was arraigned for trial. Then everybody seemed to forget the widow and orphans in their solicitude for poor George. Everything that money and influence could do was done to save him, but it all failed; he was sentenced to death. Straightway the Governor was besieged with petitions for commutation or pardon; they were brought by tearful young girls; by sorrowful old maids; by deputations of pathetic widows; by shoals of impressive orphans. But no, the Governor—for once—would not yield.

Now George Benton experienced religion. The glad news flew all around. From that time forth his cell was always full of girls and women and fresh flowers; all the day long there was prayer, and hymn-singing, and thanksgiving, and homilies, and tears, with never an interruption, except an occasional five-minute intermission for refreshments.

This sort of thing continued up to the very gallows, and George Benton went proudly home, in the black cap, before a wailing audience of the sweetest and best that the region could produce. His grave had fresh flowers on it every day, for a while, and the head-stone bore these words, under a hand pointing aloft: "He has fought the good fight."

The brave cashier's head-stone has this inscription: "Be pure, honest, sober, industrious, considerate, and you will never—"

Nobody knows who gave the order to leave it that way, but it was so given.

The cashier's family are in stringent circumstances, now, it is said; but no matter; a lot of appreciative people, who were not willing that an act so brave and true as his should go unrewarded, have collected forty-two thousand dollars—and built a Memorial Church with it.

# Frances Ellen Watkins Harper, from
# Iola Leroy, or Shadows Uplifted *(1892)*

*The idea of alcohol as a racial scourge, expressed through the description of the scene at the Bold Dragoon in Cooper's* Pioneers, *emerges in the African-American context of Frances E.W. Harper's novel,* Iola Leroy, *here in "Searching for Lost Ones," chapter XVIII. A prolific author and staunch activist for abolition, women's rights, and temperance, Harper (1825–1911) was highly esteemed in her own lifetime, but her reputation faded early in the twentieth century; recently, however, critics have rediscovered and positively reevaluated her work. Like many other reformist-minded writers of her era, both black and white, Harper produced novels, stories, and poems with a temperance agenda, such as "The Drunkard's Child," or "Signing the Pledge," two highly sentimental poems that asserted temperance ideals. At the same time, a concern with drinking emerges in those of her works not focused specifically on temperance, such as* Iola Leroy, *the eponymous protagonist of which is an educated, racially mixed young woman trying to negotiate the difficult waters of personal, ethnic, and gender identity in the United States after emancipation.*

*The excerpt below features the earthy eloquence of "Aunt Linda," an elderly black woman who condemns both white peddlers of alcohol and blacks who succumb to their blandishments. The passage begins at the point where Aunt Linda responds to the queries of Robert (Iola Leroy's future husband), who is curious about people in the neighborhood to which he has recently returned. In Aunt Linda's words, "a fool's a fool, whether he's white or black"; accordingly, she has little patience for the emancipated black who spends money on liquor, and even worse, turns into a drunkard. But her sharper condemnation is for hypocritical white temperance advocates who enlist black support for temperance while keeping their distance from black people on other issues; above all, Aunt Linda attacks white liquor peddlers—"mean white men ... tryin' to fedder dere nests sellin' licker to pore culled people." The passage is significant in showing alcohol abuse to be both a manifestation and even instrument of racial oppression, thereby anticipating later treatments of this topic, such as Richard Wright's short story, "The Man Who Killed a Shadow," from the collection* Eight Men *(1961), or N. Scott Momaday's novel,* House Made of Dawn *(1969).*

... "Do you ever go to see old Miss?" asked Robert.

"Oh, yes; I goes ebery now and den. But she's jis' fell froo. Ole Johnson jis' drunk hisself to death. He war de biggest guzzler I eber seed in my life. Why, dat man he drunk up ebery thing he could lay his han's on. Sometimes he would go 'roun' tryin' to borrer money from pore cullud folks. 'Twas rale drefful de way dat pore feller did frow hisself away. But drink did it all. I tell you, Bobby, dat drink's a drefful thing wen it gits de upper han' ob you. You'd better steer clar ob it."

"That's so," assented Robert.

"I know'd Miss Nancy's fadder and mudder. Dey war mighty rich. Some ob de real big bugs. Marse Jim used to know dem, an' come ober ter de plantation, an' eat an' drink wen he got ready, an' stay as long as he choose. Ole Cousins used to have wine at dere table ebery day, an' Marse Jim war mighty fon' ob dat wine, an' sometimes he would drink till he got quite boozy. Ole Cousins liked him bery well, till he foun' out he wanted his darter, an' den he didn't want him fer rags nor patches. But Miss Nancy war mighty headstrong, an' allers liked to hab her own way; an' dis time she got it. But didn't she step her foot inter it? Ole Johnson war mighty han'some, but when dat war said all war said. She run'd off an' got married, but wen she got down she war too spunkey to axe her pa for anything. Wen you war wid her, yer know she only took big bugs. But wen de war com'd 'roun' it tore her all ter pieces, an' now she's as pore as Job's turkey. I feel's right sorry fer her. Well, Robby, things is turned 'roun' mighty quare. Ole Mistus war up den, an' I war down; now, she's down, an' I'se up. But I pities her, 'cause she warn't so bad arter all. De wuss thing she eber did war ta sell your mudder, an' she wouldn't hab done dat but she snatched de whip out ob her han' an gib her a lickin'. Now I belieb in my heart she war 'fraid ob your mudder arter dat. But we women had ter keep 'em from whippin' us, er dey'd all de time been libin' on our bones. She had no man ter whip us 'cept dat ole drunken husband ob hern, an' he war allers too drunk ter whip hisself. He jis' wandered off, an' I reckon he died in somebody's pore-house. He warn't no 'count nohow you fix it. Weneber I goes to town I carries her some garden sass, er a little milk an' butter. An' she's mighty glad ter git it. I ain't got nothin' agin her. She neber struck me a lick in her life, an' I belieb in praising de bridge dat carries me ober. Dem Yankees set me free, an' I thinks a powerful heap ob dem. But it does rile me ter see dese mean white men comin' down yere an' settin' up dere grog-shops, tryin' to fedder dere nests sellin' licker to pore culled people. Deys de bery kine ob men dat used ter keep dorgs to ketch de runaways. I'd be chokin' fer a drink 'fore I'd eber spen' a cent wid dem, a spreadin' dere traps to git de black folks' money. You jis' go down town 'fore sun up to-morrer mornin' an' you see ef dey don't hab dem bars open to sell dere drams to dem hard workin' culled people 'fore dey goes ter work. I thinks some niggers is mighty big fools."

"Oh, Aunt Linda, don't run down your race. Leave that for the white people."

"I ain't runnin' down my people. But a fool's a fool, whether he's white or black. An' I think de nigger who will spen' his hard-earned money in dese yere new grog-shops is de biggest kine ob a fool, an' I sticks ter dat. You know we didn't hab all dese low places in slave times. An' what is dey fer, but to get the people's money. An' its a shame how dey do sling de licker 'bout 'lection times."

"But don't the temperance people want the colored people to vote the temperance ticket?"

"Yes, but some ob de culled people gits mighty skittish ef dey tries to git em to vote dare ticket 'lection time, an' keeps dem at a proper distance wen de 'lection's ober. Some ob dem say dere's a trick behine it, an' don't want to tech it. Dese white folks could do a heap wid de culled folks ef dey'd only treat em right."

"When our people say there is a trick behind it," said Robert, "I only wish they could see the trick before it—the trick of worse than wasting their money, and of keeping themselves and families poorer and more ignorant than there is any need for them to be."

"Well, Bobby, I beliebs we might be a people ef it warn't for dat mizzable drink. An' Robby, I jis' tells yer what I wants; I wants some libe man to come down yere an' splain things ter dese people. I don't mean a politic man, but a man who'll larn dese people how to bring up dere chillen, to keep our gals straight, an' our boys from runnin' in de saloons an' gamblin' dens."

"Don't your preachers do that?" asked Robert.

"Well, some ob dem does, an' some ob dem doesn't. An' wen dey preaches, I want dem to practice wat dey preach. Some ob dem says dey's called, but I jis' thinks laziness called some ob dem. An' I thinks since freedom come deres some mighty pore sticks set up for preachers. Now dere's John Anderson, Tom's brudder; you 'member Tom."

"Yes; as brave a fellow and as honest as ever stepped in shoe leather."

"Well, his brudder war mighty diffrent. He war down in de lower kentry wen de war ober. He war mighty smart, an' had a good head-piece, an' a orful glib tongue. He set up store an' sole whisky, an' made a lot ob money. Den he wanted ter go to de legislatur. Now what should he do but make out he'd got 'ligion, an' war called to preach. He had no more 'ligion dan my ole dorg. But he had money an' built a meetin' house, whar he could hole meeting, an' hab funerals; an' you know cullud folks is mighty great on funerals. Well dat jis' tuck wid de people, an' he got 'lected to de legislatur. Den he got a fine house, an' his ole wife warn't good 'nuff for him. Den dere war a young school-teacher, an' he begun cuttin' his eyes at her. But she war as deep in de mud as he war in de mire, an' he jis' gib up his ole wife and married her, a fusty thing. He war a mean ole hypocrit, an' I wouldn't sen' fer him to bury my cat. Robby, I'se down on dese kine ob preachers like a thousand bricks."

# III. Drinking and the Tavern

## William Blake, "The Little Vagabond" (1794) and Stephen Crane, from George's Mother (1896)

*Separated by just over a hundred years, Blake's poem (from the "experience" section of Blake's* Songs of Innocence and of Experience) *and Crane's short novel appear together here because they share an ironic contrast between forbidding church and welcoming tavern. The church-tavern split is widespread, appearing in many works of literature and in the warnings of the religious who saw in the tavern an all too-appealing threat and alternative to churchly authority. Horace Greeley, for example, celebrated the "working men who stick to their business ... and go on Sunday to church rather than to the grog-shop"; the American poet Edgar Lee Masters, in his* Spoon River Anthology, *inverts this perspective in describing one of his characters as "Foe of the church with its charnel darkness,/Friend of the human touch of the tavern."\* In the two selections included here, the tavern emerges as an anti-church, complete with a set of convivial customers as an alternative to the pious congregation. As so often in Blake (1757–1827), the irony of the poem (in this case, a jovial, humorous irony) strikes at the failure of religious institutions to welcome the outcast and downtrodden.*

*In Crane's text, the ironies are darker and more complex, as the comforts offered by the "little smiling saloon" are insidiously deceptive. The son of a minister-father who published* Arts of Intoxication, *a book condemning various secular pleasures, and of a temperance-supporting mother who wanted her rebellious son to attend prayer meetings, Crane (1871–1900) unflinchingly depicts both church and tavern as empty alternatives.† Beyond the obvious parallels between the two institutions as sites of human assembly and group identification, and the obvious differences (the grim propriety of the one, the inviting cheerfulness of the other), Crane suggests a deeper, more disturbing similarity between them—neither is capable of offering anything of genuine substance and support to the story's protagonist, the hapless George. To both George and his mother, tavern and church offer only the most illusory of* sanctuaries. Pessimistic as this view is, it reflects the bracing honesty (and interest in drink as a social problem) found in the work of Crane and other turn-of-the-century American Naturalist writers.

*Greeley is quoted in Joseph Gusfield, Symbolic Crusade: Status Politics and the American Temperance Movement, 2nd ed., (Urbana: University of Illinois Press, 1986), p. 3; for Masters, see his Spoon River Anthology (New York: Macmillan, 1964, (originally published 1915), p. 96.

†The notion of the tavern as a substitute for the church appeared also in nineteenth-century French culture; in the words of historian Susanna Barrows, the alcohol-dispensing French cafés became "secular churches offering comfort, rituals and solace to the dispossessed" (quoted in Gusfield, Symbolic Crusade, p. 194). Gusfield observes that Barrows' comment "applies equally to American saloons"; indeed, much the same could be said of taverns in many different times and places, as suggested by Blake's "The Little Vagabond."

## "THE LITTLE VAGABOND"

Dear Mother, dear Mother, the Church is cold,
But the Ale-house is healthy & pleasant & warm;
Besides I can tell where I am use'd well.
Such usage in heaven will never do well.

But if at the Church they would give us some Ale,
And a pleasant fire, our souls to regale:
We'd sing and we'd pray all the live-long day:
Nor ever once wish from the Church to stray.

Then the Parson might preach & drink & sing,
And we'd be as happy as birds in the spring:
And modest dame Lurch, who is always at Church,
Would not have bandy children nor fasting nor birch.

And God like a father rejoicing to see,
His children as pleasant and happy as he:
Would have no more quarrel with the Devil or the Barrel
But kiss him & give him both drink and apparel.

## GEORGE'S MOTHER, CHAPTERS I–IV

In the swirling rain that came at dusk the broad avenue glistened with that deep bluish tint which is so widely condemned when it is put into pictures. There were long rows of shops, whose fronts shone with full, golden light. Here and there, from druggists' windows, or from the red street-lamps that indicated the positions of fire-alarm boxes, a flare of uncertain, wavering crimson was thrown upon the wet pavements.

The lights made shadows, in which the buildings loomed with a new and tremendous massiveness, like castles and fortresses. There were endless processions of people, mighty hosts, with umbrellas waving, banner-like, over them. Horse-cars, aglitter with new paint, rumbled in steady array between the pillars that supported the elevated railroad. The whole street resounded with the tinkle of bells, the roar of iron-shod wheels on the cobbles, the ceaseless trample of the hundreds of feet. Above all, too, could be heard the loud screams of the tiny newsboys, who scurried in all directions. Upon the corners, standing in from the dripping eaves, were many loungers, descended from the world that used to prostrate itself before pageantry.

A brown young man went along the avenue. He held a tin lunch-pail under his arm in a manner that was evidently uncomfortable. He was puffing at a corn-cob pipe. His shoulders had a self-reliant poise, and the hang of his arms and the raised veins of his hands showed him to be a man who worked with his muscles.

As he passed a street-corner a man in old clothes gave a shout of surprise, and rushing impetuously forward, grasped his hand.

"Hello, Kelcey, ol' boy," cried the man in old clothes. "How's th' boy, anyhow? Where in thunder yeh been fer th' last seventeen years? I'll be hanged if you ain't th' last man I ever expected t' see."

The brown youth put his pail to the ground and grinned.

"Well, if it ain't ol' Charley Jones," he said, ecstatically shaking hands. "How are yeh, anyhow? Where yeh been keepin' yerself? I ain't seen yeh fer a year!"

"Well, I should say so! Why, th' last time I saw you was up in Handyville!"

"Sure! On Sunday, we———"

"Sure! Out at Bill Sickles' place. Let's go get a drink!"

They made toward a little glass-fronted saloon that sat blinking jovially at the crowds. It engulfed them with a gleeful motion of its two widely-smiling lips.

"What'll yeh take, Kelcey?"

"Oh, I guess I'll take a beer."

"Gimme little whisky, John."

The two friends leaned against the bar and looked with enthusiasm upon each other.

"Well, well, I'm thunderin' glad t' see yeh," said Jones. "Well, I guess," replied Kelcey. "Here's to yeh, ol' man." "Let 'er go."

They lifted their glasses, glanced fervidly at each other, and drank.

"Teh ain't changed much, on'y yeh've growed like th' devil," said Jones, reflectively, as he put down his glass; "I'd know yeh anywheres!"

"Certainly yeh would," said Kelcey. "An' I knew you, too, th' minute I saw yeh. Yer changed, though!"

"Yes," admitted Jones, with some complacency; "I s'pose I am." He regarded himself in the mirror that multiplied the bottles on the shelf back of the bar. He should have seen a grinning face with a rather pink nose. His derby was perched carelessly on the back part of his head. Two wisps of hair straggled down over his hollow temples. There was something very worldly and wise about him. Life did not seem to confuse him. Evidently he understood its complications. His hand thrust into his trousers-pocket, where he jingled keys, and his hat perched back on his head expressed a young man of vast knowledge. His extensive acquaintance with bar-tenders aided him materially in this habitual expression of wisdom.

Having finished he turned to the barkeeper. "John, has any of th' gang been in t'-night yet?"

"No—not yet," said the bar-keeper, "ol' Bleecker was aroun' this afternoon about four. He said if I seen any of th' boys t' tell 'em he'd be up t'-night if he could get away. I saw Connor an' that other fellah goin' down th' avenyeh about an hour ago. I guess they'll be back after awhile."

"This is th' hang-out fer a great gang," said Jones, turning to Kelcey. "They're a great crowd, I tell yeh. We own th' place when we get started. Come aroun' some night. Any night, almost—t'-night, b' jiminy. They'll almost all be here, an' I'd like t' interduce yeh. They're a great gang! Gre-e-at!"

"I'd like teh," said Kelcey.

"Well, come ahead, then," cried the other, cordially. "Yeh'd like t' know 'em. It's an outa sight crowd. Come aroun' t'-night!"

"I will if I can."

"Well, yeh ain't got anything t' do, have yeh?" demanded Jones. "Well, come along, then. Yeh might just as well spend yer time with a good crowd 'a fellahs. An' it's a great gang—great—gre-e-at!"

"Well, I must make fer home now, anyhow," said Kelcey. "It's late as blazes. What'll yeh take this time, ol' man?"

"Gimme little more whisky, John!"

"Guess I'll take another beer!"

Jones emptied the whisky into his large mouth and then put the glass upon the bar.

"Been in th' city long?" he asked. "Urn—well, three years is a good deal fer a slick man. Doin' well? Oh, well, nobody's doin' well these days." He looked down mournfully at his shabby clothes. "Father's dead, ain't 'ee? Yeh don't say so? Fell off a scaffoldin', didn't 'ee? I heard it somewheres. Mother's livin', of course? I thought she was. Fine ol' lady—fi-i-ne! Well, you're th' last of her boys. Was five of yeh onct, wasn't there? I knew four m'self. Yes, five. I thought so. An' all gone but you, hey? Well you'll have t' brace up an' be a comfort t' th' ol' mother. Well, well, well, who would 'a thought that on'y you'd be left out 'a all that mob 'a tow-headed kids. Well, well, well, it's a queer world, ain't it?"

A contemplation of this thought made him sad. He sighed and moodily watched the other sip beer.

"Well, well, it's a queer world—a damn queer world."

"Yes," said Kelcey, "I'm th' on'y one left!" There was an accent of discomfort in his voice. He did not like this dwelling upon a sentiment that was connected with himself.

"How is th' ol' lady, anyhow?" continued Jones. "Th' last time I remember she was as spry as a little ol' cricket, an' was helpeltin' aroun' the' country lecturin' before W.C.T.U.'s an' one thing an' another."

"Oh, she's pretty well," said Kelcey.

"An' outa five boys you're th' on'y one she's got left? Well, well—have another drink before yeh go."

"Oh, I guess I've had enough."

A wounded expression came into Jones's eyes. "Oh, come on," he said.

"Well, I'll take another beer!"

"Gimme little more whisky, John!"

When they had concluded this ceremony, Jones went with his friend to the door of the saloon.

"Good-bye, ol' man," he said, genially. His homely features shone with friendliness. "Come aroun', now, sure. T-night! See? They're a great crowd. Gre-e-at!"

## II

A man with a red, mottled face put forth his head from a window and cursed violently. He flung a bottle high across two backyards at a window of the opposite tenement. It broke against the bricks of the house and the fragments fell crackling upon the stones below. The man shook his fist.

A bare-armed woman, making an array of clothes on a line in one of the yards, glanced casually up at the man and listened to his words. Her eyes followed his to the other tenement. From a distant window, a youth with a pipe yelled some comments upon the poor aim. Two children, being in the proper yard, picked up the bits of broken glass and began to fondle them as new toys.

From the window at which the man raged came the sound of an old voice, singing. It quavered and trembled out into the air as if a sound-spirit had a broken wing.

"Should I be car-reed tew th' skies
O-on flow'ry be-eds of ee-ease,
While others fought tew win th' prize
An' sailed through blood-ee seas?"

The man in the opposite window was greatly enraged. He continued to swear.

A little old woman was the owner of the voice. In a fourth-story room of the red and black tenement she was trudging on a journey. In her arms she bore pots and pans, and sometimes a broom and dust-pan. She wielded them like weapons. Their weight seemed to have bended her back and crooked her arms until she walked with difficulty. Often she plunged her hands into water at a sink. She splashed about, the dwindled muscles working to and fro under the loose skin of her arms. She came from the sink, steaming and bedraggled as if she had crossed a flooded river.

There was the flurry of a battle in this room. Through the clouded dust or steam one could see the thin figure dealing mighty blows. Always her way seemed beset. Her broom was continually poised, lance-wise, at dust demons. There came clashings and clangings as she strove with her tireless foes.

It was a picture of indomitable courage. And as she went on her way her voice was often raised in a long cry, a strange war-chant, a shout of battle and defiance, that rose and fell in harsh screams, and exasperated the ears of the man with the red, mottled face.

"Should I be car-reed tew th' skies
O-on flow'ry be-eds of ee-ease—"

Finally she halted for a moment. Going to the window, she sat down and mopped her face with her apron. It was a lull, a moment of respite. Still it could be seen that she even then was planning skirmishes, charges, campaigns. She gazed thoughtfully about the room and noted the strength and position of her enemies. She was very alert.

At last, she turned to the mantel. "Five o'clock," she murmured, scrutinizing a little, swaggering, nickel-plated clock.

She looked out at chimneys growing thickly on the roofs. A man at work on one seemed like a bee. In the intricate yards below, vine-line lines had strange leaves of cloth. To her ears there came the howl of the man with the red, mottled face. He was engaged in a furious altercation with the youth who had called attention to his poor aim. They were like animals in a jungle.

In the distance an enormous brewery towered over the other buildings. Great gilt letters advertised a brand of beer. Thick smoke came from funnels and spread near it like vast and powerful wings. The structure seemed a great bird, flying. The letters of the sign made a chain of gold hanging from its neck. The little old woman looked at the brewery. It vaguely interested her, for a moment, as a stupendous affair, a machine of mighty strength.

Presently she sprang from her rest and began to buffet with her shrivelled arms. In a moment the battle was again in full swing. Terrific blows were given and received. There arose the clattering uproar of a new fight. The little intent warrior never hesitated nor faltered. She fought with a strong and relentless will. Beads and lines of perspiration stood upon her forehead.

Three blue plates were leaning in a row on the shelf back of the stove. The little old woman had seen it done somewhere. In front of them swaggered the round nickel-plated clock. Her son had stuck many cigarette pictures in the rim of a looking-glass that hung near. Occasional chromos were tacked upon the yellowed walls of the room. There was one in a gilt frame. It was quite an affair, in reds and greens. They all seemed like trophies.

It began to grow dark. A mist came winding. Rain plashed softly upon the window-sill. A lamp had been lighted in the opposite tenement; the strong orange glare revealed the man with a red, mottled face. He was seated by a table, smoking and reflecting.

The little old woman looked at the clock again. "Quarter 'a six."

She had paused for a moment, but she now hurled herself fiercely at the stove that lurked in the gloom, red-eyed, like a dragon. It hissed, and there was renewed clangor of blows. The little old woman dashed to and fro.

## III

As it grew toward seven o'clock the little old woman became nervous. She often would drop into a chair and sit staring at the little clock.

"I wonder why he don't come," she continually repeated. There was a small, curious note of despair in her voice. As she sat thinking and staring at the clock the expressions of her face changed swiftly. All manner of emotions flickered in her eyes and about her lips. She was evidently perceiving in her imagination the journey of a loved person. She dreamed for him mishaps and obstacles. Something tremendous and irritating was hindering him from coming to her.

She had lighted an oil-lamp. It flooded the room with vivid yellow glare. The table, in its oil-cloth covering, had previously appeared like a bit of bare, brown desert. It now was a white garden, growing the fruits of her labour.

"Seven o'clock," she murmured finally. She was aghast.

Then suddenly she heard a step upon the stair. She sprang up and began to bustle about the room. The little fearful emotions passed at once from her face. She seemed now to be ready to scold.

Young Kelcey entered the room. He gave a sigh of relief, and dropped his pail in a corner. He was evidently greatly wearied by a hard day of toil.

The little old woman hobbled over to him and raised her wrinkled lips. She seemed on the verge of tears and an outburst of reproaches.

"Hello!" he cried, in a voice of cheer. "Been gettin' anxious?"

"Yes," she said, hovering about him. "Where yeh been, George? What made yeh so late? I've been waitin' th' longest while. Don't throw your coat down there. Hang it up behind th' door."

The son put his coat on the proper hook, and then went to splatter water in a tin wash-basin at the sink.

"Well, yeh see, I met Jones—you remember Jones. Ol' Handyville fellah. An' we had t' stop an' talk over ol' times. Jones is quite a boy."

The little old woman's mouth set in a sudden straight line. "Oh, that Jones!" she said. "I don't like him."

The youth interrupted a flurry of white towel to give a glance of irritation. "Well, now, what's th' use of talkin' that way?" he said to her. "What do yeh know 'bout 'im? Ever spoke to 'im in yer life?"

"Well, I don't know as I ever did since he grew up," replied the little old woman. "But I know he ain't th' kind 'a man I'd like t' have you go around with. He ain't a good man. I'm sure he ain't. He drinks."

Her son began to laugh. "Th' dickens he does!"

He seemed amazed, but not shocked, at this information.

She nodded her head with the air of one who discloses a dreadful thing. "I'm sure of it! Once I saw 'im comin' outa Simpson's Hotel, up in Handyville, an' he could hardly walk. He drinks! I'm sure he drinks!"

"Holy smoke!" said Kelcey.

They sat down at the table and began to wreck the little white garden. The youth leaned back in his chair, in the manner of a man who is paying for things. His mother bended alertly forward, apparently watching each mouthful. She perched on the edge of her chair, ready to spring to her feet and run to the closet or the stove for anything that he might need. She was as anxious as a young mother with a babe. In the careless and comfortable attitude of the son there was denoted a great deal of dignity.

"Yeh ain't eatin' much t'-night, George?"

"Well, I ain't very hungry, t' tell th' truth."

"Don't yeh like yer supper, dear? Yeh must eat somethin', chile. Yeh mustn't go without."

"Well, I'm eatin' somethin', ain't I?"

He wandered aimlessly through the meal. She sat over behind the little blackened coffee-pot and gazed affectionately upon him.

After a time she began to grow agitated. Her worn fingers were gripped. It could be seen that a great thought was within her. She was about to venture something. She had arrived at a supreme moment. "George," she said, suddenly, "come t' prayer-meetin' with me t'-night."

The young man dropped his fork. "Say, you must be crazy!" he said in amazement.

"Yes, dear," she continued rapidly, in a small, pleading voice, "I'd like t' have yeh go with me onct in a while. Yeh never go with me any more, dear, an' I'd like t' have yeh go. Yeh ain't been anywheres at all with me in th' longest while."

"Well," he said—"well; but what th' blazes——"

"Ah, come on!" said the little old woman. She went to him and put her arms about his neck. She began to coax him with caresses.

The young man grinned. "Thunderation!" he said; "what would I do at a prayer-meetin'?"

The mother considered him to be consenting. She did a little antique caper.

"Well, yeh can come an' take care 'a yer mother," she cried gleefully. "It's such a long walk every Thursday night alone, an' don't yeh s'pose that when I have such a big, fine, strappin' boy I want 'im t' beau me aroun' some? Ah, I knew ye'd come!"

He smiled for a moment, indulgent of her humour. But presently his face turned a shade of discomfort. "But—" he began, protesting.

"Ah, come on!" she continually repeated.

He began to be vexed. He frowned into the air. A vision came to him of dreary blackness arranged in solemn rows. A mere dream of it was depressing.

"But—" he said again. He was obliged to make great search for an argument. Finally he concluded: "But what th' blazes would I do at prayer-meetin'?"

In his ears was the sound of a hymn, made by people who tilted their heads at a prescribed angle of devotion. It would be too apparent that they were all better than he. When he entered they would turn their heads and regard him with suspicion. This would be an enormous aggravation, since he was certain that he was as good as they.

"Well, now, y' see," he said, quite gently, "I don't wanta go, an' it wouldn't do me no good t' go if I didn't wanta go."

His mother's face swiftly changed. She breathed a huge sigh, the counterpart of ones he had heard upon like occasions. She put a tiny black bonnet on her head, and wrapped her figure in an old shawl. She cast a martyr-like glance upon her son, and went mournfully away. She resembled a limited funeral procession.

The young man writhed under it to an extent. He kicked moodily at a table-leg. When the sound of her footfalls died away he felt distinctly relieved.

## IV

That night, when Kelcey arrived at the little smiling saloon, he found his friend Jones standing before the bar engaged in a violent argument with a stout man.

"Oh, well," this latter person was saying, "you can make a lot of noise, Charley, for a man that never says anything—let's have a drink!"

Jones was waving his arms and delivering splintering blows upon some distant theories. The stout man chuckled fatly and winked at the bar-tender.

The orator ceased for a moment to say, "Gimme little whisky, John." At the same time he perceived young Kelcey. He sprang forward with a welcoming cry. "Hello, ol' man! didn't much think ye'd come." He led him to the stout man.

"Mr. Bleecker—my friend Mr. Kelcey!"

"How d'yeh do?"

"Mr. Kelcey, I'm happy to meet you, sir; have a drink."

They drew up in line and waited. The busy hands of the bar-tender made glasses clink. Mr. Bleecker, in a very polite way, broke the waiting silence.

"Never been here before, I believe, have you, Mr. Kelcey?"

The young man felt around for a high-bred reply. "Er—no—I've never had that—er—pleasure," he said.

After a time the strained and wary courtesy of their manners wore away. It became evident to Bleecker that his importance slightly dazzled the young man. He grew warmer. Obviously, the youth was one whose powers of perception were developed. Directly, then, he launched forth into a tale of bygone days, when the world was better. He had known all the great men of that age. He reproduced his conversations with them. There were traces of pride and of mournfulness in his voice. He rejoiced at the glory of the world of dead spirits. He grieved at the youth and flippancy of the present one. He lived with his head in the clouds of the past, and he seemed obliged to talk of what he saw there.

Jones nudged Kelcey ecstatically in the ribs. "You've got th' ol' man started in great shape," he whispered.

Kelcey was proud that the prominent character of the place talked at him, glancing into his eyes for appreciation of fine points.

Presently they left the bar, and going into a little rear room, took seats about a table. A gas-jet with a coloured globe shed a crimson radiance. The polished wood of walls and furniture gleamed with faint rose-coloured reflections. Upon the floor sawdust was thickly sprinkled.

Two other men presently came. By the time Bleecker had told three tales of the grand past, Kelcey was slightly acquainted with everybody.

He admired Bleecker immensely. He developed a brotherly feeling for the others, who were all gentle-spoken. He began to feel that he was passing the happiest evening of his life. His companions were so jovial and good-natured; and everything they did was marked by such courtesy.

For a time the two men who had come in late did not presume to address him directly. They would say: "Jones, won't your friend have so and so, or so and so?" And Bleecker would begin his orations: "'Now, Mr. Kelcey, don't you think——"

Presently he began to believe that he was a most remarkably fine fellow, who had at last found his place in a crowd of most remarkably fine fellows.

Jones occasionally breathed comments into his ear.

"I tell yeh, Bleecker's an ol'-timer. He was a husky guy in his day, yeh can bet. He was one 'a th' best known men in N' York onct. Yeh ought to hear him tell about——"

Kelcey listened intently. He was profoundly interested in these intimate tales of men who had gleamed in the rays of old suns.

"That O'Connor's a damn fine fellah," interjected Jones once, referring to one of the others; "he's one 'a th' best fellahs I ever knowed. He's always on th' dead level, an' he's always jest th' same as yeh see him now—good-natured an' grinnin'."

Kelcey nodded. He could well believe it.

When he offered to buy drinks there came a loud volley of protests. "No, no, Mr. Kelcey," cried Bleecker; "no, no. To-night you are our guest. Some other time——"

"Here," said O'Connor, "it's my turn now."

He called and pounded for the bar-tender. He then sat with a coin in his hand warily eying the others. He was ready to frustrate them if they offered to pay.

After a time Jones began to develop qualities of great eloquence and wit. His companions laughed. "It's the whisky talking now," said Bleecker.

He grew earnest and impassioned; he delivered speeches on various subjects. His lectures were to him very imposing. The force of his words thrilled him. Sometimes he was overcome.

The others agreed with him in all things. Bleecker grew almost tender, and considerately placed words here and there for his use. As Jones became fiercely energetic the others became more docile in agreeing. They soothed him with friendly interjections.

His mood changed directly. He began to sing popular airs with enthusiasm. He congratulated his companions upon being in his society. They were excited by his frenzy. They began to fraternize in jovial fashion. It was understood that they were true and tender spirits. They had come away from a grinding world filled with men who were harsh.

When one of them chose to divulge some place where the world had pierced him, there was a chorus of violent sympathy. They rejoiced at their temporary isolation and safety.

Once a man, completely drunk, stumbled along the floor of the saloon. He opened the door of the little room and made a show of entering. The men sprang instantly to their feet. They were ready to throttle any invader of their island. They elbowed each other in rivalry as to who should take upon himself the brunt of an encounter.

"Oh!" said the drunken individual, swaying on his legs and blinking at the party—"oh! thish private room?"

"That's what it is, Willie," said Jones. "An' you git outa here, er we'll throw yeh out."

"That's what we will," said the others.

"Oh!" said the drunken man. He blinked at them aggrievedly for an instant and then went away.

They sat down again. Kelcey felt in a way that he would have liked to display his fidelity to the others by whipping the intruder.

The bar-tender came often. "Gee, you fellahs er tanks!" he said in a jocular manner, as he gathered empty glasses and polished the table with his little towel.

Through the exertions of Jones the little room began to grow clamorous. The tobacco-smoke eddied about the forms of the men in ropes and wreaths. Near the ceiling there was a thick gray cloud.

Each man explained, in his way, that he was totally out of place in the before-mentioned world. They were possessed of various virtues which were unappreciated by those with whom they were commonly obliged to mingle—they were fitted for a tree-shaded land, where everything was peace.

Now that five of them had congregated it gave them happiness to speak their inmost thoughts without fear of being misunderstood.

As he drank more beer Kelcey felt his breast expand with manly feeling. He knew that he was capable of sublime things. He wished that some day one of his present companions would come to him for relief. His mind pictured a little scene. In it he was magnificent in his friendship.

He looked upon the beaming faces and knew that if at that instant there should come a time for a great sacrifice he would blissfully make it. He would pass tranquilly into the unknown, or into bankruptcy, amid the ejaculations of his companions upon his many virtues.

They had no bickerings during the evening. If one chose to momentarily assert himself, the others instantly submitted.

They exchanged compliments. Once old Bleecker stared at Jones for a few moments. Suddenly he broke out:

"Jones, you're one of the finest fellows I ever knew!"

A flush of pleasure went over the other's face, and then he made a modest gesture, the protest of an humble man.

"Don't flim-flam me, ol' boy," he said, with earnestness.

But Bleecker roared that he was serious about it.

The two men arose and shook hands emotionally. Jones butted against the table and knocked off a glass.

Afterward a general hand-shaking was inaugurated. Brotherly sentiments flew about the room. There was an uproar of fraternal feeling.

Jones began to sing. He beat time with precision and dignity. He gazed into the eyes of his companions, trying to call music from their souls. O'Connor joined in heartily, but with another tune. Off in a corner old Bleecker was making a speech.

The bar-tender came to the door. "Gee, you fellahs er making a row. It's time fer me t' shut up th' front th' place, an' you mugs better sit on yerselves. It's one o'clock."

They began to argue with him. Kelcey, however, sprang to his feet. "One o'clock?" he said. "Holy smoke, I mus' be flyin'!"

There came protesting howls from Jones. Bleecker ceased his oration.

"My dear boy—" he began.

Kelcey searched for his hat.

"I've gota go t' work at seven," he said.

The others watched him with discomfort in their eyes.

"Well," said O'Connor, "if one goes we might as well all go."

They sadly took their hats and filed out.

The cold air of the street filled Kelcey with vague surprise. It made his head feel hot. As for his legs, they were like willow-twigs.

A few yellow lights blinked. In front of an all-night restaurant a huge red electric lamp hung and sputtered. Horse-car bells jingled far down the street. Overhead a train thundered on the elevated road.

On the sidewalk the men took fervid leave. They clutched hands with extraordinary force and proclaimed, for the last time, ardent and admiring friendships.

When he arrived at his home Kelcey proceeded with caution. His mother had left a light burning low. He stumbled once in his voyage across the floor. As he paused to listen he heard the sound of little snores coming from her room.

He lay awake for a few moments and thought of the evening. He had a pleasurable consciousness that he had made a good impression upon those fine fellows. He felt that he had spent the most delightful evening of his life.

## *Charles Dickens, "Gin-Shops" (1836)*

*This entry from Dickens's first published book,* Sketches by Boz *(1836), speaks to the tawdry but powerful temptations offered to London's poor by the Victorian gin-palace. Appropriately enough, the original publication of "Gin-Shops" included an illustration of a gin-shop by the celebrated British caricaturist and ardent temperance supporter, George Cruikshank. But Dickens's own verbal "sketch" is notable as much for its critique of temperance as for its portrayal of alcohol's toxic effects on the community. In an 1844 letter, Dickens (1812–1870) elaborates on the view expressed at the end of "Gin-Shops" when he objects to the temperance doctrine of enforced abstinence and to what he saw as a confusion between the causes and consequences of drink: "I can no more concur in the philosophy of reducing all mankind to one total abstainment level," writes Dickens, "than I can yield to that monstrous doctrine which sets down as the consequences of Drunkenness, fifty thousand miseries which are, as all reflective persons know, and daily see, the wretched causes of it."\**

*In an interesting parallel to Dickens, Frances Willard, president of the Women's Christian Temperance Union in the United States, took in the 1890s what temperance historian Joseph Gusfield calls "a most heretical step for the advocate of Temperance; she maintained that intemperance is itself a result of social conditions: 'We are coming to the conclusion—at least I am—that we have not assigned to poverty at one end of the social scale and idleness at the other those places of prominence in the enumeration of the causes of intemperance to which they are entitled.'"†*

\**Charles Dickens,* The Letters of Charles Dickens, *ed. by Walter Dexter (Bloomsbury: Nonesuch Press, 1938), vol. I, pp. 563–6.*

†*See Joseph Gusfield,* Symbolic Crusade: Status Politics and the American Temperance Movement, *2nd ed., (Urbana: University of Illinois Press, 1986), p. 92.*

It is a remarkable circumstance, that different trades appear to partake of the disease to which elephants and dogs are especially liable, and to run stark, staring, raving mad, periodically. The great distinction between the animals and the trades, is, that the former run mad with a certain degree of propriety—they are very regular in their irregularities. We know the period at which the emergency will arise, and provide against it accordingly. If an elephant run mad, we are all ready for him—kill or cure—pills or bullets, calomel in conserve of roses, or lead in a musket-barrel. If a dog happen to look unpleasantly warm in the summer months, and to trot about the shady side of the streets with a quarter of a yard of tongue hanging out of his mouth, a thick leather muzzle, which has been previously prepared in compliance with the thoughtful injunctions of the Legislature, is instantly clapped over his head, by way of making him cooler, and he either looks remarkably unhappy for the next six weeks, or becomes legally insane, and goes mad, as it were, by Act of Parliament. But these trades are as eccentric as comets; nay, worse, for no one can calculate on the recurrence of the strange appearances which betoken the disease. Moreover, the contagion is general, and the quickness with which it diffuses itself, almost incredible.

We will cite two or three cases in illustration of our meaning. Six or eight years ago, the epidemic began to display itself among the linen-drapers and haberdashers. The primary symptoms were an inordinate love of plate-glass, and a passion for gas-lights and gilding. The disease gradually progressed, and at last attained a fearful height. Quiet, dusty old shops in different parts of town, were pulled down; spacious premises with stuccoed fronts and gold letters, were erected instead; floors were covered with Turkey carpets; roofs supported by massive pillars; doors knocked into windows; a dozen squares of glass into one; one shopman into a dozen; and there is no knowing what would have been done, if it had not been fortunately discovered, just in time, that the Commissioners of Bankruptcy were as competent to decide such cases as the Commissioners of Lunacy, and that a little confinement and gentle examination did wonders. The disease abated. It died away. A year or two of comparative tranquility ensued. Suddenly it burst out again amongst the chemists; the symptoms were the same, with the addition of a strong desire to stick the royal arms over the shop-door, and a great rage for mahogany, varnish, and expensive floor-cloth. Then, the hosiers were infected, and began to pull down their shop-fronts with frantic recklessness. The mania again died away, and the public began to congratulate themselves on its entire disappearance, when it burst forth with tenfold violence among the publicans, and keepers of "wine vaults." From that moment it has spread among them with unprecedented rapidity, exhibiting a concatenation of all the previous symptoms; onward it has rushed to every part of town, knocking down all the old public-houses, and depositing splendid mansions, stone balustrades, rosewood fittings, immense lamps, and illuminated clocks, at the corner of every street.

The extensive scale on which these places are established, and the ostentatious manner in which the business of even the smallest among them is divided into branches, is amusing. A handsome plate of ground glass in one door directs you "To the Counting-house;" another to the "Bottle Department;" a third to the "Wholesale Department;" a fourth to "The Wine Promenade;" and so forth, until we are in daily expectation of meeting with a "Brandy Bell," or a "Whiskey Entrance." Then, ingenuity is exhausted in devising attractive titles for the different descriptions of gin; and the dram-drinking portion of the community as they gaze upon the gigantic black and white announcements, which are only to be equaled in size by the figures beneath them, are left in a state of pleasing hesitation between "The Cream of the Valley," "The Out and Out," "The No Mistake," "The Good for Mixing," "The real Knock-me-down," "The celebrated Butter Gin," "The regular Flare-up," and a dozen other, equally inviting and wholesome *liqueurs*. Although places of this description are to be met with in every second street, they are invariably numerous and splendid in precise proportion to the dirt and poverty of the surrounding neighborhood. The gin-shops in and near Drury-Lane, Holborn, St. Giles's, Covent-garden, and Clare Market, are the handsomest in London. There is more of filth and squalid misery near those great thorough-fares than in any part of this mighty city.

We will endeavor to sketch the bar of a large gin-shop, and its ordinary customers, for the edification of such of our readers as may not have had opportunities of observing such scenes; and on the chance of finding one well suited to our purpose, we will make for Drury Lane, through the narrow streets and dirty courts which divide it from Oxford-street, and that classical spot adjoining the brewery at the bottom of Tottenham-court-Road, best known to the initiated as the "Rookery."

The filthy and miserable appearance of this part of London can hardly be imagined by those (and there are many such) who have not witnessed it. Wretched houses with broken windows patched with rags and paper: every room let out to a different family, and in many instances to two or even three—fruit and "sweet-stuff" manufacturers in the cellars, barbers and red-herring vendors in the front parlours, cobblers in the back; a bird-fancier in the first floor, three families on the second, starvation in the attics, Irishmen in the passage, a "musician" in the front kitchen, and a charwoman and five hungry children in the back one—filth everywhere—a gutter before the houses and a drain behind—clothes drying and slops emptying, from the windows; girls of fourteen or fifteen, with matted hair, walking about barefoot, and in white great-coats, almost their only covering; boys of all ages, in coats of all sizes and no coats at all; men and women, in every variety of scanty and dirty apparel, lounging, scolding, drinking, smoking, squabbling, fighting, and swearing.

You turn the corner. What a change! All is light and brilliancy. The hum of many voices issues from that splendid gin-shop which forms the commencement of the two streets opposite; and the gay building with the fantastically ornamented parapet, the illuminated clock, the plate-glass windows surrounded by stucco rosettes, and its profusion of gas-lights in richly-gilt burners, is perfectly dazzling when contrasted with the darkness and dirt we have just left. The interior is even gayer than the exterior. A bar of French-polished mahogany, elegantly carved, extends the whole width of the place; and there are two side-aisles of great casks, painted green and gold, enclosed within a light brass rail, and bearing such inscriptions, as "Old Tom, 549;" "Young Tom, 360;" "Samson, 1421"—the figures agreeing, we presume, with "gallons," understood. Beyond the bar is a lofty and spacious saloon, full of the same enticing vessels, with a gallery running round it, equally well furnished. On the counter, in addition to the usual spirit apparatus, are two or three little baskets of cakes and biscuits, which are carefully secured at top with wicker-work, to prevent their contents being unlawfully abstracted. Behind it, are two showily-dressed damsels with large necklaces, dispensing the spirits and "compounds." They are assisted by the ostensible proprietor of the concern, a stout, coarse fellow in a fur cap, put on very much on one side to give him a knowing air, and to display his sandy whiskers to the best advantage.

The two old washerwomen, who are seated on the little bench to the left of the bar, are rather overcome by the head-dresses and haughty demeanour of the young ladies who officiate. They receive their half-quartern of gin and peppermint, with considerable deference, prefacing a request for "one of them soft biscuits," with a "Jist be good enough, ma'am." They are quite astonished at the impudent air of the young fellow in a brown coat and bright buttons, who, ushering in his two companions, and walking up to the bar in as careless a manner as if he had been used to green and gold ornaments all his life, winks at one of the young ladies with singular coolness, and calls for a "kervorten and a three-out-glass," just as if the place were his own. "Gin for you, sir?" says the young lady when she has drawn it: carefully looking every way but the right one, to show that the wink had no effect upon her. "For me, Mary, my dear," replies the gentleman in brown. "My name an't Mary as it happens," says the young girl, rather relaxing as she delivers the change. "Well, if it an't, it ought to be," responds the irresistible one; "all the Marys as ever *I* see, was handsome gals." Here the young lady, not precisely remembering how blushes are managed in such cases, abruptly ends the flirtation by addressing the female in the faded feathers who has just entered, and who, after stating explicitly, to prevent any subsequent misunderstanding, that "this gentleman pays," calls for "a glass of port wine and a bit of sugar."

Those two old men who came in "just to have a drain," finished their third quartern a few seconds ago; they have made themselves crying drunk; and the fat comfortable-looking elderly women, who had "a glass of rum-srub" each, having chimed in with their complaints on the hardness of the times, one of the women has agreed to stand a glass round, jocularly observing that "grief never mended no broken bones, and as good people's wery scarce, what I says is, make the most on 'em, and that's all about it!" a sentiment which appears to afford unlimited satisfaction to those who have nothing to pay.

It is growing late, and the throng of men, women, and children, who have been constantly going in and out, dwindles down to two or three occasional stragglers—cold, wretched-looking creatures, in the last stage of emaciation and disease. The knot of Irish labourers at the lower end of the place, who have been alternately shaking hands with, and threatening the life of each other, for the last hour, become furious in their disputes, and finding it impossible to silence one man, who is particularly anxious to adjust the difference, they resort to the expedient of knocking him down and jumping on him afterwards. The man in the fur cap, and the potboy rush out; a scene of riot and confusion ensues; half the Irishmen get shut out, and the other half get shut in; the potboy is knocked among the tubs in no time; the landlord hits everybody, and everybody hits the landlord; the barmaids scream; the police come in; the rest is a confused mixture of arms, legs, staves, torn coats, shouting, and struggling. Some of the party are borne off to the station-house, and the remainder slink home to beat their wives for complaining, and kick the children for daring to be hungry.

We have sketched this subject very slightly, not only because our limits compel us to do so, but because, if it were pursued farther, it would be painful and repulsive. Well-disposed gentlemen, and charitable ladies, would alike turn with coldness and disgust from a description of the drunken besotted men, and wretched broken-down miserable women, who form no inconsiderable portion of the frequenters of these haunts; forgetting, in the pleasant consciousness of their own rectitude, the poverty of the one, and the temptation of the other. Gin-drinking is a great vice in England, but wretchedness and dirt are a greater; and until you improve the homes of the poor, or persuade a half-famished wretch not to seek relief in the temporary oblivion of his own misery, with the pittance which, divided among his family, would furnish a morsel of bread for each, gin-shops will increase in number and splendour. If Temperance Societies would suggest an antidote against hunger, filth, and foul air, or could establish dispensaries for the gratuitous distribution of bottles of Lethe-water, gin-palaces would be numbered among the things that were.

## James Joyce, "Counterparts" (1914)

*It is not surprising that the well-known prevalence of drinking in Irish culture is reflected in the work of Irish writers, including that of James Joyce (1882–1941). Although never the central theme of any one of his works, drinking is ubiquitous in Joyce's fiction, with important links to characterization, setting, atmosphere, and plot. In Joyce's first book, the short story collection* Dubliners, *the depiction of drink can range from realistic background detail to light-hearted comedy to, as is the case with the story included here, desperation and violence.*

*In speaking of this story, an anonymous reviewer of the first edition of* Dubliners *wrote that "In ... 'Counterparts,' is power enough to make us wish for a novel from Mr. Joyce's pen."\* That power is inextricably bound up with the tavern scenes that constitute the heart of the entire story.*

*"Counterparts" covers several hours in the life of its protagonist, a copy clerk named Farrington. The story opens at Farrington's office, where he endures ridicule and abuse from his tyrannical supervisor, Alleyne. The story closes on a parallel encounter between Farrington and his young son, at home. Flanked by these two settings is the story's lengthy central section, which shows Farrington visiting a series of pubs in which he becomes increasingly drunk. With an inexorable, almost leisurely build-up of tension, the section devoted to Farrington's pub-crawling with his cronies serves as a bridge, both in terms of theme and action, between the story's beginning and end. In his detailed account of Farrington's pub experiences, Joyce establishes the crucial—but as the story makes clear, by no means exclusive—role of alcohol and of the pub itself in the life of Farrington and of his son; thus, Joyce's tale is far removed from classic temperance fiction's use of some of the same elements: a tavern; a distraught, drunken father; an abused child. The temperance tale's dominant paradigm, exemplified by T.S. Arthur's famous "Ten Nights in a Bar-Room" (1854), or Walt Whitman's "Reuben's Last Wish" (included in the "Family" section of this volume), involves the demonization not only of liquor but of pub, bar, saloon, or tavern—in short, of any version of the public house in which liquor could be obtained. In contrast, "Counterparts" presents liquor and the pub as components in a much larger complex of economic, social, and personal factors that contribute to the pathos of Farrington's situation and to his behavior toward his child. All of these factors coalesce with Farrington's drunkenness in the story's unforgettable final scene—one of the most thought-provoking and heart-rending passages in all of Joyce.*

*\*Quoted in A. Nicholas Fargnoli and Michael Patrick Gillespie,* Critical Companion to James Joyce: A Literary Reference to His Life and Work *(New York: Facts on File, 2006), p. 80.*

The bell rang furiously and, when Miss Parker went to the tube, a furious voice called out in a piercing North of Ireland accent:

"Send Farrington here!"

Miss Parker returned to her machine, saying to a man who was writing at a desk:

"Mr Alleyne wants you upstairs."

The man muttered "*Blast* him!" under his breath and pushed back his chair to stand up. When he stood up he was tall and of great bulk. He had a hanging face, dark wine-coloured, with fair eyebrows and moustache: his eyes bulged forward slightly and the whites of them were dirty. He lifted up the counter and, passing by the clients, went out of the office with a heavy step.

He went heavily upstairs until he came to the second landing, where a door bore a brass plate with the inscription *Mr Alleyne*. Here he halted, puffing with labour and vexation, and knocked. The shrill voice cried:

"Come in!"

The man entered Mr Alleyne's room. Simultaneously Mr Alleyne, a little man wearing gold-rimmed glasses on a cleanshaven face, shot his head up over a pile of documents. The head itself was so pink and hairless it seemed like a large egg reposing on the papers. Mr Alleyne did not lose a moment:

"Farrington? What is the meaning of this? Why have I always to complain of you? May I ask you why you haven't made a copy of that contract between Bodley and Kirwan? I told you it must be ready by four o'clock."

"But Mr Shelley said, sir——"

"*Mr Shelley said, sir*.... Kindly attend to what I say and not to what *Mr Shelley says, sir*. You have always some excuse or another for shirking work. Let me tell you that if the contract is not copied before this evening I'll lay the matter before Mr Crosbie.... Do you hear me now?"

"Yes, sir."

"Do you hear me now? ... Ay and another little matter! I might as well be talking to the wall as talking to you. Understand once for all that you get a half an hour for your lunch and not an hour and a half. How many courses do you want, I'd like to know.... Do you mind me now?"

"Yes, sir."

Mr Alleyne bent his head again upon his pile of papers. The man stared fixedly at the polished skull which directed the affairs of Crosbie & Alleyne, gauging its fragility. A spasm of rage gripped his throat for a few moments and then passed, leaving after it a sharp sensation of thirst. The man recognised the sensation and felt that he must have a good night's drinking. The middle of the month was passed and, if he could get the copy done in time, Mr Alleyne might give him an order on the cashier. He stood still, gazing fixedly at the head upon the pile of papers. Suddenly Mr Alleyne began to upset all the papers, searching for something. Then, as if he had been unaware of the man's presence till that moment, he shot up his head again, saying:

"Eh? Are you going to stand there all day? Upon my word, Farrington, you take things easy!"

"I was waiting to see…"

"Very good, you needn't wait to see. Go downstairs and do your work."

The man walked heavily towards the door and, as he went out of the room, he heard Mr Alleyne cry after him that if the contract was not copied by evening Mr Crosbie would hear of the matter.

He returned to his desk in the lower office and counted the sheets which remained to be copied. He took up his pen and dipped it in the ink but he continued to stare stupidly at the last words he had written: *In no case shall the said Bernard Bodley be*…. The evening was falling and in a few minutes they would be lighting the gas: then he could write. He felt that he must slake the thirst in his throat. He stood up from his desk and, lifting the counter as before, passed out of the office. As he was passing out the chief clerk looked at him inquiringly.

"It's all right, Mr Shelley," said the man, pointing with his finger to indicate the objective of his journey.

The chief clerk glanced at the hat-rack, but, seeing the row complete, offered no remark. As soon as he was on the landing the man pulled a shepherd's plaid cap out of his pocket, put it on his head and ran quickly down the rickety stairs. From the street door he walked on furtively on the inner side of the path towards the corner and all at once dived into a doorway. He was now safe in the dark snug of O'Neill's shop, and filling up the little window that looked into the bar with his inflamed face, the colour of dark wine or dark meat, he called out:

"Here, Pat, give us a g.p., like a good fellow."

The curate brought him a glass of plain porter. The man drank it at a gulp and asked for a caraway seed. He put his penny on the counter and, leaving the curate to grope for it in the gloom, retreated out of the snug as furtively as he had entered it.

Darkness, accompanied by a thick fog, was gaining upon the dusk of February and the lamps in Eustace Street had been lit. The man went up by the houses until he reached the door of the office, wondering whether he could finish his copy in time. On the stairs a moist pungent odour of perfumes saluted his nose: evidently Miss Delacour had come while he was out in O'Neill's. He crammed his cap back again into his pocket and re-entered the office, assuming an air of absentmindedness.

"Mr Alleyne has been calling for you," said the chief clerk severely. "Where were you?"

The man glanced at the two clients who were standing at the counter as if to intimate that their presence prevented him from answering. As the clients were both male the chief clerk allowed himself a laugh.

"I know that game," he said. "Five times in one day is a little bit.... Well, you better look sharp and get a copy of our correspondence in the Delacour case for Mr Alleyne."

This address in the presence of the public, his run upstairs and the porter he had gulped down so hastily confused the man and, as he sat down at his desk to get what was required, he realised how hopeless was the task of finishing his copy of the contract before half past five. The dark damp night was coming and he longed to spend it in the bars, drinking with his friends amid the glare of gas and the clatter of glasses. He got out the Delacour correspondence and passed out of the office. He hoped Mr Alleyne would not discover that the last two letters were missing.

The moist pungent perfume lay all the way up to Mr Alleyne's room. Miss Delacour was a middle-aged woman of Jewish appearance. Mr Alleyne was said to be sweet on her or on her money. She came to the office often and stayed a long time when she came. She was sitting beside his desk now in an aroma of perfumes, smoothing the handle of her umbrella and nodding the great black feather in her hat. Mr Alleyne had swivelled his chair round to face her and thrown his right foot jauntily upon his left knee. The man put the correspondence on the desk and bowed respectfully but neither Mr Alleyne nor Miss Delacour took any notice of his bow. Mr Alleyne tapped a finger on the correspondence and then flicked it towards him as if to say: *"That's all right: you can go."*

The man returned to the lower office and sat down again at his desk. He stared intently at the incomplete phrase: *In no case shall the said Bernard Bodley be* ... and thought how strange it was that the last three words began with the same letter. The chief clerk began to hurry Miss Parker, saying she would never have the letters typed in time for post. The man listened to the clicking of the machine for a few minutes and then set to work to finish his copy. But his head was not clear and his mind wandered away to the glare and rattle of the public-house. It was a night for hot punches. He struggled on with his copy, but when the clock struck five he had still fourteen pages to write. Blast it! He couldn't finish it in time. He longed to execrate aloud, to bring his fist down on something violently. He was so enraged that he wrote *Bernard Bernard* instead of *Bernard Bodley* and had to begin again on a clean sheet.

He felt strong enough to clear out the whole office single-handed. His body ached to do something, to rush out and revel in violence. All the indignities of his life enraged him.... Could he ask the cashier privately for an advance? No, the cashier was no good, no damn good: he wouldn't give an advance.... He knew where he would meet the boys: Leonard and O'Halloran and Nosey Flynn. The barometer of his emotional nature was set for a spell of riot.

His imagination had so abstracted him that his name was called twice before he answered. Mr Alleyne and Miss Delacour were standing outside the counter and all the clerks had turn round in anticipation of something. The man got up from his desk. Mr Alleyne began a tirade of abuse, saying that two letters were missing. The man answered that he knew nothing about them, that he had made a faithful copy. The tirade continued: it was so bitter and violent that the man could hardly restrain his fist from descending upon the head of the manikin before him:

"I know nothing about any other two letters," he said stupidly.

"*You—know—nothing*. Of course you know nothing," said Mr Alleyne. "Tell me," he added, glancing first for approval to the lady beside him, "do you take me for a fool? Do you think me an utter fool?"

The man glanced from the lady's face to the little egg-shaped head and back again; and, almost before he was aware of it, his tongue had found a felicitous moment:

"I don't think, sir," he said, "that that's a fair question to put to me."

There was a pause in the very breathing of the clerks. Everyone was astounded (the author of the witticism no less than his neighbours) and Miss Delacour, who was a stout amiable person, began to smile broadly. Mr Alleyne flushed to the hue of a wild rose and his mouth twitched with a dwarf's passion. He shook his fist in the man's face till it seemed to vibrate like the knob of some electric machine:

"You impertinent ruffian! You impertinent ruffian! I'll make short work of you! Wait till you see! You'll apologise to me for your impertinence or you'll quit the office instanter! You'll quit this, I'm telling you, or you'll apologise to me!"

\* \* \*

He stood in a doorway opposite the office watching to see if the cashier would come out alone. All the clerks passed out and finally the cashier came out with the chief clerk. It was no use trying to say a word to him when he was with the chief clerk. The man felt that his position was bad enough. He had been obliged to offer an abject apology to Mr Alleyne for his impertinence but he knew what a hornet's nest the office would be for him. He could remember the way in which Mr Alleyne had hounded little Peake out of the office in order to make room for his own nephew. He felt savage and thirsty and revengeful, annoyed with himself and with everyone else. Mr Alleyne would never give him an hour's rest; his life would be a hell to him. He had made a proper fool of himself this time. Could he not keep his tongue in his cheek? But they had never pulled together from the first, he and Mr Alleyne, ever since the day Mr Alleyne had overheard him mimicking his North of Ireland accent to amuse Higgins and Miss Parker: that had been the beginning of it. He might have tried Higgins for the money, but sure Higgins never had anything for himself. A man with two establishments to keep up, of course he couldn't....

He felt his great body again aching for the comfort of the public-house. The fog had begun to chill him and he wondered could he touch Pat in O'Neill's. He could not touch him for more than a bob—and a bob was no use. Yet he must get money somewhere or other: he had spent his last penny for the g.p. and soon it would be too late for getting money anywhere. Suddenly, as he was fingering his watch-chain, he thought of Terry Kelly's pawn-office in Fleet Street. That was the dart! Why didn't he think of it sooner?

He went through the narrow alley of Temple Bar quickly, muttering to himself that they could all go to hell because he was going to have a good night of it. The clerk in Terry Kelly's said *A crown!* but the consignor held out for six shillings; and in the end the six shillings was allowed him literally. He came out of the pawn-office joyfully, making a little cylinder, of the coins between his thumb and fingers. In Westmoreland Street the footpaths were crowded with young men and women returning from business and ragged urchins ran here and there yelling out the names of the evening editions. The man passed through the crowd, looking on the spectacle generally with proud satisfaction and staring masterfully at the office-girls. His head was full of the noises of tram-gongs and swishing trolleys and his nose already sniffed the curling fumes punch. As he walked on he preconsidered the terms in which he would narrate the incident to the boys:

"So, I just looked at him—coolly, you know, and looked at her. Then I looked back at him again—taking my time, you know. 'I don't think that's a fair question to put to me,' says I."

Nosey Flynn was sitting up in his usual corner of Davy Byrne's and, when he heard the story, he stood Farrington a half-one, saying it was as smart a thing as ever he heard. Farrington stood a drink in his turn. After a while O'Halloran and Paddy Leonard came in and the story was repeated to them. O'Halloran stood tailors of malt, hot, all round and told the story of the retort he had made to the chief clerk when he was in Callan's of Fownes's Street; but, as the retort was after the manner of the liberal shepherds in the eclogues, he had to admit that it was not as clever as Farrington's retort. At this Farrington told the boys to polish off that and have another.

Just as they were naming their poisons who should come in but Higgins!

Of course he had to join in with the others. The men asked him to give his version of it, and he did so with great vivacity for the sight of five small hot whiskies was very exhilarating. Everyone roared laughing when he showed the way in which Mr. Alleyne shook his fist in Farrington's face. Then he imitated Farrington, saying, *"And here was my nabs, as cool as you please,"* while Farrington looked at the company out of his heavy dirty eyes, smiling and at times drawing forth stray drops of liquor from his moustache with the aid of his lower lip.

When that round was over there was a pause. O'Halloran had money but neither of the other two seemed to have any; so the whole party left the shop somewhat regretfully. At the corner of Duke Street Higgins and Nosey Flynn bevelled off to the left while the other three turned back towards the city. Rain was drizzling down on the cold streets and, when they reached the Ballast Office, Farrington suggested the Scotch House. The bar was full of men and loud with the noise of tongues and glasses. The three men pushed past the whining matchsellers at the door and formed a little party at the corner of the counter. They began to exchange stories. Leonard introduced them to a young fellow named Weathers who was performing at the Tivoli as an acrobat and knockabout *artiste*. Farrington stood a drink all round. Weathers said he would take a small Irish and Apollinaris. Farrington, who had definite notions of what was what, asked the boys would they have an Apollinaris too; but the boys told Tim to make theirs hot. The talk became theatrical. O'Halloran stood a round and then Farrington stood another round, Weathers protesting that the hospitality was too Irish. He promised to get them in behind the scenes and introduce them to some nice girls. O'Halloran said that he and Leonard would go, but that Farrington wouldn't go because he was a married man; and Farrington's heavy dirty eyes leered at the company in token that he understood he was being chaffed. Weathers made them all have just one little tincture at his expense and promised to meet them later on at Mulligan's in Poolbeg Street.

When the Scotch House closed they went round to Mulligan's. They went into the parlour at the back and O'Halloran ordered small hot specials all round. They were all beginning to feel mellow. Farrington was just standing another round when Weathers came back. Much to Farrington's relief he drank a glass of bitter this time. Funds were getting low but they had enough to keep them going. Presently two young women with big hats and a young man in a check suit came in and sat at a table close by. Weathers saluted them and told the company that they were out of the Tivoli. Farrington's eyes wandered at every moment in the direction of one of the young women. There was something striking in her appearance. An immense scarf of peacock-blue muslin was wound round her hat and knotted in a great bow under her chin; and she wore bright yellow gloves, reaching to the elbow. Farrington gazed admiringly at the plump arm which she moved very often and with much grace; and when, after a little time, she answered his gaze he admired still more her large dark brown eyes. The oblique staring expression in them fascinated him. She glanced at him once or twice and, when the party was leaving the room, she brushed against his chair and said "*O, pardon!*" in a London accent. He watched her leave the room in the hope that she would look back at him, but he was disappointed. He cursed his want of money and cursed all the rounds he had stood, particularly all the whiskies and Apolinaris which he had stood to Weathers. If there was one thing that he hated it was a sponge. He was so angry that he lost count of the conversation of his friends.

When Paddy Leonard called him he found that they were talking about feats of strength. Weathers was showing his biceps muscle to the company and boasting so much that the other two had called on Farrington to uphold the national honour. Farrington pulled up his sleeve accordingly and showed his biceps muscle to the company. The two arms were examined and compared and finally it was agreed to have a trial of strength. The table was cleared and the two men rested their elbows on it, clasping hands. When Paddy Leonard said "*Go!*" each was to try to bring down the other's hand on to the table. Farrington looked very serious and determined.

The trial began. After about thirty seconds Weathers brought his opponent's hand slowly down on to the table. Farrington's dark wine-coloured face flushed darker still with anger and humiliation at having been defeated by such a stripling.

"You're not to put the weight of your body behind it. Play fair," he said.

"Who's not playing fair?" said the other.

"Come on again. The two best out of three."

The trial began again. The veins stood out on Farrington's forehead, and the pallor of Weathers' complexion changed to peony. Their hands and arms trembled under the stress. After a long struggle Weathers again brought his opponent's hand slowly on to the table. There was a murmur of applause from the spectators. The curate, who was standing beside the table, nodded his red head towards the victor and said with stupid familiarity:

"Ah! that's the knack!"

"What the hell do you know about it?" said Farrington fiercely, turning on the man. "What do you put in your gab for?"

"Sh, sh!" said O'Halloran, observing the violent expression of Farrington's face. "Pony up, boys. We'll have just one little smahan more and then we'll be off."

\* \* \*

A very sullen-faced man stood at the corner of O'Connell Bridge waiting for the little Sandymount tram to take him home. He was full of smouldering anger and revengefulness. He felt humiliated and discontented; he did not even feel drunk; and he had only twopence in his pocket. He cursed everything. He had done for himself in the office, pawned his watch, spent all his money; and he had not even got drunk. He began to feel thirsty again and he longed to be back again in the hot reeking public-house. He had lost his reputation as a strong man, having been defeated twice by a mere boy. His heart swelled with fury and, when he thought of the woman in the big hat who had brushed against him and said *Pardon!* his fury nearly choked him.

His tram let him down at Shelbourne Road and he steered his great body along in the shadow of the wall of the barracks. He loathed returning to his home. When he went in by the side-door he found the kitchen empty and the kitchen fire nearly out. He bawled upstairs:

"Ada! Ada!"

His wife was a little sharp-faced woman who bullied her husband when he was sober and was bullied by him when he was drunk. They had five children. A little boy came running down the stairs.

"Who is that?" said the man, peering through the darkness.

"Me, pa."

"Who are you? Charlie?"

"No, pa. Tom."

"Where's your mother?"

"She's out at the chapel."

"That's right.... Did she think of leaving any dinner for me?"

"Yes, pa. I—"

"Light the lamp. What do you mean by having the place in darkness? Are the other children in bed?"

The man sat down heavily on one of the chairs while the little boy lit the lamp. He began to mimic his son's flat accent, saying half to himself: "*At the chapel. At the chapel, if you please!*" When the lamp was lit he banged his fist on the table and shouted:

"What's for my dinner?"

"I'm going ... to cook it, pa," said the little boy.

The man jumped up furiously and pointed to the fire.

"On that fire! You let the fire out! By God, I'll teach you to do that again!"

He took a step to the door and seized the walking-stick which was standing behind it.

"I'll teach you to let the fire out!" he said, rolling up his sleeve in order to give his arm free play.

The little boy cried "*O, pa!*" and ran whimpering round the table, but the man followed him and caught him by the coat. The little boy looked about him wildly but, seeing no way of escape, fell upon his knees.

"Now, you'll let the fire out the next time!" said the man striking at him vigorously with the stick. "Take that, you little whelp!"

The boy uttered a squeal of pain as the stick cut his thigh. He clasped his hands together in the air and his voice shook with fright.

"O, pa!" he cried. "Don't beat me, pa! And I'll ... I'll say a *Hail Mary* for you.... I'll say a *Hail Mary* for you, pa, if you don't beat me.... I'll say a *Hail Mary*...."

## *Langston Hughes, "Cocktail Sip" (1953)*

*As with most of Langston Hughes's popular stories featuring the character known as Jesse B. Semple (or, as he came to be called, Simple), "Cocktail Sip" takes place in a Harlem bar. The story's tavern setting provides Simple with a place in which to unwind the spirit and the tongue, as he confides in his friend (the more educated and somewhat stuffy narrator, loosely identified with Hughes himself). In the safe setting of the Harlem bar, far from the pressures and insults of the white world, Simple freely expounds on drink, work, race, women, money, and his own misadventures with all of the above. Although not a problem drinker, Hughes (1902–1967) was fond of taverns, including Patsy's Bar in Harlem where, according to his own account, he met the living prototype of the character he would render in dozens of stories as "Simple." In general, the bar in Hughes's work partakes of the romanticized imagery of black nightlife common in the literature of the Harlem Renaissance.\* And while an exception to Hughes's positive depiction of taverns does appear in the gloomy bar-scene depicted in his story "On the Way Home," in the present tale, the bar is a friendly, welcoming place, a haven of (largely) male camaraderie and solidarity. It is also a place of sensual promise, as suggested by the exotic Zarita, a woman who frequents the drinking establishments that Simple's lively but very proper wife-to-be, Joyce, does not. Still, for all of Zarita's sensual — and drink-enhanced — appeal, the story ends with a lightly ironic rejection of the very things that Simple seemed, at first, so much to prize in Zarita and her intoxicating world. While race is not at the forefront of this story, issues of gender, desire, drink, and the illusions of romanticized passion all subtly intersect in "Cocktail Sip."*

\**See Denise Herd, "The Paradox of Temperance: Blacks and the Alcohol Question in Nineteenth-Century America," in Susanna Barrows and Robin Room, eds., Drinking:*

Behavior and Belief in Modern History *(Berkeley and Los Angeles: University of California Press, 1991), pp. 354–375, especially p. 370.*

Along about nine o'clock Sunday evening, Simple emerged grinning from the dusky backroom of Paddy's Bar to spy me at the front. I was surprised to see him so early and so hilarious. He was half high.

"Mulberries, sweet, my Lord," he cried, "also the lips of a woman!"

"You sound like an Elizabethan," I said. "What's up?"

"Lizzie who?" asked Simple.

"Poets of long ago I studied in school."

"It must have been long ago, because you have been out of school a long time."

"I still remember some of their poems, though. For instance:
*Drink to me only with thine eyes,*
*And I will pledge with mine,*
*Or leave a kiss but in the cup*
*And I'll not ask for wine.*"*

Meanwhile, Simple was beckoning the bartender, and the juke box was blaring.

I said, "Are you listening?"

"I'm listening fluently," he protested. "But I would like some beer. Besides, these kisses I'm talking about were not in no cup."

"You're probably in your cups," I said.

"I am not," said Simple. "I am half sober. See this lipstick on my handkerchief? I just got through wiping my mouth."

"Whom, may I ask, were you kissing?"

"Zarita—in the phone booth."

"Are you running with that light-o'-love again?"

"Only occasionally," said Simple. "This evening is one of the occasions."

"If Joyce catches you, you will run *from* Zarita, not with her."

"I hope Joyce don't catch me," said Simple. "Sometimes a man likes a woman with experience."

"Then you ought to like Zarita a lot."

"I do and I don't. Zarita is strictly a after-hours gal—great when die hour is late, the wine is fine, and mellow whiskey has made you frisky."

I quoted over the juke-box blare:
*"The thirst that from the soul doth rise*
*Doth ask a drink divine...."*

"Zarita will drink anything," said Simple. "She is like me in that respect, from beer to champagne. But this Sunday, we been to a Five O'clock Cocktail Sip where they empty all the different left-over bottles on the bar into the shaker, shake it up, put in a cherry—and call it a Special. We had several Specials.

"I did not know I was going to meet Zarita there, but I did. She were unescorted, so we sipped together. Then we danced together. Then we sat together. Then I went by her house. Then she came by my house. After which, we both came here to cool. I still had to kiss her one more time in the phone booth before she shoved off. She spends every Sunday night with her foster-mama, so she has to go now. In fact, I think she already went out the side door because she does not like Buster to see her in here with me. Old funny-looking Buster standing over there thinks he likes her."

"It's a good thing you are not jealous," I said.

"I have an open mind about Zarita. I am only jealous of Joyce. I may not see Zarita again for a month. But somehow or other, her kisses make me think of mulberries—that sloe gin they colored them cocktails, I reckon."

"It's a wonder you are not rocking and reeling."

"Rocky, but not really. I feel like hey! hey! hey! Come on, have a beer!"

"On you?"

"On me," said Simple. "My generosity has come down on me! I am glad I run into you while I still have some change left. I spent Three Dollars and a Half at the Cocktail Sip, threw a Dollar to the shake dancer when the floor show come on, tipped the waiter Fifty Cents, checked out my hat—then borrowed Five Dollars from Zarita that she said Buster gave her—so it all come out even. Zarita is a good old girl. She will give you the shirt off her back, also take yours off your back. But in due time, we more than gets it back, both of us. So nobody's worried. What did you say about that kiss in the cup?"

"*Leave but a kiss within the cup/ And I'll not look for wine....*"

"I sure won't," said Simple. "Won't and don't! But lately there ain't been nary kiss in *my cup.*"

"You mean where you ring seven bells?"

"That's right," said Simple. "Joyce is still acting like she just met me—like I was a total stranger with no divorce—which maybe is why I fell into Zarita's arms today, which were wide open. You don't need a decree to relax with Zarita. You know, I usually spends Sundays with Joyce. But she said she were going to Jersey to see her godchild this afternoon. I wonder if she went? I did not ring seven to find out. Sometimes if her landlady catches me when Joyce ain't home, she just wants to talk and talk and talk, and I did not feel like talking to that woman today. So when I passed by the Heat Wave and saw that sign up—cocktail sip—I went in."

"And what did you find but sin—in the form of Zarita. 'When the cat's away, the mouse will play.'"

"Did Lizzie Beasley say that, too?"

"That's not Elizabethan, that's doggerel," I stated, "simple but true."

"Do you think I'm simple? If I wasn't drunk, I would feel bad. But I do not feel bad. I feel like if Joyce had rather go see some godchild than to see me, okay. Let the good times roll! They have rolled this evening! Look, am I wrong?"

I am neither Judge Rivers nor Judge Delany, so I will not pass judgment on you," I said.†

"I had rather go up before them than to go up before a lady judge. If my case ever got in front of any lady judge, I bet she would make me pay for Isabel's divorce. Lady judges is tight, tight, tight. But let us not mention judges this evening, partner. As long as I know what I am doing, I will never appear before one."

"You had better stop mixing your drinks then. You've been drinking cocktails, now you are drinking beer—so after a while you will not be clear as to what you are doing. Have you had your dinner yet?"

"You know I don't like restaurant cooking. And Joyce—let's not talk about her—no invite there this Sunday. I believe I will go home to bed right now, up to my Third Floor Rear. I told Zarita I might wait till she comes back, but I changed my mind. Them Specials is wearing off. Tell her I have went. If she's got any more kisses for me, tell her to leave 'em in a cup."

\*These lines appear in Ben Jonson's famous Elizabethan lyric, "Song to Celia" (1616), which was set to music as "Drink to me only with thine Eyes," an immensely popular song in Hughes' youth.

†Francis E. Rivers and Hubert T. Delany were prominent black lawyers and, at the time of this story's publication, judges in New York City, their accomplishments being well-publicized throughout Harlem's African-American community.

## Nicolás Guillén, "Bars" (1958)

*Celebration has not been a hallmark of the passages in this section. Blake's "Little Vagabond" serves more to criticize the church's social failures than to praise the ale-house as such; the Crane and Dickens selections show taverns in a negative light, as does Joyce's "Counterparts," where pub-crawling leads to drunkenness and violence. For Hughes, the bar provides atmosphere and a vivid setting, but it is not the main focus of his "Cocktail Sip." In contrast, the poem "Bares" ("Bars"), by Nicolás Guillén (1902–1989) is a genuinely celebratory, joyful text about the subject of its title, paralleling such texts as Keats's tribute to a famous literary* inn, "Lines on the Mermaid Tavern," also reprinted in this section, or Raymond Chandler's eloquent riff on bars in his detective novel, The Long Goodbye.*

Moreover, Guillén's poem ties in with a major dimension of tavern history, as indicated in the introduction: the traditional associations of the public house with popular solidarity and democratic impulses. In the time of the American Revolution, taverns were perceived as "seed beds of the Revolution"; in France, cafés were traditionally recognized as, in Balzac's phrase, "parliaments of the people"; in late nineteenth and early twentieth-century Germany, labor organizations were closely linked with drinking establishments.† Himself a Cuban political activist who was jailed in 1936–37 for publishing "subversive material," and who was expelled from Cuba for opposition to Batista's regime in 1953, Guillén eventually returned to Cuba to become the president of that country's Writers and Artists Union, a post he held until his death in 1989. His poetry, which ranges from the overtly political to the intensely personal, reflects truly international and multicultural influences: Afro-Cuban speech and song elements; Caribbean Francophone poetry; the classical Spanish literary tradition; and the Harlem Renaissance. In its evocation of parallels between seemingly unrelated, distant places, in its exuberantly subversive tone, and in the way it links human fellowship to the world of nature (twice the poet says that the "bares y tavernas" are "junto al mar"— "near the sea"), this poem typifies the subject matter and style of Guillén's poetry.‡ The translation here is by Roberto Márquez and David Arthur McMurray.

*"I like bars just after they open for the evening.... I like the neat bottles on the back bar and the lovely shining glasses and the anticipation. I like to watch the man mix the first one of the evening and put it down on a crisp mat and put the little folded napkin beside it.... The first quiet drink of the evening in a quiet bar—that's wonderful" (Terry Lennox, speaking to the narrator, Philip Marlowe, in Raymond Chandler, The Long Good-Bye (New York: Random House, 1953), p. 17.

†On American taverns, see W.J. Rorabaugh, The Alcoholic Republic: An American Tradition (New York: Oxford University Press, 1979), p. 35; on French cafés and German taverns, see, respectively, Susanna Barrows, "Parliaments of the People," in Barrows and Room, eds., Drinking, pp. 87–88, and James S. Roberts, "The Tavern and Politics," also in Drinking, pp. 98–111.

‡A striking irony here is that the lifelong Marxist Guillén's romanticized seaside bars of the people contrast sharply with traditional Marxist discourses of alcohol. In an 1844 manuscript, Marx described the gin-shops of England as "symbolical embodiments of private property" quoted in Brian Harrison, Drink and the Victorians (Pittsburgh: University of Pittsburgh Press, 1971), p. 394, while in The Condition of the Working Class, "the consumption of alcohol was one of Engels's benchmarks for the increasing exploitation of laborers, the breakdown of communal life, and the demoralization of the working class" (Susanna Barrows and Robin Room, "Introduction," in Barrows and Room, eds., Drinking, p. 3). In personal terms, however, Marx "was no stranger to alehouses," and even served as "co-president of the Trier Tavern Club, a society of about thirty university students from his home town [Trier]..."; see Francis Wheen, Karl Marx: A Life (New York: W.W. Norton & Co., 2001), p. 16.

How I love the bars and taverns
near the sea,
where people drink and talk
just to talk and drink.
Where John Nobody comes and calls
for an ordinary drink,
and in come John Harshvoice, John Straightrazor,
John Spadenose, and even John Simple
... plain and simple
John.

That's where a white wave foams with friendship;
a people's friendship, one without rhetoric:
a wave of "Hey," of "What's happening?"
That's where it smells of fish,
mangrove, rum, salt,
and a sweaty shirt out drying in the sun.

So come by, brother, and you'll find me
(in La Habana, Oporto,
Jacmel, Shanghai)
with ordinary people
who just to drink and talk
people the bars and taverns
near the sea.

## *John Keats, "Lines on the Mermaid Tavern" (1818) and E.E. Cummings, "i was sitting in mcsorley's" (1922)*

*Many works of literature include a fictional bar or tavern as the setting for drinking, refer in passing to actual taverns, or focus on the nature of public drinking establishments in general, whether in praise (as in Blake's "The Little Vagabond") or condemnation (as in Dickens's "Gin-Shops"). Yet another trend in the depiction of the tavern appears in the two poems reprinted below—the evocation of an actual public house.*

*The first poem, by John Keats (1795–1821), celebrates London's venerable Mermaid Tavern (no longer in existence), which was rich in literary associations* *already long before Keats's time. As a number of critics have pointed out, Keats's poem continues a tradition of literary evocations of the Mermaid Tavern that began in Elizabethan times, when the tavern was originally founded, and reputedly served as a meeting-place for such dramatists as Francis Beaumont, John Fletcher, Ben Jonson, and possibly even Shakespeare. The Mermaid is briefly mentioned in Ben Jonson's poem, "Inviting a Friend to Supper," and is celebrated for its atmosphere and literary associations at more length in Beaumont's verse "Letter to Ben Jonson"; these Elizabethan literary associations of the Mermaid Tavern were doubtless in Keats's mind since the letter to his friend John Reynolds, in which the poem on the Mermaid Tavern first appeared, speaks nostalgically and admiringly of Elizabethan literature and legends. A tavern frequented by some of England's great writers of the past would have a double appeal for Keats, linking his devotion to poetry with his oft-proclaimed love of wine—a love reflected in the wine imagery found throughout his work.\**

*The second poem, by E.E. Cummings (1894–1962), was written in 1922, and published in 1923, during Cummings' immersion in the artistic life of New York and his burgeoning literary creativity following his return from World War I. The tavern evoked in Cummings' poem, McSorley's, was established in the nineteenth century, and enjoyed a venerable reputation among New York taverns by the time Cummings wrote his poem, a reputation that contributes to the tavern's current status as a tourist hot spot in Greenwich Village. In the poem, McSorley's provides the poet with a pretext for describing in a kind of verbal collage of imagery the sounds, sights, and smells of the busy tavern, and also the varying states of inebriety—including, perhaps, the poet's own—that occur within its "snug and evil" interior.†*

\*For a helpful account of Keats's drinking habits and attitudes toward alcohol, see W. Jackson Bate, John Keats *(Cambridge: Harvard University Press, 1963), pp. 463–64.*

†Two decades after Cummings' poem appeared, an entire book devoted to McSorley's was published by journalist and New Yorker *contributor Joseph Mitchell. In a possible echo of Cummings' line about drinking McSorley's "ale which never lets you grow old," Mitchell described the aged patrons of McSorley's departing at the end of the day: "they yawn, stretch, and start for home, insulated with ale against the dreadful loneliness of the old"; see Joseph Mitchell,* McSorley's Wonderful Saloon *(New York: Duell, Sloan, and Pearce, 1943), p. 19.*

### John Keats, "Lines on the Mermaid Tavern"

Souls of Poets dead and gone,
What Elysium have ye known,
Happy field or mossy cavern,
Choicer than the Mermaid Tavern?
Have ye tippled drink more fine

Than mine host's Canary wine?
Or are fruits of Paradise
Sweeter than those dainty pies
Of venison? O generous food!
Drest as though bold Robin Hood
Would, with his maid Marian,
Sup and bowse from horn and can.
I have heard that on a day
Mine host's sign-board flew away,
Nobody knew whither, till
An astrologer's old quill
To a sheepskin gave the story,
Said he saw you in your glory,
Underneath a new old sign
Sipping beverage divine,
And pledging with contented smack
The Mermaid in the Zodiac.
Souls of poets dead and gone,
What Elysium have ye known,
Happy field or mossy cavern,
Choicer than the Mermaid Tavern?

### E.E. Cummings, "i was sitting in mcsorleys"

i was sitting in mcsorley's.   outside it was New York and beautifully snowing.

Inside snug and evil.   the slobbering walls filthily push witless creases of screaming warmth chuck pillows are noise funnily swallows swallowing revolvingly pompous a the swallowed mottle with smooth or a but of rapidly goes gobs the and of flecks of and a chatter sobbings intersect with which distinct disks of graceful oath,upsoarings the break on      ceiling-flatness.

The Bar.tinking luscious jigs dint of ripe silver with warmlyish
wetflat splurging smells waltz the glush of squirting taps plus slush
of foam knocked off and a faint piddle-of-drops she says I ploc spittle
what the lands thaz me kid in no sir hopping sawdust you kiddo he's a
palping wreaths of badly Yep cigars who jim him why gluey grins topple
together eyes pout gestures stickily point made glints squinting who's
a wink bum-nothing and money fuzzily mouths take big wobbly foot-steps
every goggle cent of it get out ears dribbles soft right old feller
belch the chap hic summore eh chuckles skulch....

and i was sitting in the din thinking drinking the ale, which never
lets you grow old blinking at the low ceiling my being pleasantly was
punctuated by the always retchings of a worthless lamp.

when With a minute terrif     iceffort one dirty squeal of soiling light
yanking from bushy obscurity a bald greenish foetal head established
It suddenly upon the huge neck around whose unwashed sonorous muscle
the filth of a collar hung gently.

(spattered) by this instant of semiluminous nausea A vast wordless
nondescript genie of trunk trickled firmly in to one exactly-mutilated
ghost of a chair,

a;domeshaped interval of complete plasticity, shoulders, sprouted the
extraordinary arms through an angle of ridiculous velocity commenting
upon an unclearn table,and,whose distended immense Both paws slowly
loved a dinted mug

gone Darkness     it was so near to me, i ask of shadow won't you
have a drink?

(the eternal perpetual question)

Inside snugandevil.     i was sitting in mcsorley's     It, did not
answer.

outside (it was New York and beautifully, snowing....

# IV. Drinking and the Family

## *Walt Whitman, "Reuben's Last Wish" (1856)*

*One of the staples of temperance literature in its nineteenth-century heyday was drink's dangers to family life. Both verbal and visual works extolling temperance, such as T.S. Arthur's enormously popular novelette,* Ten Nights in a Barroom, and What I Saw There *(1855), and the temperance engravings of George Cruikshank, e.g., "The Bottle" (1848) and "The Drunkard's Children" (1847), reveled in depictions of the economic, physical, and psychological evils caused by excessive drinking. Such works often paid particular attention to a drinker's suffering family members—usually neglected parents and starved, even beaten wife and children, with the occasional portrait of the husband of a female drinker. Long before he became a great American poet and, indeed, American cultural icon, the writer we now know as Walt Whitman (1819–1892) was Walter Whitman, author of various pieces of journalism, poetry, and fiction, including tales furthering the cause of the mid nineteenth-century temperance movements. The most famous and the longest of these temperance works is the novel* Franklin Evans; or, The Inebriate. *Here, however, I include "Reuben's Last Wish," a shorter piece representative of Whitman's early temperance writing, and indeed of temperance literature's emphasis on the family, especially children, as the most immediate victims of drunkenness. The conventional, somewhat stilted prose and unabashedly sentimental attitude of this story are a far cry, both stylistically and thematically, from the bold pages of Whitman's later poetic masterpiece,* Leaves of Grass, *or from the vigor of Melville's temperance-inflected chapter from* Moby-Dick *reprinted above, in "Effects of Drinking." That said, "Reuben's Last Wish" stands here as an example of the contextualization of drinking in terms of family life, and of the temperance movement's tendency to emphasize children as both innocent victims of their elders' drinking, and as potential reformers of those elders—as the tale shows, Reuben, the son of drunkard Franklin Slade, calls to his father even to embrace temperance—a plea made all the more moving or melodramatic, depending upon one's point of view, by the fact that the plea is made with Reuben's dying breath.*

*One curious detail about this story is the name of the heavily drinking father, Franklin Slade. The name appears to conflate the first name and last names of two horrific drinkers from earlier texts: Franklin Evans, the protagonist of Whitman's own 1842 novel, mentioned above, and Simon Slade, the infamous drunkard from T.S. Arthur's* Ten Nights in a Barroom. *Slade's name may well have been on Whitman's mind during the composition of "Reuben's Last Wish" since, published in 1856, Whitman's story appeared only a year after the public met Arthur's villainous Simon Slade.*

*The whole phenomenon of drinking was one which, said Whitman, deserved serious study in literature. Late in his life (1888), Whitman made a statement that seems to represent his own views about drink more accurately—or at least maturely—than the rather sensationalistic and simplistic treatment of the drunkard in "Reuben's Last Wish," or in his jocular statements about only having been able to get through the writing of* Franklin Evans *by drinking copious amounts of port and, in some versions of the anecdote, gin! In an interview with his biographer, Horace Traubel, Whitman asserted that "the influence of drink in literature might also be written about—would also be instructive: it has so many sides, noble, devilish: it would need to be rightly interpreted—not by a puritan, not by a toper (the puritan is only another kind of toper). I have almost made up my mind to make some use of the themes myself, though I don't know as I'll ever get to them—so many physical obstacles drop into my pathway these years."\**

\**Quoted in Horace Traubel,* With Walt Whitman in Camden, *Vol. 1, 1906, pp. 146–47 (from The Walt Whitman Archive, ed. Ed Folsom and Kenneth M. Price, at www.whitmanarchive.org). Brief but helpful comments on the development of the undistinguished Walter Whitman into the legendary Walt Whitman appear in Thomas L. Brasher's "Introduction" to his edition of* Walt Whitman: The Early Poems and the Fiction *(New York: New York University Press, 1963) pp. xv–xviii; on Whitman's own drinking and attitudes toward temperance, see Brasher's headnote to* Franklin Evans *in the above volume, pp. 124–125, as well as David S. Reynolds,* Beneath the American Renaissance: the Subversive Imagination in the Age of Emerson and Melville *(New York: Alfred A. Knopf, 1988), passim.*

If the reader supposes that I am going to tell a story full of plot, interest, and excitement, let him peruse no farther than these two or three lines—for he will be disappointed. A simple tale—a narration not half so strange as people frequently see exemplified in their ordinary walks—is all I have to offer. Yet, as the greatest and profoundest truths are often most plain to the senses of men—in the same resemblance, my "Reuben" may haply teach a moral and plant a seed of wholesome instruction.

Not many weeks since, I happened to be in a country village, sixty miles, more or less, to the north of our great new world metropolis, New York. Towards sundown, I heard from the keeper of the inn where I was staying, that there was to be a temperance lecture in the place that night. The scene of the meeting was the school house; and having no other means of employing my time, I determined to attend.

At the appointed hour, I did so. The lecture itself was rather a prosy affair, but fortunately short; when it concluded, several persons, apparently residents thereabout, rose and made remarks, partly advice and partly transcripts of facts which had come under their observation. One of the speakers, a man considerably advanced in life, I listened to with much interest. After the exercises were over, I took occasion to introduce myself, and converse for some time with this man; and upon what I heard him say in the public meeting—the particulars he furnished me at our private interview—and, also, the additional facts I gathered from the people of the place, the subsequent day—I have based the narrative which follows.

Franklin Slade, a handsome, healthy American farmer, possessed at the age of thirty years, a comfortable estate, a fair reputation, a tolerably well filled purse—and could boast that he owed no debts which he was not able to pay on the instant. He had a prudent, good tempered wife, and two children, sons, one eight years old and the other three.

Through one of the thousand painted snares, which ministers of sin ever stand ready to tempt frailty withal, Slade, about this period, fell into a habit of tippling. At first, he would indulge himself but rarely, and that to a limited degree; but the fatal taste grew upon him, and in the course of years, the man was a *drunkard*, habitual and confirmed.

Franklin Slade, a bloated, red faced fellow, at the age of forty years, had his estate mortgaged for half its value—no man cared for his good will—his purse held not a dollar—and creditors insulted him daily. The once ruddy cheek of his wife was withered and pale from much sorrow; and her eye had lost its accustomed brightness. His eldest son, Slade had struck in a fit of drunken passion; the boy was high tempered—he left his father's house— shipped as a sailor to some far distant port—and thenceforward they never heard of him again. Little Reuben, the other son, was an invalid, and, (the bitter truth may as well be told,) an invalid through his father's wretched sensuality. Some time previous, the child being with Slade several miles away, the farmer drank so deeply, that he soon felt in no condition to get home. Reuben was kept out the whole night—a cold, rainy one. He was naturally delicate, and the exposure produced an effect on him from which he never recovered.

There is something very solemn in the sickness of children. The ashiness, and the moisture on the brow, and the film over the eye balls—what man can look upon the sight, and not feel his heart awed within him? Children, I have noticed too, increase in beauty as their illness deepens. The angels, it may be, are already vesting them with the garments they shall wear in the Pleasant Land.

Slade, to do him justice, was deeply grieved that the fruits of his folly fell thus upon the innocent Reuben, whom he loved much. Yet his infatuation had rooted so deeply, that he desisted in no respect from his dissolute practices. He scoffed at the efforts of the temperance advocates, who were becoming numerous and successful in the town—as they occasionally strove to bring him to their faith, and besought him to sign the pledge. His son very often joined his voice for the same purpose; entreaties and arguments, however, were alike futile.

Visiting, whenever his strength permitted, the meetings of the Temperance people, and reading and talking frequently upon the subject, Reuben before long entered with much enthusiasm into the new movement. He was an intelligent lad—and that he had seen what an evil thing drunkenness was, may well be imagined from the facts already given.

"I would," said the child one day to his mother, "I would have this paper bordered prettily with silk, and a fine ribbon bow at the top."

He held in his hand a Temperance pledge, with a picture at the top, and a blank space at the bottom for the names of signers.

"You are whimsical, my dear," said the matron, as she took the paper; "why do you desire so needless a thing done?"

"I hardly know myself," answered he, "yet please do it, mother. Ask me not why—let it be a whim."

And he smiled faintly.

And the sickening thought came over the woman's soul, that ere long she would probably not have the pleasant trouble of listening to the poor fellow's vagaries. She stepped hastily from the room, weeping.

In a day or two the Temperance pledge was edged tastily with a border of blue silk, and at each end, a piece of ribbon of the same color. The child was pleased: he took it and put it aside.

Days, months rolled on. The dwelling of Slade was a substantial old farm-house, a pleasant place, in the rear of which stretched a large garden. As it was now the season of advanced spring, the trees began to bud out and bloom there—the flowers to put forth their beautiful tints—and the grass donned its darkest green. Birds sang there too—the robin, and the black bird, and the fanciful bob-o-link. In the middle of the garden was a fine, grassy patch, shaded by a stupendous tree: leaning against the trunk of the tree had been built a long, wide, rustic seat. It was very fair, that spot—dreamy, warm, and free from annoyance of any kind.

Reuben, frequently walking here among the flowers and shrubs, would admire this grass plot, and stop, and resting himself on the seat, would remain a long hour enjoying the delight of the scene—not such delight as children are generally fond of, romping, and playing, and laughing—but a noiseless, motionless delight, in keeping with the place.

Still the days rolled on—and Reuben grew no better, but worse. Physicians seemed of little benefit. The only method of producing a favorable effect upon his spirits—and that was merely temporary—seemed to be to let him have quite his own way in all his fancies and his actions. Still he was never querulous or fretful.

One notion of the sick boy—though an odd one, they acquiesced in it—was to have a kind of couch made for him; and when he was too weak for walking about, to have it carried in the garden, on the favorite grass plot, that he might rest on it there.

For a time they kept somebody by him while he lay thus, lest his illness might take a fatal turn.—As, however, nothing of that kind occurred, and he lingered day after day without alteration, they relaxed somewhat from having a watcher by his garden bed. Now and then they would leave him, though not long—for a mother's affection is to her child like a needle to its magnet—though it may vibrate aside a little on occasions, it ever settles back again, truly and constantly.

Reuben, indeed, preferred being alone. He would get them to bring him large bunches of flowers, roses, and the fragrant carnation, and the delicate lily—which he would arrange fancifully about him: then, when he grew tired of such simple pastime, he would sink back, and lie long, long minutes, gazing on the bright sky above, and watching the changes of the clouds as they melted from tint to tint, and changed from form to form.

It grew at length to be, that the very birds, that had their nests thereabout, or sought fruit from the neighboring trees, became accustomed to the presence of Reuben, and hopped down upon his couch, and would rest upon his extended hand. They sometimes sat upon the branches over him, and would sing blithely and long—which was very sweet to the little invalid.

One morning it happened that the child fell asleep while he lay alone upon his bed in the garden. And while he slept, he dreamed a beautiful dream. He thought that he, after passing, he could not tell how, for a great way through the air, landed at last on the borders of a fair country, where he wandered about for some time. The place was more delightful than ever entered the imagination of man, with fadeless verdure, and bright day, and summer eternal. By and by he entered a city, thronged with people, such as it charmed his eyes to behold—all clothed in raiment like the fleecy clouds, and each with a glittering star upon his forehead. Here he was accosted by a Being, even more splendid than the others, and told in tones of soft music, that he should not be sick any more as on earth, but be taken to the presence of the Great King. Then he was conducted by the Being, who led the way, holding his hand, through many bright avenues and shining halls—and at last ushered into a mighty space, whose limits the gazer's eye could not scan, filled with millions of the winged ones—and in the midst a throne, whence light flashed like double lightning.

And then the sleeper awoke.

Several persons were standing around him. One, the village doctor, had apparently been holding his wrist—for he let it fall as soon as Reuben opened his eyes. The boy felt strangely faint, yet he smiled as he saw his parents, and briefly told them his vision. His mother was sobbing aloud.

"My son," she cried, in uncontrollable agony; "my son! you die!"

And the father bowed him low, as a tree by the tempest—and thick tears rippled between the fingers which he held before his eyes. O, it is a fearful thing to see a *man* in desperate grief!

Reuben comprehended the truth; else why that cloud—that dark consciousness shadowing his soul? He lay drowsily; a few drops of sweat started upon his forehead, and he began to grow insensible to perception or feeling of any kind. It was a state somewhat resembling sleep, yet different from it—it was without pain—it was Death.

For what moved the child thus uneasily and sped his eyes from one to another? With some effort he turned himself, raised his arm to his pillow, and drew something from underneath it, he unrolled a paper edged with silk, of the hue of the clouds overhead.

All was the silence of the grave. The dying boy slowly lifted the tremulous forefinger of his right hand, as he held the document in his left—that finger quivered for a moment in the air—the eyes of the child, now becoming glassy with death damp, were fixedly cast toward his father's face; he smiled pleasantly—and as an indistinct gurgle sounded from his throat, the uplifted finger calmly settled downward, and rested, pointing upon the blank space at the bottom of the Temperance pledge.

And so he passed away.

When the solemnity of the scene, and the impressiveness of the closing incident, which for a while awed them motionless and silent, allowed other influences to act, they looked, and saw Reuben lying before them a cold corpse. His finger was pointed still. A gentle look lingered upon his face; the perfume of flowers filled the air; and from the western sky came a ray of light, left by the departing sun, investing the spot, as it were, with a halo of glory.

## *Émile Zola, from* L'Assommoir (The Dram-Shop) *(1877)*

*Raised in modest circumstances, Émile Zola (1840–1902) gained wealth and fame through the publication of* L'Assommoir, *a novel focusing on the alcohol-soaked squalor of a group of impoverished Parisian workers. Because of its grim subject-matter, frank descriptions, and bold use of workers' slang,* L'Assommoir *became one of the most controversial and influential of nineteenth-century French novels. The book epitomizes many of the chief features of naturalism, the literary school emphasizing the roles of heredity and environment in human behavior, and drawing extensively on scientific, medical, and sociological materials. The book's title suggests the richly multi-layered quality of Zola's approach to his subject: "assommoir" refers to a dram shop or tavern, but the word can also mean a club or bludgeon. As David Baguley observes, the usual English translations of Zola's title (e.g.,* Drink, The Dram Shop, The Gin Palace*), fail to capture the suggestiveness and ambiguity of the original French, in which the dram-shop serves as a bludgeon or, as Baguley suggests, a "sap" with which to batter the novel's degraded characters, unable to extricate themselves from a cycle of poverty and alcoholism.\**

*As for his novel's purpose, Zola himself explicitly pointed to its demonstration of the moral and physical effects of alcoholism, especially in conjunction with the ignorance, penury, and brutalizing labor of the French working class. In his preface to the book, Zola writes, "I have sought to picture the fatal downfall of a family of workpeople, in the pestilental atmosphere of our faubourgs. After drunkenness and sloth come the loosening of family ties, filth engendered by promiscuity, progressive forgetfulness of all upright sentiments, and then, as finish, shame and death. The book is simply a lesson in morality." Although the title* L'Assommoir *suggests, on the surface, that the novel might belong in the section of this anthology dealing with the tavern, Zola's primary concern in the book, as indicated in his preface and as demonstrated throughout the novel itself, is less with the specific locale and influence of the "dramshop" than it is with alcohol's broader relation to human relations, particularly within the family—the main theme of the series of novels of which* L'Assommoir *is a part.*

*In the selection reprinted here, from chapter VIII, "The Wiles of the Tempter," the novel's protagonist, Gervaise, finds herself torn in three directions by the other inhabitants of her home: her feckless, drunken husband, Coupeau, her erstwhile lover, Lantier (whom the unsuspecting Coupeau treats as a trusted friend), and her neglected, semi-wild daughter, Nana, who will eventually grow into a life of prostitution, recounted in detail in Zola's later novel,* Nana. *In this tangle of competing forces, Zola zeroes in on alcohol's role in familial disintegration. The selec-*

*tion epitomizes the "fatal downfall of a family" mentioned above and, as such, reflects Zola's concern not just with alcoholism as a problem for the drinker, or as a social annoyance, but as a truly toxic phenomenon whose victims include not only individuals, but the stabilizing, protective structure within society that, for Zola, the family can and should be. Implicitly, then, respectable and powerful members of society who tolerate the poverty and abuse that constitute the lower-class environment, are indirectly guilty of fomenting alcoholism and, ultimately, alcoholism's destruction of family life. The translator of this passage and of the selection from Zola's preface mentioned above, Ernest Alfred Vizetelly (1853–1922), was a contemporary and devotee of Zola who did much to promote his fiction in the English-speaking world. It was a 1915 edition of the Vizetelly translation of* L'Assommoir *that Jack London, another prominent novelist in the naturalistic tradition of Zola, owned. While Vizetelly's translations, as he himself acknowledged, softened Zola's slangy French for late Victorian English readers, his work did much to advance Zola's reputation. Vizetelly essentially constituted a one-man public relations service for Zola with the English-speaking public, both through translation and journalism on behalf of the French author who was notorious for both his subject-matter (drunkenness, violence, sex), and for the frank realism of his style.*

*\*David Baguley,* Émile Zola, "L'Assommoir" *(Cambridge: Cambridge University Press, 1992), pp. 2, 73.*

It should be said that Coupeau and Lantier were forever junketing together. Lantier would now borrow money of Gervaise—ten francs, twenty francs at a time, whenever he smelt that there was money in the house. And on those occasions he would keep Coupeau away from work, talk of some distant errand, and take him off; and then, seated opposite each other in a snug corner of some neighbouring restaurant, they would treat themselves to dishes which one cannot get at home, and wash them down with bottles of high-class wine. The zinc-worker would have preferred a booze in the hail-fellow-well-met style; but he was impressed by the aristocratic tastes of the hatter, who would search the bill of fare for sauces with the most extraordinary names. One could never have imagined a man with a palate so delicate and so hard to please. But they are all like that, it seems, in the South of Prance. Lantier, for his part, would have nothing heating; he discussed each dish from a hygienic point of view, and even sent it away when he thought it too salt or too peppery. It was worse still if there was a draught in the restaurant; draughts filled him with mortal dread; he abused the whole establishment if a door was left ajar. Withal, he was very stingy, only giving the waiter a couple of sous after a meal costing seven or eight francs. Nevertheless, people trembled before him, and the pair were well-known along the outer Boulevards, from Batignolles to Belleville. They would go to the Grande Eue des Batignolles to eat tripe *d la mode de Caen,* which was served to them on metal warmers heated with charcoal. Down below Montmartre, at the "Town of Bar-le-Duc," they obtained the best oysters in the neighbourhood. When they ventured to the top of the height, as far as the "Galette Windmill," they had a rabbit *sauté.* Then the "Lilacs" in the Bue des Martyrs had a reputation for calf's head; whilst the restaurants of the "Golden Lion" and the "Two Chestnut Trees," on the Chaussee Clignancourt, served them the finest of stewed kidneys. But they more often turned to the left towards Belleville, where there was always a table kept for them at the "Vintages of Burgundy," the "Blue Dial," and the "Capuchin"—reliable establishments, where one could order whatever one pleased with one's eyes shut. And these were sly little parties, which they covertly talked of on the morrow, whilst trifling with Gervaise's fried potatoes. One day when they feasted at the "Galette Windmill," Lantier actually brought a female acquaintance with him.

It is of course impossible to guttle and work at the same time, and so, since the hatter had made one of the family, the zinc-worker, already lazy enough, had got to the point of never touching a tool. Whenever he was tired of knocking about and let himself be prevailed upon to start a job, his mate would look him up, chaff him unmercifully at finding him hanging to his knotted cord like a smoked ham, and call to him to come down and have a glass of wine. That settled it: the zinc-worker would send the job to blazes, and start on a drinking bout which lasted for days and weeks. Oh, it was a famous bout, a general review of all the dram-shops of the neighbourhood, the intoxication of the morning slept off at midday, and renewed in the evening; the goes of "vitriol" fast following one upon another, all count of them being lost in the depths of the night, through which they stretched away like the Venetian lanterns of an illumination, until the last candle disappeared with the last glass. But that rogue of a hatter never kept on to the end. He allowed the other to get elevated, then gave him the slip, and returned home smiling in his pleasant way. He coloured his own nose decently, without people noticing it. When one got to know him well, one could only tell it by his half-closed eyes and forwardness with the fair sex. The zinc-worker, on the contrary, became disgusting, ho could no longer drink without putting himself into the most dreadful state imaginable.

In this wise, towards the beginning of November, Coupeau went in for a bout which ended abominably, both for himself and others. On the previous day he had been offered a job. Lantier this time was full of fine sentiments; he lauded work because work ennobles man. In the morning he even rose before daylight, for he gravely declared that he wished to accompany his friend to the workshop, honouring in him the workman really worthy of the name. But when they reached the "Little Civet," which was just opening, they went in just to have a plum in brandy, only one, by way of toasting the firm observance of a good resolution. However, they there found Bibi-the-Smoker who, with a sulky look on his face, and his pipe in his mouth, was seated on a bench opposite the counter.

"Hallo! here's Bibi having a snooze," said Coupeau. "Have you got a lazy fit on, old man?"

"No, no," replied the other, stretching his arms. "It's the employers who disgust me. I sent mine to the right about yesterday. They're all blackguards, all scoundrels."

And then Bibi-the-Smoker accepted a plum. He had, no doubt, been waiting for some one to stand him a drink. Lantier, however, took the part of the employers; they often had very hard times, as he, who had been in business himself, well knew. Workmen were a bad lot! always on the booze, not caring a hang for their work, but leaving one in the lurch at some pressing moment, and only putting in an appearance again when their money was all gone. For instance, there had been a little fellow from Picardy in his employ, whose fad was to go driving about in cabs; yes, the moment he had got his week's screw, he took cabs for days together. Was that a taste worthy of the worker? But all at once Lantier also began to attack the employers. Oh, he saw things clearly, he told everyone what he thought of them. And, after all, employers were a dirty race, fellows without the least shame, regular man-eaters. He, thank heaven, could sleep with an easy conscience, for he had always treated his men as friends, and had preferred not to make millions by grinding down the poor as others did.

"Let's be off, my boy," he added, turning to Coupeau. "We must be good or we shall be late."

Bibi-the-Smoker followed them, swinging his arms. Outside, the sun was scarcely rising, and the pale half-light seemed dirtied by the muddy reflection of the pavement. Some rain had fallen the night before, and the temperature was very mild. The gas lamps had just been turned out; the Rue des Poissonniers, in which shreds of night rent by the houses still floated about, was gradually filling with the dull tramp of workmen, descending towards Paris. Coupeau, with his tool-bag slung over his shoulder, walked along in the bouncing manner of a fellow who for once in a way feels equal to any amount of work. But all at once he turned round and asked: "Bibi, are you game for a job? The governor told me to bring a pal if I could."

"Thanks," answered Bibi-the-Smoker; "I'm taking medicine. You should ask My-Boots, who was looking out for a crib yesterday. Wait a minute. My-Boots is most likely in there."

And as they reached the bottom of the street, they indeed caught sight of My-Boots inside old Colombe's. Early as was the hour, the "Assommoir" was flaring, the shutters down and the gas lighted. Lantier remained at the door, telling Coupeau to make haste, as they had only ten minutes left.

"What! you're going to that rascal Bourguignon's?" yelled My-Boots, when the zinc-worker had spoken to him. "You'll never catch me in his hutch again! No, I'd rather go till next year with my tongue hanging out of my mouth. As for you, old fellow, you won't stay there three days, it's I who tell you so."

"Really, now, is it such a dirty hole?" asked Coupeau anxiously.

"Oh, the very dirtiest. You can't move there. The ape's for ever on your back. And such high and mighty ways, too—a missus who always says you're drunk, a shop where you mustn't even spit. I sent 'em to the right about the first night, you understand."

"Good; now I'm warned. I sha'n't stop there forever. I'll just try it this morning; but if the governor bothers me, I'll collar him and plump him down on his missus, and bang them together like a pair of soles!"

Then the zinc-worker shook his comrade's hand to thank him for his warning; and he was moving off, when My-Boots flew into a temper. What! was that fellow Bourguignon going to prevent them from having a drink together? Were men no longer men, then? The ape could very well wait for five minutes. Thereupon Lantier entered to join in the drink, and the four men stood up in front of the bar. My-Boots, with his shoes trodden down at heel, his blouse black with filth, and his cap flattened on his head, yelled and rolled his eyes as though the whole "Assommoir" belonged to him.

"I say, you Borgia," he called to old Colombe, "give us some of your yellow stuff, number one quality!"

When old Colombe, pale and quiet in his blue, knitted waistcoat, had filled the four glasses, the gentlemen tossed off the liquor so as not to let it get flat.

"That does one some good all the same," murmured Bibi-the-Smoker.

However, that animal My-Boots began to tell them something awfully comical. He had been so drunk on the previous Friday, that some of his comrades had fixed his pipe in his mouth with a handful of cement. Anyone else would have died of it; but he merely drew himself up and strutted about as usual.

"Do you gentlemen require anything more?" asked old Colombe in his oily voice.

"Yes, fill up again," said Lantier. "It's my turn."

They were now talking of women. Bibi-the-Smoker said that he had taken his girl to an aunt's at Montrouge on the previous Sunday; and Coupeau asked for news of the "Indian Mail," a washerwoman of Chaillot, who was known in the establishment. However, they were about to drink, when My-Boots shouted to Goujet and Lorilleux, who were passing by. They came to the door, but would not enter. The blacksmith, for his part, did not care to take anything. As for the chain-maker who, pale and shivering, had his hand in his pocket, grasping the gold chains which he was going to deliver, he coughed, and asked them to excuse him, as the smallest drop of brandy always laid him up.

"There are hypocrites for you!" grunted My-Boots. "I bet they have their drinks on the sly."

However, when he had poked his nose in his glass, he attacked old Colombe. "You old villain," said he, "you've changed the bottle! You know, it's no good your trying to doctor your vitriol with me!"

The dawn was now spreading, and a kind of half-light lit up the "Assommoir," where the landlord was turning out the gas. Coupeau had begun to offer excuses for his brother-in-law, who really could not stand drink, which after all was no crime. And he approved even of Goujet's behaviour, for it was a real blessing never to be thirsty. Then he talked of going off to work, but Lantier, putting on his grand air, sharply gave him a lesson. A man should at least stand treat in his turn before sneaking off; he ought not to leave his friends like a prig, even when it was a question of going to his duty.

"Is he going to badger us much longer about his work?" cried My-Boots.

"So this is your turn, sir?" asked old Colombe of Coupeau.

The zinc-worker paid. But when it came to the turn of Bibi-the-Smoker, the latter whispered to the landlord, who refused with a shake of the head. My-Boots understood what was up, and again began to abuse that old Jew, Colombe. What! a rascal like him dared to behave in that way to a comrade! Everywhere else one could get a drink on tick! It was only in such low pepperboxes that one got insulted! However, the landlord remained quite calm, resting his big fists on the edge of the counter, and politely saying: "Lend the gentleman some money—that will be far simpler."

"Thunder! yes, I'll lend him some," yelled My-Boots. "Here, Bibi, throw his money in his face!"

Then, fairly started, and annoyed by the sight of the bag slung over Coupeau's shoulder, he continued, speaking to the zinc-worker: "You look like a wet-nurse. Drop your brat. It'll give you a hump-back."

Coupeau hesitated for an instant; and then, quietly, as though he had only made up his mind after considerable reflection, he set his bag on the floor, saying: "It's too late now. I'll go to Bourguignon's after lunch. I'll tell him that the missus was ill. Listen, old Colombe, I'll leave my tools under this seat, and I'll call for them at twelve o'clock."

Lantier nodded his approval of this arrangement. A man must work, no doubt; only, when he is with friends, politeness passes before everything. An inclination for a spree had gradually overcome the four of them, and they stood there with heavy hands, and exchanging questioning glances. And as soon as they realised that they had five hours' idleness before them, they were suddenly seized with a noisy joy, catching each other friendly slaps, and bawling affectionate words in each other's faces. Coupeau, who in particular felt much relieved and even younger, called the others "old bricks!" They had one more round of drinks, and then moved off to the "Sniffing Flea," a low dram-shop which possessed a billiard table. The hatter at first made a grimace, for it was not a very clean-looking crib; the brandy there cost a franc the quart, ten sous a pint in two glasses, and the customers had so soiled the billiard table that the balls fairly stuck to it. However, when once the game had begun, the hatter, who was an extremely expert player, recovered his good temper and graciousness, thrusting his chest forward and wriggling his hips at each cannon he made.

When lunch time came, Coupeau had an idea. He stamped his feet and exclaimed: "We must go to fetch Salted-Chops. I know where he works. We'll take him to Mother Louis's to have some stewed pettitoes."

The idea was greeted with acclamations. Yes, Salted Chops, otherwise Drink-without-Thirst, must be in want of some pettitoes. So they started off. The streets were yellowish, and a fine rain was falling. But the tipplers were already too warm internally to feel a slight watering of their limbs. Coupeau led the others to the bolt factory in the Eue Marcardet, and as they arrived there a good half hour before the time when the workmen usually came out, he gave a lad a couple of sous to go in and tell Salted-Chops that his wife was ill and wanted him at once. The blacksmith made his appearance, strutting along but looking very calm, and already scenting a tuck-out.

"Ah! you jokers!" said he, as soon as he caught sight of the others hiding in a doorway. "I guessed as much. Well! what are we going to eat?"

Once at Mother Louis's, whilst they sucked the little bones of the pettitoes, they again fell to abusing the employer class. Salted-Chops, otherwise Drink-without-Thirst, related that at his crib they just then had a most pressing order to execute. So the boss was fairly pleasant for the time being. One might be late, and he dared say nothing; he no doubt considered himself lucky when the men did turn up. Besides, there was no fear that any one would ever dare to give Salted-Chops the sack, for it was no longer possible to find fellows of his talent in the bolt-forging line. Then, the pettitoes having been disposed of, the company ordered an omelet. Each drank his quart of wine. Mother Louis had her wine sent to her from Auvergne—it was of blood-like hue, and could almost be cut with a knife. Things were now beginning to get amusing; the carouse was going apace.

"What do you think is the boss's latest?" cried Salted Mouth at dessert. "Why, he's been and put a bell up in his crib! A bell, indeed! that's good for slaves. Ah well! it can ring to-day! They won't catch me at the anvil again! I've been sticking there for five days past, and may well give myself a rest. If he has the cheek to fine me, I'll send him to blazes."

"For my part," said Coupeau, with an important air, "I'm obliged to leave you; I'm off to work. Yes, I promised my wife. Amuse yourselves; my heart, you know, remains with my pals."

The others chaffed him. But he seemed so decided that at last they all accompanied him on his way to fetch his tools from old Colombe's. He there took his bag from under the seat and laid it on the floor before him, whilst they had a final drink. But at one o'clock the party was still standing glasses round. Then Coupeau, with a gesture of boredom, once more deposited the tools under the seat. They were in his way; he could not get near the counter without stumbling against them. It was all too absurd to think of working that day; he would go to Bourguignon's on the morrow. The other four, who meantime were quarrelling over the question of salaries, were not at all surprised when the zinc-worker, without any explanation, proposed a little stroll along the Boulevard, just to stretch their legs. It had left off raining, but the little stroll resolved itself into their trudging along for a couple of hundred paces all in a row and swinging their arms. They no longer found a word to say, incommoded as they were by the fresh air, and bored at being out of doors. And without even having to nudge one another by way of consultation, they slowly and instinctively ascended the Eue des Poissonniers, and entered Francois's tavern to drink a glass of bottle wine. They really needed it to pull them together again. The streets were altogether too depressing; it was so muddy in them, that one wouldn't willingly have turned even a "copper" out of doors. Lantier pushed his comrades inside the private room at the back of the tavern; a narrow crib, containing but one table, and separated from the shop proper by a glazed partition. The hatter usually preferred to colour his nose in private rooms, because it was more respectable. Were they not all very comfortable in there? One could almost think oneself at home, and have indulged in a nap without scruple. He, however, called for the newspaper, spread it out open before him, and began to look through it, frowning the while. Coupeau and My-Boots had started a game of piquet. Two bottles of wine and five glasses were scattered about the table.

"Well! what do they say in that rag?" asked Bibi-the-Smoker of the hatter. Lantier, after an interval, replied without raising his eyes: "I'm reading the report of the Chamber. They're not republicans at all, those lazy scoundrels of the Left! Are they elected by the people merely to swill sugar and water? Here's one who believes in Providence, and makes advances to those dirty ministers! If I were elected, I'd get into the tribune and say "Rot" to their faces. Yes, nothing more, that sums up my opinion!"

"You know that Badinguet's had a fight with his missus, before the whole court, don't you?" responded Salted-Chops, otherwise Drink-without-Thirst. "Pon my honour it's true! And all about nothing, just a little wrangle. But Badinguet was a bit screwed."

"Shut up with your politics!" cried the zinc-worker. "Read us the murders, they're much more amusing."

And reverting to his game, he declared a tierce from the nine and three queens as follows: "I've a tierce from the sewer and three doves. The crinolines stick to me."

They emptied their glasses, and then Lantier read out: "A frightful crime has just spread consternation throughout the locality of Gaillon, in the Department of Seine-et-Marne. A son has hacked his father to death with a spade, in order to rob him of thirty sous."

They all uttered a cry of horror. There was one, dash it all! whom they would have taken great pleasure in seeing guillotined! In fact, the guillotine was not severe enough; he deserved to be cut into mincemeat. The story of an infanticide likewise aroused their indignation; but the hatter in highly moral language found excuses for the woman, and cast all the blame on her seducer. However, they waxed enthusiastic on hearing of the exploits of the Marquis de T—, who, leaving a ball at two o'clock in the morning, had defended himself against three ruffians on the Boulevard des Invalides. Without even taking off his gloves, he had rid himself of two of the men by butting them in the stomach, and had then led the third by the ear to the nearest police station. Ah! there was a smart fellow for you! What a pity he was an aristocrat!

"Listen to this, now," continued Lantier, "Here's some news of the toffs. The Countess de Bretigny is giving her eldest daughter in marriage to the young Baron de Valancay, aide-de-camp to His Majesty. The wedding trousseau will contain more than three hundred thousand francs' worth of lace."

"What's that to us?" interrupted Bibi-the-Smoker. "What do we care for her lace?"

Then as Lantier seemed about to continue his reading, Salted-Chops, otherwise Drink-without-Thirst, took the newspaper from him, and sat upon it, declaring that papers were merely so much rot.

Meanwhile, My-Boots, who had been looking at his hand, triumphantly banged his fist on the table. He was just scoring ninety-three. "I've the Revolution," he shouted. "A quint in clubs. That's twenty, isn't it? Then tierce major in diamonds, twenty-three; three kings, twenty-six; three jacks, twenty-nine; three aces, ninety-two. And I play year one of the Republic, ninety-three."

"You're done for, old boy," cried the others to Coupeau.

They ordered two fresh bottles. The glasses were now refilled as soon as they were emptied; the drinking bout waxed fast and furious. Towards five o'clock, things even began to get disgusting, so much so, that Lantier kept very quiet and began to think of how he might give the others the slip; brawling and throwing wine about was not his style. Just then, as it happened, Coupeau stood up to make the drunkard's sign of the cross. "Montparnasse," said he, as he touched his head; "Menilmonte," as he brought his hand to his right shoulder; "La Courtille," as he moved it to the left one, and "Bagnolet," as he dealt himself a blow in the stomach. And finally hitting his chest, he shouted, "Stewed rabbit!" three times in succession. Then, the hatter, taking advantage of the clamour which greeted the performance of this feat, quietly made for the door. His comrades did not even notice his departure. He himself had already had a good dose. But, once outside, he shook himself and regained his self-possession; and quietly made for the shop, where he told Gervaise that Coupeau was with some friends.

Two days went by. The zinc-worker had not returned. He was reeling about the neighbourhood, but no one knew exactly where. Various persons, however, asserted that they had seen him at Mother Baquet's, at the "Butterfly," and at the "Little Old Man with a Cough." Only, some said that he was alone, whilst others affirmed that he was in the company of seven or eight drunkards like himself. Gervaise shrugged her shoulders in a resigned sort of way. All she had to do was to get used to it. She never ran about after her old man; if she caught sight of him inside a wine-shop, she even retraced her steps and went whither she was bound by some circuitous route, so that he might not imagine she was spying on him; and she quietly waited at home till he returned, listening at night-time to ascertain if he were snoring outside the door. He, however, would sleep on a rubbish heap, or a bench, or in a piece of vacant land, or even across a gutter. On the morrow, having but imperfectly slept off his carouse of the day before, he would set out again, knocking at the doors of all the consolation dealers, plunging afresh into a furious batter, amidst nips of spirits, glasses and quarts of wine, losing his friends, and then finding them again, going long journeys, whence he returned in a state of stupor, seeing the streets dance before his eyes, the night fall, and the dawn appear, without any other thought than that of drinking, and sleeping off the effects wheresoever he might be. When in the latter state, the world was ended so far as he was concerned. Nevertheless, on this occasion, on the second day, Gervaise went to old Colombe's "Assommoir" to inquire about him; he had been there another five times, she heard, but they were unable to tell her anything more. All she could do was to take away his tools, which he had left under the seat.

In the evening, Lantier, seeing that the laundress seemed very much worried, offered to take her to a music-hall, just by way of passing a pleasant hour or two. She refused at first, for she was in no mood for laughing. Otherwise, she would not have declined, for the hatter had made the proposal in too straightforward a manner for her to mistrust him. He seemed to feel for her in quite a paternal way. Frequent as were Coupeau's bouts he had never before slept out two nights in succession. And so every ten minutes, in spite of herself, she would go to the door, iron in hand, and look up and down the street to see if her man was coming. She tingled, she said, in such a way that she could not keep still. Coupeau might very likely get a limb broken, or fall under some vehicle and stay there, which all considered would be a good riddance, for she could no longer entertain the least affection for such a disgusting individual. But it was becoming extremely annoying to have to ask oneself incessantly, day after day, whether he would return that night or not. And at last, when the gas lamps were lighted, and Lantier again proposed the music-hall, Gervaise accepted his offer. After all, she was very stupid to refuse herself some enjoyment, when for three days past her husband had been leading such a harum-scarum life. As he didn't come home, she would go out in her turn. The show might burn down if it liked. She was ready to set it on fire herself, for the troubles of life were beginning to disgust her with everything.

They ate their dinner quickly; and on going off at eight o'clock, arm-in-arm with the hatter, Gervaise told Mother Coupeau and Nana to go to bed at once. The shop was shut. She left by the door opening into the courtyard and gave Madame Boche the key, asking her to have the kindness to put her pig to bed should he happen to come home. The hatter, meantime, waited for her under the porch, arrayed in his best, and whistling a tune. Gervaise was wearing her silk dress; and they went slowly along the pavement, walking close to one another, and lighted by the flashes from the shop windows, which showed them smiling and chatting in low tones.

The music-hall was on the Boulevard de Eochechouart; it had originally been a little cafe, enlarged by the erection of a kind of wooden shed in the courtyard. At the door, a string of glass globes simulated a luminous porch. Tall posters pasted upon boards stood on the ground, close to the gutter.

"Here we are," said Lantier. "To-night, first appearance of Mademoiselle Amanda, serio-comic."

However, just then he caught sight of Bibi-the-Smoker, who was also reading the poster. Bibi had a black eye; some knock which he had run up against on the previous day.

"Well, and where's Coupeau?" inquired the hatter, looking about him. "Have you lost Coupeau, then?"

"Oh! long ago, since yesterday," replied the other. "There was a bit of a mill on leaving Mother Baquet's. I don't care for fisticuffs. But there was a row, you know, with Mother Baquet's potboy, because he wanted to make us pay for a quart twice over. And then I sloped and went to have a snooze."

He was still gaping, though he had slept ten hours at a stretch. But on the other hand he was quite sobered. His jacket was covered with fluff; no doubt he had tumbled into bed with his clothes on.

"And you don't know where my husband is, sir?" asked the laundress.

"Well, no, not a bit. It was five o'clock when we left Mother Baquet's. That's all I know about it. Perhaps he went down the street. Yes, I fancy now that I saw him go to the 'Butterfly' with a coachman. Oh! how stupid it all is! Really, we deserve to be shot!"

Lantier and Gervaise spent a very pleasant evening at the music-hall. At eleven o'clock, when the place closed, they strolled home without hurrying. It was rather chilly, the spectators were going off in parties, and there were girls laughing under the trees, at the pleasantries of the men who accompanied them. Lantier, between his teeth, sang one of Mademoiselle Amanda's songs, "It's in the nose that it tickles me," and Gervaise, who was in a giddy state, as though intoxicated, took up the chorus. She had felt very warm all the evening. Moreover, the two drinks which she had had, the tobacco smoke, and the odour of so many people crowded together had helped to upset her. Nevertheless, she came away with a very lively impression of Mademoiselle Amanda. She herself would never have dared to appear before the public in so scanty a toilet. Still she had to admit that the lady had a very fine figure, and she listened with curiosity to various particulars concerning her, which Lantier began to retail.

"Every one's asleep," exclaimed Gervaise, when they had reached the house and had rung the bell three times, without getting the Boches to pull the string by which the door was opened.

At length, however, it did open, but all was dark under the porch, and when the young woman knocked at the window of the doorkeeper's room to ask for her key, Madame Boche, who was half asleep, called out some rigmarole of which she could at first make nothing. She eventually understood that Poisson, the policeman, had brought Coupeau home in a frightful state, and that the key was no doubt in the lock.

"Good heavens!" murmured Lantier, when they had gone in, "whatever has he been up to here? The smell is abominable."

When Gervaise, who had been looking for the matches, at last succeeded in lighting a candle, a horrible, a loathsome sight greeted their eyes. Coupeau was on the floor, having fallen no doubt from the bed, where Poisson had thrown him, and there he lay snoring amidst unmentionable filth, like a hog wallowing in the mire.

"Oh! the pig! the pig!" repeated Gervaise, indignant and exasperated. "He's dirtied everything. No, a dog wouldn't have done such a thing, a dead dog is cleaner."

Never before had the zinc-worker come home in such a state; never before had he turned the place into such a pigstye. The sight dealt a great blow to such affection as his wife still had for him. In the earlier days, when he had returned elevated or even tipsy, she had shown herself kind, without appearance of disgust. But this time it was too much, her whole being revolted. She would not have touched him with a pair of tongs. And she shivered with repugnance at the thought that this disgusting sot was her husband, and she his wife.

"I must go to bed, however," she murmured. "I can't sleep in the street. Oh! I'll tread on him sooner."

She tried to step over the drunkard, but had to catch hold of the chest of drawers to save herself from slipping. Coupeau quite blocked the way to the bed. Then, Lantier, silently laughing to himself, took hold of her hand, and said in a low and ardent voice: "Gervaise; listen, Gervaise."

But she had understood. She freed herself, and in her bewilderment addressed him familiarly as in former days. "No, leave me. I implore you, Auguste, go away."

"Don't be foolish, Gervaise," he resumed. "It's too abominable; you can't remain here."

She struggled, and energetically shook her head. And in her confusion, as though to show that she intended to remain there, she divested herself of her silk gown and flung it on a chair. Then twice again she tried to find a clear space to enable her to get past the prostrate Coupeau. But Lantier was there, ever seeking to restrain her. Ah! she was in a terrible position, with a hog of a husband in front of her, and an unscrupulous knave in the rear, whose only thought was to take advantage of her misfortune! As the hatter raised his voice, she implored him to keep quiet. And then she listened, with her ear inclined towards the little room occupied by Nana and Mother Coupeau. They were no doubt asleep, for one could hear a heavy breathing. Then again she begged Lantier to be gone. He no longer spoke, but stood there smiling; and he slowly kissed her on the ear, just as he had often done in olden time in order to tease her. At this her strength deserted her; she felt a great buzzing in her ears, and a violent tremor shook her. Yet, she took another step forward; and she was again obliged to draw back. It was not possible, her disgust was too great.

And this was the outcome of Drink, this was one example of the results of the passion for strong liquor: Man degraded to bestiality, filling the woman who had loved him with horror and loathing, rending the last shred of affection felt for him, snapping every remaining tie. Coupeau, lying there as comfortably as on a bed of down, was sleeping off his debauch, with lifeless limbs, and mouth all awry. And around him were nameless horrors.

"So much the worse for him," stammered Gervaise at last, "it's his fault, his fault! Ah! good heavens! ah! good heavens! he himself drives me away; it's all his fault."

She trembled, and lost her head. And as Lantier was drawing her away, Nana's face, pale with sleep, appeared at the glass door of her little chamber. The child had just awoke. She was very grave, and gazed at the others with dilated, wondering eyes.

## *Mark Twain (Samuel Langhorne Clemens)*, The Adventures of Huckleberry Finn *(1885)*

*One of the many remarkable things about* The Adventures of Huckleberry Finn *is Twain's harrowing account of delirium tremens experienced by Pap, Huck's alcoholic father. In part, Twain (1835–1910) uses Pap's alcoholism to mock the sentimentality and naïveté of nineteenth-century temperance activists, as when Pap "reforms" early in the novel, only to fall off the wagon and alarm his stuffily respectable, sanctimonious rescuers. But in the scene below, Twain also demonstrates the insecurity and fear of a child abused by an alcoholic parent, as well as the horrifying effects of alcoholic withdrawal. Here, for all of his mistreatment of Huck, Pap emerges as a figure of enormous pity, his mind and body ravaged by the alcohol he has consumed over a lifetime. Brief as it is, this scene powerfully presents the pathos of a man whose drinking has reached such a point that he can neither live with alcohol nor without it. Although drawing on a then-popular staple of temperance diatribes against liquor—i.e., the "mania a potu" or state of delirium tremens—Twain's portrayal of Pap avoids the over-the-top tone of most such accounts. At the same time, the passage fully retains both the terror experienced by the hallucinating Pap, and the terror felt by Huck, who is, after all, not only the narrator of the book, but a son watching his father disintegrate before his very eyes. As such, the passage is striking not only for its vivid presentation of delirium tremens, but for being written from the perspective of the drunkard's own child;*

*for its complete avoidance of the distracting sentimentality of most temperance treatments of a similar theme (as in Whitman's temperance tale, "Reuben's Last Wish"); and for its inclusion of the repulsive Pap's own terror and powerlessness in the face of his alcoholic debilitation. The scene occurs in Chapter 6, where Pap takes to drinking after railing at the "govment"; the humor of the preceding scenes, where an outraged Pap knocks his shins against the salt pork tub, modulates to the terrifying scene of his violent drunkenness.*

After supper pap took the jug, and said he had enough whisky there for two drunks and one delirium tremens. That was always his word. I judged he would be blind drunk in about an hour, and then I would steal the key, or saw myself out, one or t'other. He drank and drank, and tumbled down on his blankets by and by; but luck didn't run my way. He didn't go sound asleep, but was uneasy. He groaned and moaned and thrashed around this way and that for a long time. At last I got so sleepy I couldn't keep my eyes open all I could do, and so before I knowed what I was about I was sound asleep, and the candle burning.

I don't know how long I was asleep, but all of a sudden there was an awful scream and I was up. There was pap looking wild, and skipping around every which way and yelling about snakes. He said they was crawling up his legs; and then he would give a jump and scream, and say one had bit him on the cheek—but I couldn't see no snakes. He started and run round and round the cabin, hollering "Take him off! take him off! he's biting me on the neck!" I never see a man look so wild in the eyes. Pretty soon he was all fagged out, and fell down panting; then he rolled over and over wonderful fast, kicking things every which way, and striking and grabbing at the air with his hands, and screaming and saying there was devils a-hold of him. He wore out by and by, and laid still a while, moaning. Then he laid stiller, and didn't make a sound. I could hear the owls and the wolves away off in the woods, and it seemed terrible still. He was laying over by the corner. By and by he raised up part way and listened, with his head to one side. He says, very low:

"Tramp—tramp—tramp; that's the dead; tramp—tramp—tramp; they're coming after me; but I won't go. Oh, they're here! don't touch me—don't! hands off—they're cold; let go. Oh, let a poor devil alone!"

Then he went down on all fours and crawled off, begging them to let him alone, and he rolled himself up in his blanket and wallowed in under the old pine table, still a-begging; and then he went to crying. I could hear him through the blanket.

By and by he rolled out and jumped up on his feet looking wild, and he see me and went for me. He chased me round and round the place with a clasp-knife, calling me the Angel of Death, and saying he would kill me, and then I couldn't come for him no more. I begged, and told him I was only Huck; but he laughed *such* a screechy laugh, and roared and cussed, and kept on chasing me up. Once when I turned short and dodged under his arm he made a grab and got me by the jacket between my shoulders, and I thought I was gone; but I slid out of the jacket quick as lightning, and saved myself. Pretty soon he was all tired out, and dropped down with his back against the door, and said he would rest a minute and then kill me. He put his knife under him, and said he would sleep and get strong, and then he would see who was who.

So he dozed off pretty soon. By and by I got the old split-bottom chair and clumb up as easy as I could, not to make any noise, and got down the gun. I slipped the ramrod down it to make sure it was loaded, then I laid it across the turnip barrel, pointing towards pap, and set own behind it to wait for him to stir. And how slow and still the time did drag along.

## *Carson McCullers, "A Domestic Dilemma" (1951)*

*This unusual story is by one of the United States' most accomplished southern writers of fiction, whose best-known works include the short story, "The Ballad of the Sad Café," and the novels,* Member of the Wedding, Reflections in a Golden Eye, *and* The Heart Is a Lonely Hunter, *all of which were turned into successful films. In "A Domestic Dilemma," McCullers (1817–1967) stands some familiar motifs on their head as her narrative depicts not a long-suffering wife and mother pining away for a drunken, derelict husband, but rather a young father struggling to maintain familial order as his depressed wife, drunkenly inattentive to her children, sinks further and further into a sherry-sipping alcoholism. The use of alcohol to fill a spiritual void, the fine line between "social drinking" and "problem drinking," the network of familial relations affected by the alcoholism of one family member, and a subtle inversion of gender stereotypes mark this tightly narrated, haunting tale which is at once a story by and about a woman, a family story, a love story. What makes "A Domestic Dilemma" all the more fresh and moving is the way that it implicitly acknowledges yet turns away from the double standard long associated with the drinking woman, especially the drinking mother. It is this double standard that the anthropologist Margaret Mead referred to when, in an article on drinking women, she noted that "men shudder at the task of protecting an alcoholic wife or mother or daughter"* an emotion that Emily's husband expe-*

riences, even as he also shows a far more complex range of attitudes and responses to his wife's drunkenness.

McCullers herself often drank heavily, famously sipping from a sherry-filled thermos while working at the writer's colony at Yaddo; the author seems to have portrayed aspects of herself and of her own tippling mother in the figure of Emily Meadows.† An easily overlooked detail is that the caretaker-husband's name, Martin Meadows, may allude to St. Martin, patron saint of drunkards.

*Quoted in Thelma McCormack, "The 'Wets' and the 'Drys': Binary Images of Women and Alcohol in Popular Culture," Communication *(9, 1986), 55.*

†See the excellent biographies of McCullers by Josyane Savigneau, Carson McCullers: A Life, *trans. Joan E. Howard (Boston: Houghton-Mifflin, 2001), and Virginia Spencer Carr,* The Lonely Hunter: A Biography of Carson McCullers *(Athens: University of Georgia Press 2003), both of which frankly deal with the role of drinking in McCullers' life.*

On Thursday Martin Meadows left the office early enough to make the first express bus home. It was the hour when the evening lilac glow was fading in the slushy streets, but by the time the bus had left the Mid-town terminal the bright city night had come. On Thursdays the maid had a half-day off and Martin liked to get home as soon as possible, since for the past year his wife had not been—well. This Thursday he was very tired and, hoping that no regular commuter would single him out for conversation, he fastened his attention to the newspaper until the bus had crossed the George Washington Bridge. Once on 9-W Highway Martin always felt that the trip was halfway done, he breathed deeply, even in cold weather when only ribbons of draught cut through the smoky air of the bus, confident that he was breathing country air. It used to be that at this point he would relax and being to think with pleasure of his home. But in this last year nearness brought only a sense of tension and he did not anticipate the journey's end. This evening Martin kept his face close to the window and watched the barren fields and lonely lights of the passing townships. There was a moon, pale on the dark earth and areas of late, porous snow; to Martin the countryside seemed vast and somehow desolate that evening. He took his hat from the rack and put his folded newspaper in the pocket of his overcoat a few minutes before time to pull the cord.

The cottage was a block from the bus stop, near the river but not directly on the shore; from the living-room window you could look across the street and opposite yard and see the Hudson. The cottage was modern, almost too white and new on the narrow plot of yard. In summer the grass was soft and bright and Martin carefully tended a flower border and a rose trellis. But during the cold, fallow months the yard was bleak and the cottage seemed naked. Lights were on that evening in all the rooms in the little house and

Martin hurried up the front walk. Before the steps he stopped to move a wagon out of the way.

The children were in the living room, so intent on play that the opening of the front door was at first unnoticed. Martin stood looking at his safe, lovely children. They had opened the bottom drawer of the secretary and taken out the Christmas decorations. Andy had managed to plug in the Christmas tree lights and the green and red bulbs glowed with out-of-season festivity on the rug of the living room. At the moment he was trying to trail the bright cord over Marianne's rocking horse. Marianne sat on the floor pulling off an angel's wings. The children wailed a startling welcome. Martin swung the fat little baby girl up to his shoulder and Andy threw himself against his father's legs.

"Daddy, Daddy, Daddy!"

Martin set down the little girl carefully and swung Andy a few times like a pendulum. Then he picked up the Christmas tree cord.

"What's all this stuff doing out? Help me put it back in the drawer. You're not to fool with the light socket. Remember I told you that before. I mean it, Andy."

The six-year-old child nodded and shut the secretary drawer. Martin stroked his fair soft hair and his hand lingered tenderly on the nape of the child's frail neck.

"Had supper yet, Bumpkin?"

"It hurt. The toast was hot."

The baby girl stumbled on the rug and, after the first surprise of the fall, began to cry; Martin picked her up and carried her in his arms back to the kitchen.

"See, Daddy," said Andy. "The toast—"

Emily had laid the children's supper on the uncovered porcelain table. There were two plates with the remains of cream-of-wheat and eggs and silver mugs that had held milk. There was also a platter of cinnamon toast, untouched except for one tooth-marked bite. Martin sniffed the bitten piece and nibbled gingerly. Then he put the toast into the garbage pail.

"Hoo—phui—What on earth!"

Emily had mistaken the tin of cayenne for the cinnamon.

"I like to have burnt up," Andy said. "Drank water and ran outdoors and opened my mouth. Marianne didn't eat none."

"Any," corrected Martin. He stood helpless, looking around the walls of the kitchen. "Well, that's that, I guess," he said finally. "Where is your mother now?"

"She's up in you all's room."

Martin left the children in the kitchen and went up to his wife. Outside the door he waited for a moment to still his anger. He did not knock and once inside the room he closed the door behind him.

Emily sat in the rocking chair by the window of the pleasant room. She had been drinking something from a tumbler and as he entered she put the glass hurriedly on the floor behind the chair. In her attitude there was confusion and guilt which she tried to hide by a show of spurious vivacity.

"Oh, Marty! You home already? The time slipped up on me. I was just going down—" She lurched to him and her kiss was strong with sherry. When he stood unresponsive she stepped back a pace and giggled nervously.

"What's the matter with you? Standing there like a barber pole. Is anything wrong with you?"

"Wrong with *me*?" Martin bent over the rocking chair and picked up the tumbler from the floor. "If you could only realize how sick I am—how bad it is for all of us."

Emily spoke in a false, airy voice that had become too familiar to him. Often at such times she affected a slight English accent, copying perhaps some actress she admired. "I haven't the vaguest idea what you mean. Unless you are referring to the glass I used for a spot of sherry. I had a finger of sherry—maybe two. But what is the crime in that, pray tell me? I'm quite all right. Quite all right."

"So anyone can see."

As she went into the bathroom Emily walked with careful gravity. She turned on the cold water and dashed some on her face with her cupped hands, then patted herself dry with the corner of the bath towel. Her face was delicately featured and young, unblemished.

"I was just going down to make dinner." She tottered and balanced herself by holding to the door frame.

"I'll take care of dinner. You stay up here. I'll bring it up."

"I'll do nothing of the sort. Why, whoever heard of such a thing?"

"Please," Martin said.

"Leave me alone. I'm quite all right. I was just on the way down—"

"Mind what I say."

"Mind your grandmother."

She lurched toward the door, but Martin caught her by the arm. "I don't want the children to see you in this condition. Be reasonable."

"Condition!" Emily jerked her arm. Her voice rose angrily. "Why, because I drink a couple of sherries in the afternoon you're trying to make me out a drunkard. Condition! Why, I don't even touch whiskey. As well you know, *I* don't swill liquor at bars. And that's more than you can say. I don't even have a cocktail at dinnertime. I only sometimes have a glass of sherry. What, I ask you, is the disgrace of that? Condition!"

Martin sought words to calm his wife. "We'll have a quiet supper by ourselves up here. That's a good girl." Emily sat on the side of the bed and he opened the door for a quick departure.

"I'll be back in a jiffy."

As he busied himself with the dinner downstairs he was lost in the familiar question as to how this problem had come upon his home. He himself had always enjoyed a good drink. When they were still living in Alabama they had served long drinks or cocktails as a matter of course. For years they had drunk one or two—possibly three drinks before dinner, and at bedtime a long nightcap. Evenings before holidays they might get a buzz on, might even become a little tight. But alcohol had never seemed a problem to him, only a bothersome expense that with the increase in the family they could scarcely afford. It was only after his company had transferred him to New York that Martin was aware that certainly his wife was drinking too much. She was tippling, he noticed, during the day.

The problem acknowledged, he tried to analyze the source. The change from Alabama to New York had somehow disturbed her; accustomed to the idle warmth of a small Southern town, the matrix of the family and cousinship and childhood friends, she had failed to accommodate herself to the stricter, lonelier mores of the North. The duties of motherhood and housekeeping were onerous to her. Homesick for Paris City, she had made no friends in the suburban town. She read only magazines and murder books. Her interior life was insufficient without the artifice of alcohol.

The revelations of incontinence insidiously undermined his previous conceptions of his wife. There were times of unexplainable malevolence, times when the alcoholic fuse caused an explosion of unseemly anger. He encountered a latent coarseness in Emily, inconsistent with her natural simplicity. She lied about drinking and deceived him with unsuspected stratagems.

Then there was an accident. Coming home from work one evening about a year ago, he was greeted with screams from the children's room. He found Emily holding the baby, wet and naked from her bath. The baby had been dropped, her frail, frail skull striking the table edge, so that a thread of blood was soaking into the gossamer hair. Emily was sobbing and intoxicated. As Martin cradled the hurt child, so infinitely precious at that moment, he had an affrighted vision of the future.

The next day Marianne was all right. Emily vowed that never again would she touch liquor, and for a few weeks she was sober, cold and downcast. Then gradually she began—not whiskey or gin—but quantities of beer, or sherry, or outlandish liqueurs; once he had come across a hatbox of empty créme de menthe bottles. Martin found a dependable maid who managed the household competently. Virgie was also from Alabama and Martin had never dared tell Emily the wage scale customary in New York. Emily's drinking was entirely secret now, done before he reached the house. Usually the effects were almost imperceptible—a looseness of movement or the heavy-lidded eyes. The times of irresponsibilities, such as the cayenne-pepper toast, were rare, and Martin could dismiss his worries when Virgie was at the house. But, nevertheless, anxiety was always latent, a threat of indefined disaster that underlaid his days.

"Marianne!" Martin called, for even the recollection of that time brought the need for reassurance. The baby girl, no longer hurt, but no less precious to her father, came into the kitchen with her brother. Martin went on with the preparations for the meal. He opened a can of soup and put two chops in the frying pan. Then he sat down by the table and took his Marianne on his knees for a pony ride. Andy watched them, his fingers wobbling the tooth that had been loose all that week.

"Andy-the-candyman!" Martin said. "Is that old critter still in your mouth? Come closer, let Daddy have a look."

"I got a string to pull it with." The child brought from his pocket a tangled thread. "Virgie said to tie it to the tooth and tie the other end to the doorknob and shut the door real suddenly."

Martin took out a clean handkerchief and felt the loose tooth carefully. "That tooth is coming out of my Andy's mouth tonight. Otherwise I'm awfully afraid we'll have a tooth tree in the family."

"A what?"

"A tooth tree," Martin said. "You'll bite into something and swallow that tooth. And the tooth will take root in poor Andy's stomach and grow into a tooth tree with sharp little teeth instead of leaves."

"Shoo, Daddy," Andy said. But he held the tooth firmly between his grimy little thumb and forefinger. "There ain't any tree like that. I never seen one."

"There *isn't* any tree like that and I never *saw* one."

Martin tensed suddenly. Emily was coming down the stairs. He listened to the fumbling footsteps, his arm embracing the little boy with dread. When Emily came into the room he saw from her movements and her sullen face that she had again been at the sherry bottle. She began to yank open drawers and set the table.

"Condition!" she said in a furry voice. "You talk to me like that. Don't think I'll forget. I remember every dirty lie you say to me. Don't you think for a minute that I forget."

"Emily!" he begged. "The children—"

"The children—yes! Don't think I don't see through your dirty plots and schemes. Down here trying to turn my own children against me . Don't think I don't see and understand."

"Emily! I beg you—please go upstairs."

"So you can turn my children—my very own children—" Two large tears coursed rapidly down her cheeks. "Trying to turn my little boy, my Andy, against his own mother."

With drunken impulsiveness Emily knelt on the floor before the startled child. Her hands on his shoulders balanced her. "Listen, my Andy,—you wouldn't listen to any lies you father tells you? You wouldn't believe what he says? Listen, Andy, what was your father telling you before I came downstairs?" Uncertain, the child sought his father's face. "Tell me. Mama wants to know."

"About the tooth tree."

"What?"

The child repeated the words and she echoed them with unbelieving terror. "The tooth tree!" She swayed and renewed her grasp on the child's shoulder. "I don't know what you're talking about. But listen, Andy, Mama is all right, isn't she?" The tears were spilling down her face and Andy drew back from her, for he was afraid. Grasping the table edge, Emily stood up.

"See! You have turned my child against me."

Marianne began to cry, and Martin took her in his arms.

"That's all right, you can take *your* child. You have always shown partiality from the very first. I don't mind, but at least you can leave me my little boy."

Andy edged close to his father and touched his leg. "Daddy," he wailed.

Martin took the children to the foot of the stairs. "Andy, you take up Marianne and Daddy will follow you in a minute."

"But Mama?" the child asked, whispering.

"Mama will be all right. Don't worry."

Emily was sobbing at the kitchen table, her face buried in the crook of her arm. Martin poured a cup of soup and set it before her. Her rasping sobs unnerved him; the vehemence of her emotion, irrespective of the source, touched in him a strain of tenderness. Unwillingly he laid his hand on her dark hair. "Sit up and drink the soup." Her face as she looked up at him was chastened and imploring. The boy's withdrawal or the touch of Martin's hand had turned the tenor of her mood.

"Ma-Martin," she sobbed. "I'm so ashamed."

"Drink the soup."

Obeying him, she drank between gasping breaths. After a second cup she allowed him to lead her up to their room. She was docile now and more restrained. He laid her nightgown on the bed and was about to leave the room when a fresh round of grief, the alcoholic tumult, came again.

"He turned away. My Andy looked at me and turned away."

Impatience and fatigue hardened his voice, but he spoke warily. "You forget that Andy is still a little child—he can't comprehend the meaning of such scenes."

"Did I make a scene? Oh, Martin, did I make a scene before the children?"

Her horrified face touched and amused him against his will. "Forget it. Put on your nightgown and go to sleep."

"My child turned away from me. Andy looked at his mother and turned away. The children—"

She was caught in the rhythmic sorrow of alcohol. Martin withdrew from the room saying: "For God's sake go to sleep. The children will forget by tomorrow."

As he said this he wondered if it was true. Would the scene glide so easily from memory—or would it root in the unconscious to fester in the after-years? Martin did not know, and the last alternative sickened him. He thought of Emily, foresaw the morning-after humiliation: the shards of memory, the lucidities that glared from the obliterating darkness of shame. She would call the New York office twice—possibly three or four times. Martin anticipated his own embarrassment, wondering if the others at the office could possibly suspect. He felt that his secretary had divined the trouble long ago and that she pitied him. He suffered a moment of rebellion against his fate; he hated his wife.

Once in the children's room he closed the door and felt secure for the first time that evening. Marianne fell down on the floor, picked herself up and calling: "Daddy, watch me," fell again, got up, and continued the falling-calling routine. Andy sat in the child's low chair, wobbling the tooth. Martin ran the water in the tub, washed his own hands in the lavatory, and called the boy into the bathroom.

"Let's have another look at that tooth." Martin sat on the toilet, holding Andy between his knees. The child's mouth gaped and Martin grasped the tooth. A wobble, a quick twist and the nacreous milk tooth was free. Andy's face was for the first moment split between terror, astonishment, and delight. He mouthed a swallow of water and spat into the lavatory.

"Look, Daddy! It's blood. Marianne!"

Martin loved to bathe his children, loved inexpressibly the tender, naked bodies as they stood in the water so exposed. It was not fair of Emily to say that he showed partiality. As Martin soaped the delicate boy-body of his son he felt that further love would be impossible. Yet he admitted the difference in the quality of his emotions for the two children. His love for his daughter was graver, touched with a strain of melancholy, a gentleness that was akin to pain. His pet names for the little boy were the absurdities of daily inspiration—he called the little girl always Marianne, and his voice as he spoke it was a caress. Martin patted dry the fat baby stomach and the sweet little genital fold. The washed child faces were radiant as flower petals, equally loved.

"I'm putting my tooth under my pillow. I'm supposed to get a quarter."

"What for?"

"*You* know, Daddy. Johnny got a quarter for his tooth."

"Who puts the quarter there?" asked Martin. "I used to think the fairies left it in the night. It was a dime in my day, though."

"That's what they say in kindergarten."

"Who does put it there?"

"Your parents," Andy said. "You!"

Martin was pinning the cover on Marianne's bed. His daughter was already asleep. Scarcely breathing, Martin bent over and kissed her forehead, kissed again the tiny hand that lay palm-upward, flung in slumber beside her head.

"Good night, Andy-man."

The answer was only a drowsy murmur. After a minute Martin took out his change and slid a quarter underneath the pillow. He left a night light in the room. As Martin prowled about the kitchen making a late meal, it occurred to him that the children had not once mentioned their mother or the scene that must have seemed to them incomprehensible. Absorbed in the instant—the tooth, the bath, the quarter—the fluid passage of child-time had borne these weightless episodes like leaves in the swift current of a shallow stream while the adult enigma was beached and forgotten on the shore. Martin thanked the Lord for that.

But his own anger, repressed and lurking, arose again. His youth was being frittered by a drunkard's waste, his very manhood subtly undermined. And the children, once the immunity of incomprehension passed—what would it be like in a year or so? With his elbows on the table he ate his food brutishly, untasting. There was no hiding the truth—soon there would be gossip in the office and in the town; his wife was a dissolute woman. Dissolute. And he and his children were bound to a future of degradation and slow ruin.

Martin pushed away from the table and stalked into the living room. He followed the lines of a book with his eyes but his mind conjured miserable images: he saw his children drowned in the river, his wife a disgrace on the public street. By bedtime the dull, hard anger was like a weight upon his chest and his feet dragged as he climbed the stairs.

The room was dark except for the shafting light from the half-opened bathroom door. Martin undressed quietly. Little by little, mysteriously, there came in him a change. His wife was asleep, her peaceful respiration sounding gently in the room. Her high-heeled shoes with the carelessly dropped stockings made to him a mute appeal. Her underclothes were flung in disorder on the chair. Martin picked up the girdle and the soft, silk brassiére and stood for a moment with them in his hands. For the first time that evening he looked at his wife. His eyes rested on the sweet forehead, the arch of the fine brow. The brow had descended to Marianne, and the tilt at the end of the delicate nose. In his son he could trace the high cheekbones and pointed chin. Her body was full-bosomed, slender and undulant. As Martin watched the tranquil slumber of his wife the ghost of the old anger vanished. All thoughts of blame or blemish were distant from him now. Martin put out the bathroom light and raised the window. Careful not to awaken Emily he slid into the bed. By moonlight he watched his wife for the last time. His hand sought the adjacent flesh and sorrow paralleled desire in the immense complexity of love.

# V. Drinking and Gender

## George Eliot (Mary Anne Evans), from "Janet's Repentance" (1857)

**Best known for such major Victorian novels as** Middlemarch, The Mill on the Floss, *and* Adam Bede, *Mary Ann Evans (1819–1880), using the pen name of George Eliot, came to the writing of fiction slowly. She was already 38 when her first published fiction, the collection of stories entitled* Scenes of Clerical Life, *appeared in the prestigious* Blackwood's Magazine. *Included in this collection, the story "Janet's Repentance" was unusual, even shocking, for its unvarnished presentation of small-town English life, and for its depiction of female alcoholism. Although he admired much in the story, the magazine's editor, John Blackwood, expressed reservations that "the poor wife's sufferings should have driven her to so unsentimental a resource as beer;" a few years later, even the sophisticated Henry James wrote of "Janet's Repentance" that "it would be difficult for what is called realism to go further than in the adoption of a heroine stained with the vice of intemperance. The theme is unpleasant; the author chose it at her peril." Responding to Blackwood (who did not know her true identity), Eliot stuck to her guns: some alterations to the text were possible, but if she could not be true to her own "conceptions of life and character," she would rather "close the series [of tales she was writing] for the Magazine now." Blackwood's anxious response to the then unknown author whose genius, however, he recognized, has become famous: "I do not fall in with George Eliots every day and the idea of stopping the Series as suggested in your letter gave me 'quite a turn.'" ... As a result, the story appeared, with some excisions and rephrasing, in the November, 1857 issue of* Blackwoods.\*

*Written at a time when the notion of female alcoholism was almost taboo in polite literature, "Janet's Repentance" is not limited to the theme of drink. In fact, the story's depiction of drinking is all the more realistic and complex for contextualizing the use and abuse of alcohol in relation to other aspects of life; Eliot blends the depiction of female intemperance with such topics as male drinking patterns* (especially that of Dempster, Janet's husband); gender roles in Victorian England; the battle between self-control and the power of addiction; the nuances of male-female friendship; the tragedy and complexity of domestic violence; controversies involving religious faith; and marital disintegration. Yet running through the dark fabric of this story are strands of light and hope that emerge at the story's end, when the repentance alluded to in the title entails also regeneration for its protagonist, Janet.

The selections reprinted below are from the third and fourth chapters of "Janet's Repentance." In the selection from Chapter III, Eliot depicts the gossipy, catty conversation among four genteel female residents of the provincial town of Milby, where the story takes place—Miss Linnet, Miss Pratt, Miss Pratt's niece, Eliza, and their friend, Mrs. Pettifer. The selection opens with the characters discussing Janet's unhappy marriage to Robert Dempster, and reveals a range of attitudes toward female drinking—attitudes tinged with irony, given that the speakers themselves are all women. The selection from Chapter IV shows the violent confrontation between drunken husband and drunken wife, as the first comes home and, enraged by his wife's drinking, proceeds to beat her for being in the same condition as himself. The motif of Janet's mother's suffering over her daughter's unhappiness appears in both selections. The story will be clearer if we know that its overall context is religious factionalism in Milby, with Robert Dempster leading the resistance against the town's new young clergyman, Mr. Tryan, who will later befriend and help Janet deal with both her unfortunate marriage and her alcoholism. Janet is occasionally referred to by her maiden name, Raynor; the character called Mrs. Raynor is Janet's mother. The "row" in Chapter IV refers to a mob organized by Janet's husband, an anti-evangelical lawyer who is bitterly opposed to Mr. Tryan.

*For the background of the story's publication, see Gordon Haight, *George Eliot: A Biography (New York: Oxford University Press, 1968), pp. 234–37. For Henry James's comments, see Haight, ed.,* A Century of George Eliot Criticism *(Boston: Houghton Mifflin, 1965), p. 46.*

### From Chapter III of "Janet's Repentance"

"Well, poor thing," said Mrs Pettifer, "you know she stands up for everything her husband says and does. She never will admit to anybody that he's not a good husband."

"That is her pride," said Miss Pratt. "She married him in opposition to the advice of her best friends, and now she is not willing to admit that she was wrong. Why, even to my brother—and a medical attendant, you know, can hardly fail to be acquainted with family secrets—she has always pretended to have the highest respect for her husband's qualities. Poor Mrs Raynor, however, is well aware that every one knows the real state of things. Latterly, she has not even avoided the subject with me. The very last time I called on her she said, 'Have you been to see my poor daughter?' and burst into tears."

"Pride or no pride," said Mrs Pettifer, "I shall always stand up for Janet Dempster. She sat up with me night after night when I had that attack of rheumatic fever six years ago. There's great excuses for her. When a woman can't think of her husband coming home without trembling, it's enough to "make her drink something to blunt her feelings—and no children either, to keep her from it. You and me might do the same, if we were in her place."

"Speak for yourself, Mrs Pettifer," said Miss Pratt. "Under no circumstances can I imagine myself resorting to a practice so degrading. A woman should find support in her own strength of mind."

"I think," said Rebecca, who considered Miss Pratt still very blind in spiritual things, notwithstanding her assumption of enlightenment, "she will find poor support if she trusts only to her own strength. She must seek aid elsewhere than in herself."

Happily the removal of the tea-things just then created a little confusion, which aided Miss Pratt to repress her resentment at Rebecca's presumption in correcting her—a person like Rebecca Linnet! who six months ago was as flighty and vain a woman as Miss Pratt had ever known—so very unconscious of her unfortunate person!

## From Chapter IV of "Janet's Repentance"

Mr. Tryan was right in saying that the "row" in Milby had been preconcerted by Dempster. The placards and the caricature were prepared before the departure of the delegates; and it had been settled that Mat Paine, Dempster's clerk, should ride out on Thursday morning to meet them at Whitlow, the last place where they would change horses, that he might gallop back and prepare an ovation' for the triumvirate in case of their success. Dempster had determined to dine at Whitlow: so that Mat Paine was in Milby again two hours before the entrance of the delegates, and had time to send a whisper up the back streets that there was promise of a "spree" in the Bridge Way, as well as to assemble two knots of picked men—one to feed the flame of orthodox zeal with gin-and-water, at the Green Man, near High Street; the other to solidify their church principles with heady beer at the Bear and Ragged Staff, in the Bridge Way.

The Bridge Way was an irregular straggling street, where the town fringed off raggedly into the Whitlow road: rows of new red-brick houses, in which ribbon-looms were rattling behind long lines of window, alternating with old, half-thatched, half-died cottages—one of those dismal wide streets where dirt and misery have no long shadows thrown on them to soften their ugliness. Here, about half-past five o'clock, Silly Caleb, an idiot well known in Dog Lane, but more of a stranger in the Bridge Way, was seen slouching along with a string of boys hooting at his heels; presently another group, for the most part out at elbows, came briskly in the same direction, looking round them with an air of expectation; and at no long interval, Deb Traunter, in a pink flounced gown and floating ribbons, was observed talking with great affability to two men in seal-skin caps and fustian, who formed her cortege. The Bridge Way began to have a presentiment of something in the wind. Phib Cook left her evening wash-tub and appeared at her door in soap-suds, a bonnet-poke, and general dampness; three narrow-chested ribbon-weavers, in rusty black streaked with shreds of many-coloured silk, sauntered out with their hands in their pockets; and Molly Beale, a brawny old virago, descrying wiry Dame Ricketts peeping out from her entry, seized the opportunity of renewing the morning's skirmish. In short, the Bridge Way was in that state of excitement which is understood to announce a "demonstration" on the part of the British public; and the afflux of remote townsmen increasing, there was soon so large a crowd that it was time for Bill Powers, a plethoric Goliath, who presided over the knot of beer-drinkers at the Bear and Ragged Staff, to issue forth with his companions, and, like the enunciator of the ancient myth, make the assemblage distinctly conscious of the common sentiment that had drawn them together. The expectation of the delegates' chaise, added to the fight between Molly Beale and Dame Ricketts, and the ill-advised appearance of a lean bull-terrier, were a sufficient safety-valve to the popular excitement during the remaining quarter of an hour; at the end of which, the chaise was seen approaching along the Whitlow road, with oak boughs ornamenting the horses' heads, and, to quote the account of this interesting scene which was sent to the *Rotherby Guardian*, "loud cheers immediately testified to the sympathy of the honest fellows collected there, with the public-spirited exertions of their fellow-townsmen." Bill Powers, whose bloodshot eyes, bent hat, and protuberant altitude, marked him out as the natural leader of the assemblage, undertook to interpret the common sentiment by stopping the chaise, advancing to the door with raised hat, and begging to know of Mr Dempster, whether the Rector had forbidden the "canting lecture."

"Yes, yes," said Mr Dempster. "Keep up a jolly good hurray."

No public duty could have been more easy and agreeable to Mr Powers and his associates, and the chorus swelled all the way to the High Street, where, by a mysterious coincidence often observable in these spontaneous "demonstrations," large placards on long poles were observed to shoot upwards from among the crowd, principally in the direction of Tucker's Lane, where the Green Man was situated. One bore, "Down with the Tryanites!"

another, "No Cant!" another, "Long live our venerable Curate!" and one in still larger letters, "Sound Church Principles and no Hypocrisy!" But a still more remarkable impromptu was a huge caricature of Mr Tryan in gown and band, with an enormous aureole of yellow hair and upturned eyes, standing on the pulpit stairs and trying to pull down old Mr Crewe. Groans, yells, and hisses—hisses, yells, and groans—only stemmed by the appearance of another caricature representing Mr Tryan being pitched head-foremost from the pulpit stairs by a hand which the artist, either from subtilty of intention or want of space, had left unindicated. In the midst of the tremendous cheering that saluted this piece of symbolical art, the chaise had reached the door of the Red Lion, and loud cries of "Dempster for ever!" with a feebler cheer now and then for Tomlinson and Budd, were presently responded to by the appearance of the public-spirited attorney at the large upper window, where also were visible a little in the background the small sleek head of Mr Budd, and the blinking countenance of Mr Tomlinson.

Mr Dempster held his hat in his hand, and poked his head forward with a butting motion by way of bow. A storm of cheers subsided at last into dropping sounds of "Silence!" "Hear him!" "Go it, Dempster!" and the lawyer's rasping voice became distinctly audible.

"Fellow-townsmen! It gives us the sincerest pleasure—I speak for my respected colleagues as well as myself—to witness these strong proofs of your attachment to the principles of our excellent Church, and your zeal for the honour of our venerable pastor. But it is no more than I expected of you. I know you well. I've known you for the last twenty years to be as honest and respectable a set of ratepayers as any in this county. Your hearts are sound to the core! No man had better try to thrust his cant and hypocrisy down *your* throats. You're used to wash them with liquor of a better flavour. This is the proudest moment in my own life, and I think I may say in that of my colleagues, in which I have to tell you that our exertions in the cause of sound religion and manly morality have been crowned with success. Yes, my fellow-townsmen! I have the gratification of announcing to you thus formally what you have already learned indirectly. The pulpit from which our venerable pastor has fed us with sound doctrine for half a century is not to be invaded by a fanatical, sectarian, double-faced, Jesuitical interloper! We are not to have our young people demoralized and corrupted by the temptations to vice, notoriously connected with Sunday evening lectures! We are not to have a preacher obtruding himself upon us, who decries good works, and sneaks into our homes perverting the faith of our wives and daughters! We are not to be poisoned with doctrines which damp every innocent enjoyment, and pick a poor man's pocket of the sixpence with which he might buy himself a cheerful glass after a hard day's work, under pretence of paying for bibles to send to the Chicktaws!

"But I'm not going to waste your valuable time with unnecessary words. I am a man of deeds" ("Aye, damn you, that you are, and you charge well for 'em too," said a voice from the crowd, probably that of a gentleman who was immediately afterwards observed with his hat crushed over his head.) "I shall always be at the service of my fellow-townsmen, and whoever dares to hector over you, or interfere with your innocent pleasures, shall have an account to settle with Robert Dempster.

"Now, my boys! you can't do better than disperse and carry the good news to all your fellow-townsmen, whose hearts are as sound as your own. Let some of you go one way and some another, that every man, woman, and child in Milby may know what you know yourselves. But before we part, let us have three cheers for True Religion, and down with Cant!"

When the last cheer was dying, Mr Dempster closed the window, and the judiciously instructed placards and caricatures moved off in divers directions, followed by larger or smaller divisions of the crowd. The greatest attraction apparently lay in the direction of Dog Lane, the outlet towards Paddiford Common, whither the caricatures were moving; and you foresee, of course, that those works of symbolical art were consumed with a liberal expenditure of dry gorse-bushes and vague shouting.

After these great public exertions, it was natural that Mr Dempster and his colleagues should feel more in need than usual of a little social relaxation; and a party of their friends was already beginning to assemble in the large parlour of the Red Lion, convened partly by their own curiosity, and partly by the invaluable Mat Paine. The most capacious punch-bowl was put in requisition; and that born gentleman, Mr Lowme, seated opposite Mr Dempster as "Vice," undertook to brew the punch, defying the criticisms of the envious men out of office, who, with the readiness of irresponsibility, ignorantly suggested more lemons. The social festivities were continued till long past midnight, when several friends of sound religion were conveyed home with some difficulty, one of them showing a dogged determination to seat himself in the gutter.

Mr Dempster had done as much justice to the punch as any of the party; and his friend Boots, though aware that the lawyer could "carry his liquor like Old Nick," with whose social demeanour Boots seemed to be particularly well acquainted, nevertheless thought it might be as well to see so good a customer in safety to his own door, and walked quietly behind his elbow out of the inn-yard. Dempster, however, soon became aware of him, stopped short, and, turning slowly round upon him, recognized the well-known drab waistcoat sleeves, conspicuous enough in the starlight.

"You twopenny scoundrel! What do you mean by dogging a professional man's footsteps in this way? I'll break every bone in your skin if you attempt to track me, like a beastly cur sniffing at one's pocket. Do you think a gentleman will make his way home any the better for having the scent of your blacking-bottle thrust up his nostrils?"

Boots slunk back, in more amusement than ill-humour, thinking the lawyer's "rum talk" was doubtless part and parcel of his professional ability; and Mr Dempster pursued his slow way alone.

His house lay in Orchard Street, which opened on the prettiest outskirt of the town—the church, the parsonage, and a long stretch of green fields. It was an old-fashioned house, with an overhanging upper storey; outside, it had a face of rough stucco, and casement windows with green frames and shutters; inside, it was full of long passages, and rooms with low ceilings. There was a large heavy knocker on the green door, and though Mr Dempster carried a latch-key, he sometimes chose to use the knocker. He chose to do so now. The thunder resounded through Orchard Street, and, after a single minute, there was a second clap louder than the first. Another minute, and still the door was not opened; whereupon Mr Dempster, muttering, took out his latch-key, and, with less difficulty than might have been expected, thrust it into the door. When he opened the door the passage was dark.

"Janet!" in the loudest rasping tone, was the next sound that rang through the house.

"Janet!" again—before a slow step was heard on the stairs, and a distant light began to flicker on the wall of the passage.

Yet another few seconds, and the figure of a tall woman, holding aslant a heavy-plated drawing-room candlestick, appeared at the turning of the passage that led to the broader entrance.

She had on a light dress which sits loosely about her figure, but did not disguise its liberal, graceful outline. A heavy mass of straight jet-black hair has escaped from its fastening, and hangs over her shoulders. Her grandly-cut features, pale with the natural paleness of a brunette, have premature lines about them, telling that the years had been lengthened by sorrow, and the delicately-curved nostril, which seemed made to quiver with the proud consciousness of power and beauty, must have quivered to the heart-piercing griefs which had given that worn look to the corners of the mouth. Her wide open black eyes had a strangely fixed, sightless gaze, as she paused at the turning, and stood silent before her husband.

"I'll teach you to keep me waiting in the dark, you pale staring fool!" he said, advancing with his slow drunken step. "What, you've been drinking again, have you? I'll beat you into your senses."

He laid his hand with a firm grip on her shoulder, turned her round, and pushed her slowly before him along the passage and through the dining-room door which stood open on their left hand.

There was a portrait of Janet's mother, a grey-haired, dark-eyed old woman, in a neatly-fluted cap, hanging over the mantelpiece. Surely the aged eyes take on a look of anguish as they see Janet—not trembling, no! it would be better if she trembled—standing stupidly unmoved in her great beauty, while the heavy arm is lifted to strike her. The blow falls—another—and another. Surely the mother hears that cry—"O Robert! pity! pity!"

Poor grey-haired woman! Was it for this you suffered a mother's pangs in your lone widowhood five-and-thirty years ago? Was it for this you kept the little worn morocco shoes Janet had first run in, and kissed them day by day when she was away from you, a tall girl at school? Was it for this you looked proudly at her when she came back to you in her rich pale beauty, like a tall white arum that has just unfolded its grand pure curves to the sun?

The mother lies sleepless and praying in her lonely house, weeping the hard tears of age, because she dreads this may be a cruel night for her child.

She too has a picture over her mantelpiece, drawn in chalk by Janet long years ago. She looked at it before she went to bed. It is a head bowed beneath a cross, and wearing a crown of thorns.

## *Willa Cather, "On the Divide" (1896)*

*Born in the same year as the Women's Christian Temperance Union (WCTU), Willa Cather (1873–1947) grew up surrounded by conflicts and controversies about the topic of drinking in America.\* As a young woman, she witnessed the formation of yet another powerful, national temperance organization, the Anti-Saloon League (founded 1893), and as a mature, celebrated author, lived through Prohibition (1920–1933). Familiar with the heavy-drinking practices of Scandinavian immigrants and many others who lived on the Nebraska plains where she spent her childhood, Cather also knew well the arguments for abstinence that loomed so large in American society of the late 19th and early 20th centuries. Neither a teetotaler nor a heavy drinker herself, Cather showed an awareness of the issues surrounding drinking throughout her work, from such early stories as "On the Divide," reprinted here (the story was originally published in 1896 in* The Overland Monthly*), through her late fiction. Without sentimentalizing drink or drinkers, Cather's work reveals a tolerant, matter-of-fact tone in dealing with these subjects. In many of Cather's novels and stories, drinking simply figures casually as part of the overall setting. At times, however, alcohol connects to larger questions* of characterization or social commentary. Thus, in the short story, "A Sculptor's Funeral" (1905), one of the dead sculptor's few sincere admirers is the drunken Jim Laird—a far more sympathetic character than the respectable hypocrites who surround him. In another short story, "Coming, Aphrodite" (1920), drink is briefly but intriguingly featured in relation to gender, as the freethinking protagonist, Eden Bower, shows a casual familiarity with wine unusual among female fictional characters of the time. In the novel A Lost Lady, published in 1923, three years into Prohibition's "noble experiment," we see that Miriam Forrester, the "lost lady" of the title, gets drunk, but the novel's narrator views Mrs. Forrester sympathetically, implicitly seeming to excuse her intoxications as an expression of her more general joie de vivre. Moreover, the novel shows Mrs. Forrester's good taste and capacity for enjoying life's pleasures partly through her knowledge about fine drink and its accompanying rituals.

In the story below, drinking—indeed, desperate, reckless intoxication—becomes part of the very essence of the male protagonist, the taciturn Canute Canuteson. Yet, while "a mystery and a terror" to those who know him, Canute never devolves, in Cather's hands, into the stereotypical "drunken brute" of so much fiction that pits vicious male against helpless female. That male drinking figures in the physical and emotional abuse of women and children is undeniable, and central to both the plot and theme of works like George Eliot's "Janet's Repentance," Walt Whitman's "Reuben's Last Wish," and James Joyce's "Counterparts," found elsewhere in this volume. But without diminishing Canute's potential for violence, Cather reveals his drunkenness to be part of a deeper spiritual yearning that is connected to his loneliness as well as to the creative force that emerges in the strange, gargoyle-like figures that he carves in his cabin.

In terms of gender relations, alcohol seems to fuel the wildness in Canute that erupts in his abduction of the neighboring farm girl Lena. But by the story's end, Cather swerves her characters and us, the readers, away from any predictable scenario we might imagine between the male and female forces represented by Canute and Lena. These forces, and the third force of alcohol, which almost becomes personified here, are potent elements within this tale. Yet Cather's finale points not toward any explicit moral about drinking and gender, but rather toward the dark and tangled regions of human desire.

*The founding date of the WCTU as a national organization is November 1874. However, as the historical portion of the WCTU website indicates, it was in December of 1873 that the local parent of this organization, meeting in Fredonia, New York, called itself the Women's Christian Temperance Union.

Near Rattlesnake Creek, on the side of a little draw stood Canute's shanty. North, east, south, stretched the level Nebraska plain of long rust-red grass that undulated constantly in the wind. To the west the ground was broken and rough, and a narrow strip of timber wound along the turbid, muddy little stream that had scarcely ambition enough to crawl over its black bottom. If it had not been for the few stunted cottonwoods and elms that grew along its banks, Canute would have shot himself years ago. The Norwegians are a timber-loving people, and if there is even a turtle pond with a few plum bushes around it they seem irresistibly drawn toward it.

As to the shanty itself, Canute had built it without aid of any kind, for when he first squatted along the banks of Rattlesnake Creek there was not a human being within twenty miles. It was built of logs split in halves, the chinks stopped with mud and plaster. The roof was covered with earth and was supported by one gigantic beam curved in the shape of a round arch. It was almost impossible that any tree had ever grown in that shape. The Norwegians used to say that Canute had taken the log across his knee and bent it into the shape he wished. There were two rooms, or rather there was one room with a partition made of ash saplings interwoven and bound together like big straw basket work. In one corner there was a cook stove, rusted and broken. In the other a bed made of unplaned planks and poles. it was fully eight feet long, and upon it was a heap of dark bed clothing. There was a chair and a bench of colossal proportions. There was an ordinary kitchen cupboard with a few cracked dirty dishes in it, and beside it on a tall box a tin washbasin. Under the bed was a pile of pint flasks, some broken, some whole, all empty. On the wood box lay a pair of shoes of almost incredible dimensions. On the wall hung a saddle, a gun, and some ragged clothing, conspicuous among which was a suit of dark cloth, apparently new, with a paper collar carefully wrapped in a red silk handkerchief and pinned to the sleeve. Over the door hung a wolf and a badger skin, and on the door itself a brace of thirty or forty snake skins whose noisy tails rattled ominously every time it opened. The strangest things in the shanty were the wide windowsills. At first glance they looked as though they had been ruthlessly hacked and mutilated with a hatchet, but on closer inspection all the notches and holes in the wood took form and shape. There seemed to be a series of pictures. They were, in a rough way, artistic, but the figures were heavy and labored, as though they had been cut very slowly and with very awkward instruments. There were men plowing with little horned imps sitting on their shoulders and on their horses' heads. There were men praying with a skull hanging over their heads and little demons behind them mocking their attitudes. There were men fighting with big serpents, and skeletons dancing together. All about these pictures were blooming vines and foliage such as never grew in this world, and coiled among the branches of the vines there was always the scaly body of a serpent, and behind every flower there was a serpent's head. It was a veritable Dance of Death by one who had felt its sting. In the wood box lay some boards, and every inch of them was cut up in the same manner. Sometimes the work was very rude and careless, and looked as though the hand of the workman had trembled. It would sometimes have been hard to distinguish the men from their evil geniuses but for one fact, the men were always grave and were either toiling or praying, while the devils were always smiling and dancing. Several of these boards had been split for kindling and it was evident that the artist did not value his work highly.

It was the first day of winter on the Divide. Canute stumbled into his shanty carrying a basket of cobs, and after filling the stove, sat down on a stool and crouched his seven foot frame over the fire, staring drearily out of the window at the wide gray sky. He knew by heart every individual clump of bunch grass in the miles of red shaggy prairie that stretched before his cabin. He knew it in all the deceitful loveliness of its early summer, in all the bitter barrenness of its autumn. He had seen it smitten by all the plagues of Egypt. He had seen it parched by drought, and sogged by rain, beaten by hail, and swept by fire, and in the grasshopper years he had seen it eaten as bare and clean as bones that the vultures have left. After the great fires he had seen it stretch for miles and miles, black and smoking as the floor of hell.

He rose slowly and crossed the room, dragging his big feet heavily as though they were burdens to him. He looked out of the window into the hog corral and saw the pigs burying themselves in the straw before the shed. The leaden gray clouds were beginning to spill themselves, and the snow flakes were settling down over the white leprous patches of frozen earth where the hogs had gnawed even the sod away. He shuddered and began to walk, trampling heavily with his ungainly feet. He was the wreck of ten winters on the Divide and he knew what that meant. Men fear the winters of the Divide as a child fears night or as men in the North Seas fear the still dark cold of the polar twilight. His eyes fell upon his gun, and he took it down from the wall and looked it over. He sat down on the edge of his bed and held the barrel towards his face, letting his forehead rest upon it, and laid his finger on the trigger. He was perfectly calm, there was neither passion nor despair in his face, but the thoughtful look of a man who is considering. Presently he laid down the gun, and reaching into the cupboard, drew out a pint bottle of raw white alcohol. Lifting it to his lips, he drank greedily. He washed his face in the tin basin and combed his rough hair and shaggy blond beard. Then he stood in uncertainty before the suit of dark clothes that hung on the wall. For the fiftieth time he took them in his hands and tried to summon courage to put them on. He took the paper collar that was pinned to the sleeve of the coat and cautiously slipped it under his rough beard, looking with timid expectancy into the cracked, splashed glass that hung over the bench. With a short laugh he threw it down on the bed, and pulling on his old black hat, he went out, striking off across the level.

It was a physical necessity for him to get away from his cabin once in a while. He had been there for ten years, digging and plowing and sowing, and reaping what little the hail and the hot winds and the frosts left him to reap. Insanity and suicide are very common things on the Divide. They come on like an epidemic in the hot wind season. Those scorching dusty winds that blow up over the bluffs from Kansas seem to dry up the blood in men's veins as they do the sap in the corn leaves. Whenever the yellow scorch creeps down over the tender inside leaves about the ear, then the coroners prepare for active duty; for the oil of the country is burned out and it does not take long for the flame to eat up the wick. It causes no great sensation there when a Dane is found swinging to his own windmill tower, and most of the Poles after they have become too careless and discouraged to shave themselves keep their razors to cut their throats with.

It may be that the next generation on the Divide will be very happy, but the present one came too late in life. It is useless for men that have cut hemlocks among the mountains of Sweden for forty years to try to be happy in a country as flat and gray and naked as the sea. It is not easy for men that have spent their youth fishing in the Northern seas to be content with following a plow, and men that have served in the Austrian army hate hard work and coarse clothing on the loneliness of the plains, and long for marches and excitement and tavern company and pretty barmaids. After a man has passed his fortieth birthday it is not easy for him to change the habits and conditions of his life. Most men bring with them to the Divide only the dregs of the lives that they have squandered in other lands and among other peoples.

Canute Canuteson was as mad as any of them, but his madness did not take the form of suicide or religion but of alcohol. He had always taken liquor when he wanted it, as all Norwegians do, but after his first year of solitary life he settled down to it steadily. He exhausted whisky after a while, and went to alcohol, because its effects were speedier and surer. He was a big man and with a terrible amount of resistant force, and it took a great deal of alcohol even to move him. After nine years of drinking, the quantities he could take would seem fabulous to an ordinary drinking man. He never let it interfere with his work, he generally drank at night and on Sundays. Every night, as soon as his chores were done, he began to drink. While he was able to sit up he would play on his mouth harp or hack away at his window sills with his jackknife. When the liquor went to his head he would lie down on his bed and stare out of the window until he went to sleep. He drank alone and in solitude not for pleasure or good cheer, but to forget the awful loneliness and level of the Divide. Milton made a sad blunder when he put mountains in hell. Mountains postulate faith and aspiration. All mountain peoples are religious. It was the cities of the plains that, because of their utter lack of spirituality and the mad caprice of their vice, were cursed of God.

Alcohol is perfectly consistent in its effects upon man. Drunkenness is merely an exaggeration. A foolish man drunk becomes maudlin; a bloody man, vicious; a coarse man, vulgar. Canute was none of these, but he was morose and gloomy, and liquor took him through all the hells of Dante. As he lay on his giant's bed all the horrors of this world and every other were laid bare to his chilled senses. He was a man who knew no joy, a man who toiled in silence and bitterness. The skull and the serpent were always before him, the symbols of eternal futileness and of eternal hate.

When the first Norwegians near enough to be called neighbors came, Canute rejoiced, and planned to escape from his bosom vice. But he was not a social man by nature and had not the power of drawing out the social side of other people. His new neighbors rather feared him because of his great strength and size, his silence and his lowering brows. Perhaps, too, they knew that he was mad, mad from the eternal treachery of the plains, which every spring stretch green and rustle with the promises of Eden, showing long grassy lagoons full of clear water and cattle whose hoofs are stained with wild roses. Before autumn the lagoons are dried up, and the ground is burnt dry and hard until it blisters and cracks open.

So instead of becoming a friend and neighbor to the men that settled about him, Canute became a mystery and a terror. They told awful stories of his size and strength and of the alcohol he drank.

They said that one night, when he went out to see to his horses just before he went to bed, his steps were unsteady and the rotten planks of the floor gave way and threw him behind the feet of a fiery young stallion. His foot was caught fast in the floor, and the nervous horse began kicking frantically. When Canute felt the blood trickling down into his eyes from a scalp wound in his head, he roused himself from his kingly indifference, and with the quiet stoical courage of a drunken man leaned forward and wound his arms about the horse's hind legs and held them against his breast with crushing embrace. All through the darkness and cold of the night he lay there, matching strength against strength. When little Jim Peterson went over the next morning at four o'clock to go with him to the Blue to cut wood, he found him so, and the horse was on its fore knees, trembling and whinnying with fear. This is the story the Norwegians tell of him, and if it is true it is no wonder that they feared and hated this Holder of the Heels of Horses.

One spring there moved to the next "eighty" a family that made a great change in Canute's life. Ole Yensen was too drunk most of the time to be afraid of any one, and his wife Mary was too garrulous to be afraid of any one who listened to her talk, and Lena, their pretty daughter, was not afraid of man nor devil. So it came about that Canute went over to take his alcohol with Ole oftener than he took it alone. After a while the report spread that he was going to marry Yensen's daughter, and the Norwegian girls began to tease Lena about the great bear she was going to keep house for. No one could quite see how the affair had come about, for Canute's tactics of courtship were somewhat peculiar. He apparently never spoke to her at all: he would sit for hours with Mary chattering on one side of him and Ole drinking on the other and watch Lena at her work. She teased him, and threw flour in his face and put vinegar in his coffee, but he took her rough jokes with silent wonder, never even smiling. He took her to church occasionally, but the most watchful and curious people never saw him speak to her. He would sit staring at her while she giggled and flirted with the other men.

Next spring Mary Lee went to town to work in a steam laundry. She came home every Sunday, and always ran across to Yensens to startle Lena with stories of ten cent theaters, firemen's dances, and all the other esthetic delights of metropolitan life. In a few weeks Lena's head was completely turned, and she gave her father no rest until he let her go to town to seek her fortune at the ironing board. From the time she came home on her first visit she began to treat Canute with contempt. She had bought a plush cloak and kid gloves, had her clothes made by the dress maker, and assumed airs and graces that made the other women of the neighborhood cordially detest her. She generally brought with her a young man from town who waxed his mustache and wore a red necktie, and she did not even introduce him to Canute.

The neighbors teased Canute a good deal until he knocked one of them down. He gave no sign of suffering from her neglect except that he drank more and avoided the other Norwegians more carefully than ever. He lay around in his den and no one knew what he felt or thought, but little Jim Peterson, who had seen him glowering at Lena in church one Sunday when she was there with the town man, said that he would not give an acre of his wheat for Lena's life or the town chap's either; and Jim's wheat was so wondrously worthless that the statement was an exceedingly strong one.

Canute had bought a new suit of clothes that looked as nearly like the town man's as possible. They had cost him half a millet crop; for tailors are not accustomed to fitting giants and they charge for it. He had hung those clothes in his shanty two months ago and had never put them on, partly from fear of ridicule, partly from discouragement, and partly because there was something in his own soul that revolted at the littleness of the device.

Lena was at home just at this time. Work was slack in the laundry and

Mary had not been well, so Lena stayed at home, glad enough to get an opportunity to torment Canute once more.

She was washing in the side kitchen, singing loudly as she worked. Mary was on her knees, blacking the stove and scolding violently about the young man who was coming out from town that night. The young man had committed the fatal error of laughing at Mary's ceaseless babble and had never been forgiven.

"He is no good, and you will come to a bad end by running with him! I do not see why a daughter of mine should act so. I do not see why the Lord should visit such a punishment upon me as to give me such a daughter. There are plenty of good men you can marry."

Lena tossed her head and answered curtly, "I don't happen to want to marry any man right away, and so long as Dick dresses nice and has plenty of money to spend, there is no harm in my going with him."

"Money to spend? Yes, and that is all he does with it I'll be bound. You think it very fine now, but you will change your tune when you have been married five years and see your children running naked and your cupboard empty. Did Anne Hermanson come to any good end by marrying a town man?"

"I don't know anything about Anne Hermanson, but I know any of the laundry girls would have Dick quick enough if they could get him."

"Yes, and a nice lot of store clothes huzzies you are too. Now there is Canuteson who has an 'eighty' proved up and fifty head of cattle and—"

"And hair that ain't been cut since he was a baby, and a big dirty beard, and he wears overalls on Sundays, and drinks like a pig. Besides he will keep. I can have all the fun I want, and when I am old and ugly like you he can have me and take care of me.

The Lord knows there ain't nobody else going to marry him."

Canute drew his hand back from the latch as though it were red hot. He was not the kind of man to make a good eavesdropper, and he wished he had knocked sooner. He pulled himself together and struck the door like a battering ram. Mary jumped and opened it with a screech.

"God! Canute, how you scared us! I thought it was crazy Lou—he has been tearing around the neighborhood trying to convert folks. I am afraid as death of him. He ought to be sent off, I think. He is just as liable as not to kill us all, or burn the barn, or poison the dogs. He has been worrying even the poor minister to death, and he laid up with the rheumatism, too! Did you notice that he was too sick to preach last Sunday? But don't stand there in the cold, come in. Yensen isn't here, but he just went over to Sorenson's for the mail; he won't be gone long. Walk right in the other room and sit down."

Canute followed her, looking steadily in front of him and not noticing Lena as he passed her. But Lena's vanity would not allow him to pass unmolested. She took the wet sheet she was wringing out and cracked him across the face with it, and ran giggling to the other side of the room. The blow stung his cheeks and the soapy water flew in his eyes, and he involuntarily began rubbing them with his hands. Lena giggled with delight at his discomfiture, and the wrath in Canute's face grew blacker than ever. A big man humiliated is vastly more undignified than a little one. He forgot the sting of his face in the bitter consciousness that he had made a fool of himself. He stumbled blindly into the living room, knocking his head against the door jamb because he forgot to stoop. He dropped into a chair behind the stove, thrusting his big feet back helplessly on either side of him.

Ole was a long time in coming, and Canute sat there, still and silent, with his hands clenched on his knees, and the skin of his face seemed to have shriveled up into little wrinkles that trembled when he lowered his brows. His life had been one long lethargy of solitude and alcohol, but now he was awakening, and it was as when the dumb stagnant heat of summer breaks out into thunder.

When Ole came staggering in, heavy with liquor, Canute rose at once.

"Yensen," he said quietly, "I have come to see if you will let me marry your daughter today."

"Today!" gasped Ole.

"Yes, I will not wait until tomorrow. I am tired of living alone."

Ole braced his staggering knees against the bedstead, and stammered eloquently: "Do you think I will marry my daughter to a drunkard? a man who drinks raw alcohol? a man who sleeps with rattle snakes? Get out of my house or I will kick you out for your impudence." And Ole began looking anxiously for his feet.

Canute answered not a word, but he put on his hat and went out into the kitchen. He went up to Lena and said without looking at her, "Get your things on and come with me!"

The tones of his voice startled her, and she said angrily, dropping the soap, "Are you drunk?"

"If you do not come with me, I will take you—you had better come," said Canute quietly.

She lifted a sheet to strike him, but he caught her arm roughly and wrenched the sheet from her. He turned to the wall and took down a hood and shawl that hung there, and began wrapping her up. Lena scratched and fought like a wild thing. Ole stood in the door, cursing, and Mary howled and screeched at the top of her voice. As for Canute, he lifted the girl in his arms and went out of the house. She kicked and struggled, but the helpless wailing of Mary and Ole soon died away in the distance, and her face was held down tightly on Canute's shoulder so that she could not see whither he was taking her. She was conscious only of the north wind whistling in her ears, and of rapid steady motion and of a great breast that heaved beneath her in quick, irregular breaths. The harder she struggled the tighter those iron arms that had held the heels of horses crushed about her, until she felt as if they would crush the breath from her, and lay still with fear. Canute was striding across the level fields at a pace at which man never went before, drawing the stinging north winds into his lungs in great gulps. He walked with his eyes half closed and looking straight in front of him, only lowering them when he bent his head to blow away the snow flakes that settled on her hair. So it was that Canute took her to his home, even as his bearded barbarian ancestors took the fair frivolous women of the South in their hairy arms and bore them down to their war ships. For ever and anon the soul becomes weary of the conventions that are not of it, and with a single stroke shatters the civilized lies with which it is unable to cope, and the strong arm reaches out and takes by force what it cannot win by cunning.

When Canute reached his shanty he placed the girl upon a chair, where she sat sobbing. He stayed only a few minutes. He filled the stove with wood and lit the lamp, drank a huge swallow of alcohol and put the bottle in his pocket. He paused a moment, staring heavily at the weeping girl, then he went off and locked the door and disappeared in the gathering gloom of the night.

Wrapped in flannels and soaked with turpentine, the little Norwegian preacher sat reading his Bible, when he heard a thundering knock at his door, and Canute entered, covered with snow and his beard frozen fast to his coat.

"Come in, Canute, you must be frozen," said the little man, shoving a chair towards his visitor.

Canute remained standing with his hat on and said quietly, "I want you to come over to my house tonight to marry me to Lena Yensen."

"Have you got a license, Canute?"

"No, I don't want a license. I want to be married."

"But I can't marry you without a license, man. It would not be legal."

A dangerous light came in the big Norwegian's eye. "I want you to come over to my house to marry me to Lena Yensen."

"No, I can't, it would kill an ox to go out in a storm like this, and my rheumatism is bad tonight."

"Then if you will not go I must take you," said Canute with a sigh.

He took down the preacher's bearskin coat and bade him put it on while he hitched up his buggy. He went out and closed the door softly after him.

Presently he returned and found the frightened minister crouching before the fire with his coat lying beside him. Canute helped him put it on and gently wrapped his head in his big muffler. Then he picked him up and carried him out and placed him in his buggy. As he tucked the buffalo robes around him be said: "Your horse is old, he might flounder or lose his way in this storm. I will lead him."

The minister took the reins feebly in his hands and sat shivering with the cold. Sometimes when there was a lull in the wind, he could see the horse struggling through the snow with the man plodding steadily beside him. Again the blowing snow would hide them from him altogether. He had no idea where they were or what direction they were going. He felt as though he were being whirled away in the heart of the storm, and he said all the prayers he knew. But at last the long four miles were over, and Canute set him down in the snow while he unlocked the door. He saw the bride sitting by the fire with her eyes red and swollen as though she had been weeping. Canute placed a huge chair for him, and said roughly,—

"Warm yourself."

Lena began to cry and moan afresh, begging the minister to take her home. He looked helplessly at Canute. Canute said simply,

"If you are warm now, you can marry us."

"My daughter, do you take this step of your own free will?" asked the minister in a trembling voice.

"No, sir, I don't, and it is disgraceful he should force me into it! I won't marry him."

"Then, Canute, I cannot marry you," said the minister, standing as straight as his rheumatic limbs would let him.

"Are you ready to marry us now, sir?" said Canute, laying one iron hand on his stooped shoulder. The little preacher was a good man, but like most men of weak body he was a coward and had a horror of physical suffering, although he had known so much of it. So with many qualms of conscience he began to repeat the marriage service. Lena sat sullenly in her chair, staring at the fire. Canute stood beside her, listening with his head bent reverently and his hands folded on his breast. When the little man had prayed and said amen, Canute began bundling him up again.

"I will take you home, now," he said as he carried him out and placed him in his buggy, and started off with him through the fury of the storm, floundering among the snow drifts that brought even the giant himself to his knees.

After she was left alone, Lena soon ceased weeping. She was not of a particularly sensitive temperament, and had little pride beyond that of vanity. After the first bitter anger wore itself out, she felt nothing more than a healthy sense of humiliation and defeat. She had no inclination to run away, for she was married now, and in her eyes that was final and all rebellion was useless. She knew nothing about a license, but she knew that a preacher married folks. She consoled herself by thinking that she had always intended to marry Canute someday, anyway.

She grew tired of crying and looking into the fire, so she got up and began to look about her. She had heard queer tales about the inside of Canute's shanty, and her curiosity soon got the better of her rage. One of the first things she noticed was the new black suit of clothes hanging on the wall. She was dull, but it did not take a vain woman long to interpret anything so decidedly flattering, and she was pleased in spite of herself. As she looked through the cupboard, the general air of neglect and discomfort made her pity the man who lived there.

"Poor fellow, no wonder he wants to get married to get somebody to wash up his dishes. Batchin's pretty hard on a man."

It is easy to pity when once one's vanity has been tickled. She looked at the windowsill and gave a little shudder and wondered if the man were crazy. Then she sat down again and sat a long time wondering what her Dick and Ole would do.

"It is queer Dick didn't come right over after me. He surely came, for he would have left town before the storm began and he might just as well come right on as go back. If he'd hurried he would have gotten here before the preacher came. I suppose he was afraid to come, for he knew Canuteson could pound him to jelly, the coward!" Her eyes flashed angrily.

The weary hours wore on and Lena began to grow horribly lonesome. It was an uncanny night and this was an uncanny place to be in. She could hear the coyotes howling hungrily a little way from the cabin, and more terrible still were all the unknown noises of the storm. She remembered the tales they told of the big log overhead and she was afraid of those snaky things on the windowsills. She remembered the man who had been killed in the draw, and she wondered what she would do if she saw crazy Lou's white face glaring into the window. The rattling of the door became unbearable, she thought the latch must be loose and took the lamp to look at it. Then for the first time she saw the ugly brown snake skins whose death rattle sounded every time the wind jarred the door.

"Canute, Canute!" she screamed in terror.

Outside the door she heard a heavy sound as of a big dog getting up and shaking himself. The door opened and Canute stood before her, white as a snow drift.

"What is it?" he asked kindly.

"I am cold," she faltered.

He went out and got an armful of wood and a basket of cobs and filled the stove. Then he went out and lay in the snow before the door. Presently he heard her calling again.

"What is it?" he said, sitting up.

"I'm so lonesome, I'm afraid to stay in here all alone."

"I will go over and get your mother." And he got up.

"She won't come."

"I'll bring her," said Canute grimly.

"No, no. I don't want her, she will scold all the time."

"Well, I will bring your father."

She spoke again and it seemed as though her mouth was close up to the key-hole. She spoke lower than he had ever heard her speak before, so low that he had to put his ear up to the lock to hear her.

"I don't want him either, Canute;—I'd rather have you."

For a moment she heard no noise at all, then something like a groan. With a cry of fear she opened the door, and saw Canute stretched in the snow at her feet, his face in his hands, sobbing on the doorstep.

## *Jack London, from* John Barleycorn *(1913)*

*The following passages from London's "alcoholic memoirs,"* John Barleycorn, *reflect the interplay of gender—both male and female—and the role of alcohol in American history. The first passage is London's account of his increasing use of alcohol as a sign of manliness and male camaraderie along the Oakland waterfront where London grew up; the second passage, toward the end of the book, articulates London's view that the evils of alcohol—for which London uses the old personification of "John Barleycorn" (see the poem of that title by Robert Burns in the section "Effects of Drinking")—can only be removed through the political action of women.*

*Many historians have noted the major role played by women in furthering the temperance cause in the United States; the Women's Christian Temperance Union, for example, founded in 1873–1874, lobbied energetically for prohibition, and saw success finally in the passage of the Eighteenth Amendment to the Constitution in 1920 (only to witness prohibition's repeal, of course, thirteen years later). Keenly aware of drink as a largely masculine activity, and of American women's tendency to support temperance and even prohibition, Jack London (1876–1916) voices his support in the passage below for women's suffrage as a crucial step in the battle with "John Barleycorn"; for London, giving women the vote was the likeliest path for men like himself to escape the ravages of drink. Despite London's support, how-*

ever, national female suffrage was, ironically, not passed until after Prohibition, when the Nineteenth Amendment granting the vote to women was ratified in August of 1920. On issues of masculine identity and the literary depiction of alcohol in London and other modern writers, see John W. Crowley, The White Logic: Alcoholism and Gender in American Modernist Fiction *(Amherst: University of Massachusetts Press, 1994).*

## Chapter VI

But the time was rapidly drawing near when I was to begin my second series of bouts with John Barleycorn. When I was fourteen, my head filled with the tales of the old voyagers, my vision with tropic isles and far sea-rims, I was sailing a small centreboard skiff around San Francisco Bay and on the Oakland Estuary. I wanted to go to sea. I wanted to get away from monotony and the commonplace. I was in the flower of my adolescence, a-thrill with romance and adventure, dreaming of wild life in the wild man-world. Little I guessed how all the warp and woof of that man-world was entangled with alcohol.

So, one day, as I hoisted sail on my skiff, I met Scotty. He was a husky youngster of seventeen, a runaway apprentice, he told me, from an English ship in Australia. He had just worked his way on another ship to San Francisco; and now he wanted to see about getting a berth on a whaler. Across the estuary, near where the whalers lay, was lying the sloop-yacht Idler. The caretaker was a harpooner who intended sailing next voyage on the whale ship Bonanza. Would I take him, Scotty, over in my skiff to call upon the harpooner?

Would I! Hadn't I heard the stories and rumours about the Idler?—the big sloop that had come up from the Sandwich Islands where it had been engaged in smuggling opium. And the harpooner who was caretaker! How often had I seen him and envied him his freedom. He never had to leave the water. He slept aboard the Idler each night, while I had to go home upon the land to go to bed. The harpooner was only nineteen years old (and I have never had anything but his own word that he was a harpooner); but he had been too shining and glorious a personality for me ever to address as I paddled around the yacht at a wistful distance. Would I take Scotty, the runaway sailor, to visit the harpooner, on the opium-smuggler Idler? WOULD I!

The harpooner came on deck to answer our hail, and invited us aboard. I played the sailor and the man, fending off the skiff so that it would not mar the yacht's white paint, dropping the skiff astern on a long painter, and making the painter fast with two nonchalant half-hitches.

We went below. It was the first sea-interior I had ever seen. The clothing on the wall smelled musty. But what of that? Was it not the sea-gear of men?—leather jackets lined with corduroy, blue coats of pilot cloth, sou'westers, sea-boots, oilskins. And everywhere was in evidence the economy of space—the narrow bunks, the swinging tables, the incredible lockers. There were the tell-tale compass, the sea-lamps in their gimbals, the blue-backed charts carelessly rolled and tucked away, the signal-flags in alphabetical order, and a mariner's dividers jammed into the woodwork to hold a calendar. At last I was living. Here I sat, inside my first ship, a smuggler, accepted as a comrade by a harpooner and a runaway English sailor who said his name was Scotty.

The first thing that the harpooner, aged nineteen, and the sailor, aged seventeen, did to show that they were men was to behave like men. The harpooner suggested the eminent desirableness of a drink, and Scotty searched his pockets for dimes and nickels. Then the harpooner carried away a pink flask to be filled in some blind pig, for there were no licensed saloons in that locality. We drank the cheap rotgut out of tumblers. Was I any the less strong, any the less valiant, than the harpooner and the sailor? They were men. They proved it by the way they drank. Drink was the badge of manhood. So I drank with them, drink by drink, raw and straight, though the damned stuff couldn't compare with a stick of chewing taffy or a delectable "cannon-ball." I shuddered and swallowed my gorge with every drink, though I manfully hid all such symptoms.

Divers times we filled the flask that afternoon. All I had was twenty cents, but I put it up like a man, though with secret regret at the enormous store of candy it could have bought. The liquor mounted in the heads of all of us, and the talk of Scotty and the harpooner was upon running the Easting down, gales off the Horn and pamperos off the Plate, lower topsail breezes, southerly busters, North Pacific gales, and of smashed whaleboats in the Arctic ice.

"You can't swim in that ice water," said the harpooner confidentially to me. "You double up in a minute and go down. When a whale smashes your boat, the thing to do is to get your belly across an oar, so that when the cold doubles you you'll float."

"Sure," I said, with a grateful nod and an air of certitude that I, too, would hunt whales and be in smashed boats in the Arctic Ocean. And, truly, I registered his advice as singularly valuable information, and filed it away in my brain, where it persists to this day.

But I couldn't talk—at first. Heavens! I was only fourteen, and had never been on the ocean in my life. I could only listen to the two sea-dogs, and show my manhood by drinking with them, fairly and squarely, drink and drink.

The liquor worked its will with me; the talk of Scotty and the harpooner poured through the pent space of the Idler's cabin and through my brain like great gusts of wide, free wind; and in imagination I lived my years to come and rocked over the wild, mad, glorious world on multitudinous adventures.

We unbent. Our inhibitions and taciturnities vanished. We were as if we had known each other for years and years, and we pledged ourselves to years of future voyagings together. The harpooner told of misadventures and secret shames. Scotty wept over his poor old mother in Edinburgh—a lady, he insisted, gently born—who was in reduced circumstances, who had pinched herself to pay the lump sum to the ship-owners for his apprenticeship, whose sacrificing dream had been to see him a merchantman officer and a gentleman, and who was heartbroken because he had deserted his ship in Australia and joined another as a common sailor before the mast. And Scotty proved it. He drew her last sad letter from his pocket and wept over it as he read it aloud. The harpooner and I wept with him, and swore that all three of us would ship on the whaleship Bonanza, win a big pay-day, and, still together, make a pilgrimage to Edinburgh and lay our store of money in the dear lady's lap.

And, as John Barleycorn heated his way into my brain, thawing my reticence, melting my modesty, talking through me and with me and as me, my adopted twin brother and alter ego, I, too, raised my voice to show myself a man and an adventurer, and bragged in detail and at length of how I had crossed San Francisco Bay in my open skiff in a roaring southwester when even the schooner sailors doubted my exploit. Further, I—or John Barleycorn, for it was the same thing—told Scotty that he might be a deep-sea sailor and know the last rope on the great deep-sea ships, but that when it came to small-boat sailing I could beat him hands down and sail circles around him.

The best of it was that my assertion and brag were true. With reticence and modesty present, I could never have dared tell Scotty my small-boat estimate of him. But it is ever the way of John Barleycorn to loosen the tongue and babble the secret thought.

Scotty, or John Barleycorn, or the pair, was very naturally offended by my remarks. Nor was I loath. I could whip any runaway sailor seventeen years old. Scotty and I flared and raged like young cockerels, until the harpooner poured another round of drinks to enable us to forgive and make up. Which we did, arms around each other's necks, protesting vows of eternal friendship—just like Black Matt and Tom Morrisey, I remembered, in the ranch kitchen in San Mateo. And, remembering, I knew that I was at last a man—despite my meagre fourteen years—a man as big and manly as those two strapping giants who had quarrelled and made up on that memorable Sunday morning of long ago.

By this time the singing stage was reached, and I joined Scotty and the harpooner in snatches of sea songs and chanties. It was here, in the cabin of the Idler, that I first heard "Blow the Man Down," "Flying Cloud," and "Whisky, Johnny, Whisky." Oh, it was brave. I was beginning to grasp the meaning of life. Here was no commonplace, no Oakland Estuary, no weary round of throwing newspapers at front doors, delivering ice, and setting up ninepins. All the world was mine, all its paths were under my feet, and John Barleycorn, tricking my fancy, enabled me to anticipate the life of adventure for which I yearned.

We were not ordinary. We were three tipsy young gods, incredibly wise, gloriously genial, and without limit to our powers. Ah!—and I say it now, after the years—could John Barleycorn keep one at such a height, I should never draw a sober breath again. But this is not a world of free freights. One pays according to an iron schedule—for every strength the balanced weakness; for every high a corresponding low; for every fictitious god-like moment an equivalent time in reptilian slime. For every feat of telescoping long days and weeks of life into mad magnificent instants, one must pay with shortened life, and, oft-times, with savage usury added.

Intenseness and duration are as ancient enemies as fire and water. They are mutually destructive. They cannot co-exist. And John Barleycorn, mighty necromancer though he be, is as much a slave to organic chemistry as we mortals are. We pay for every nerve marathon we run, nor can John Barleycorn intercede and fend off the just payment. He can lead us to the heights, but he cannot keep us there, else would we all be devotees. And there is no devotee but pays for the mad dances John Barleycorn pipes.

Yet the foregoing is all in after wisdom spoken. It was no part of the knowledge of the lad, fourteen years old, who sat in the Idler's cabin between the harpooner and the sailor, the air rich in his nostrils with the musty smell of men's sea-gear, roaring in chorus: "Yankee ship come down de ribber—pull, my bully boys, pull!"

We grew maudlin, and all talked and shouted at once. I had a splendid constitution, a stomach that would digest scrap-iron, and I was still running my marathon in full vigour when Scotty began to fail and fade. His talk grew incoherent. He groped for words and could not find them, while the ones he found his lips were unable to form. His poisoned consciousness was leaving him. The brightness went out of his eyes, and he looked as stupid as were his efforts to talk. His face and body sagged as his consciousness sagged. (A man cannot sit upright save by an act of will.) Scotty's reeling brain could not control his muscles. All his correlations were breaking down. He strove to take another drink, and feebly dropped the tumbler on the floor. Then, to my amazement, weeping bitterly, he rolled into a bunk on his back and immediately snored off to sleep.

The harpooner and I drank on, grinning in a superior way to each other over Scotty's plight. The last flask was opened, and we drank it between us, to the accompaniment of Scotty's stertorous breathing. Then the harpooner faded away into his bunk, and I was left alone, unthrown, on the field of battle.

I was very proud, and John Barleycorn was proud with me. I could carry my drink. I was a man. I had drunk two men, drink for drink, into unconsciousness. And I was still on my two feet, upright, making my way on deck to get air into my scorching lungs. It was in this bout on the Idler that I discovered what a good stomach and a strong head I had for drink—a bit of knowledge that was to be a source of pride in succeeding years, and that ultimately I was to come to consider a great affliction. The fortunate man is the one who cannot take more than a couple of drinks without becoming intoxicated. The unfortunate wight is the one who can take many glasses without betraying a sign, who must take numerous glasses in order to get the "kick."

The sun was setting when I came on the Idler's deck. There were plenty of bunks below. I did not need to go home. But I wanted to demonstrate to myself how much I was a man. There lay my skiff astern. The last of a strong ebb was running out in channel in the teeth of an ocean breeze of forty miles an hour. I could see the stiff whitecaps, and the suck and run of the current was plainly visible in the face and trough of each one.

I set sail, cast off, took my place at the tiller, the sheet in my hand, and headed across channel. The skiff heeled over and plunged into it madly. The spray began to fly. I was at the pinnacle of exaltation. I sang "Blow the Man Down" as I sailed. I was no boy of fourteen, living the mediocre ways of the sleepy town called Oakland. I was a man, a god, and the very elements rendered me allegiance as I bitted them to my will.

The tide was out. A full hundred yards of soft mud intervened between the boat-wharf and the water. I pulled up my centreboard, ran full tilt into the mud, took in sail, and, standing in the stern, as I had often done at low tide, I began to shove the skiff with an oar. It was then that my correlations began to break down. I lost my balance and pitched head-foremost into the ooze. Then, and for the first time, as I floundered to my feet covered with slime, the blood running down my arms from a scrape against a barnacled stake, I knew that I was drunk. But what of it? Across the channel two strong sailormen lay unconscious in their bunks where I had drunk them. I WAS a man. I was still on my legs, if they were knee-deep in mud. I disdained to get back into the skiff. I waded through the mud, shoving the skiff before me and yammering the chant of my manhood to the world.

I paid for it. I was sick for a couple of days, meanly sick, and my arms were painfully poisoned from the barnacle scratches. For a week I could not use them, and it was a torture to put on and take off my clothes.

I swore, "Never again!" The game wasn't worth it. The price was too stiff. I had no moral qualms. My revulsion was purely physical. No exalted moments were worth such hours of misery and wretchedness. When I got back to my skiff, I shunned the Idler. I would cross the opposite side of the channel to go around her. Scotty had disappeared. The harpooner was still about, but him I avoided. Once, when he landed on the boat-wharf, I hid in a shed so as to escape seeing him. I was afraid he would propose some more drinking, maybe have a flask full of whisky in his pocket.

And yet—and here enters the necromancy of John Barleycorn—that afternoon's drunk on the Idler had been a purple passage flung into the monotony of my days. It was memorable. My mind dwelt on it continually. I went over the details, over and over again. Among other things, I had got into the cogs and springs of men's actions. I had seen Scotty weep about his own worthlessness and the sad case of his Edinburgh mother who was a lady. The harpooner had told me terribly wonderful things of himself. I had caught a myriad enticing and inflammatory hints of a world beyond my world, and for which I was certainly as fitted as the two lads who had drunk with me. I had got behind men's souls. I had got behind my own soul and found unguessed potencies and greatnesses.

Yes, that day stood out above all my other days. To this day it so stands out. The memory of it is branded in my brain. But the price exacted was too high. I refused to play and pay, and returned to my cannon-balls and taffy-slabs. The point is that all the chemistry of my healthy, normal body drove me away from alcohol. The stuff didn't agree with me. It was abominable. But, despite this, circumstance was to continue to drive me toward John Barleycorn, to drive me again and again, until, after long years, the time should come when I would look up John Barleycorn in every haunt of men—look him up and hail him gladly as benefactor and friend. And detest and hate him all the time. Yes, he is a strange friend, John Barleycorn.

## Chapter XXXVIII

The foregoing is a sample roaming with the White Logic* through the dusk of my soul. To the best of my power I have striven to give the reader a glimpse of a man's secret dwelling when it is shared with John Barleycorn. And the reader must remember that this mood, which he has read in a quarter of an hour, is but one mood of the myriad moods of John Barleycorn, and that the procession of such moods may well last the clock around through many a day and week and month.

My alcoholic reminiscences draw to a close. I can say, as any strong, chesty drinker can say, that all that leaves me alive to-day on the planet is my unmerited luck—the luck of chest, and shoulders, and constitution. I dare to say that a not large percentage of youths, in the formative stage of fifteen to seventeen, could have survived the stress of heavy drinking that I survived between my fifteenth and seventeenth years; that a not large percentage of men could have punished the alcohol I have punished in my manhood years and lived to tell the tale. I survived, through no personal virtue, but because I did not have the chemistry of a dipsomaniac and because I possessed an organism unusually resistant to the ravages of John Barleycorn. And, surviving, I have watched the others die, not so lucky, down all the long sad road.

It was my unmitigated and absolute good fortune, good luck, chance, call it what you will, that brought me through the fires of John Barleycorn. My life, my career, my joy in living, have not been destroyed. They have been scorched, it is true; like the survivors of forlorn hopes, they have by unthinkably miraculous ways come through the fight to marvel at the tally of the slain.

And like such a survivor of old red war who cries out, "Let there be no more war!" so I cry out, "Let there be no more poison-fighting by our youths!" The way to stop war is to stop it. The way to stop drinking is to stop it. The way China stopped the general use of opium was by stopping the cultivation and importation of opium. The philosophers, priests, and doctors of China could have preached themselves breathless against opium for a thousand years, and the use of opium, so long as opium was ever accessible and obtainable, would have continued unabated. We are so made, that is all.

We have with great success made a practice of not leaving arsenic and strychnine, and typhoid and tuberculosis germs lying around for our children to be destroyed by. Treat John Barleycorn the same way. Stop him. Don't let him lie around, licensed and legal, to pounce upon our youth. Not of alcoholics nor for alcoholics do I write, but for our youths, for those who possess no more than the adventure-stings and the genial predispositions, the social man-impulses, which are twisted all awry by our barbarian civilisation which feeds them poison on all the corners. It is the healthy, normal boys, now born or being born, for whom I write.

It was for this reason, more than any other, and more ardently than any other, that I rode down into the Valley of the Moon, all a-jingle, and voted for equal suffrage. I voted that women might vote, because I knew that they, the wives and mothers of the race, would vote John Barleycorn out of existence and back into the historical limbo of our vanished customs of savagery. If I thus seem to cry out as one hurt, please remember that I have been sorely bruised and that I do dislike the thought that any son or daughter of mine or yours should be similarly bruised.

The women are the true conservators of the race. The men are the wastrels, the adventure-lovers and gamblers, and in the end it is by their women that they are saved. About man's first experiment in chemistry was the making of alcohol, and down all the generations to this day man has continued to manufacture and drink it. And there has never been a day when the women have not resented man's use of alcohol, though they have never had the power to give weight to their resentment. The moment women get the vote in any community, the first thing they proceed to do is to close the saloons. In a thousand generations to come men of themselves will not close the saloons. As well expect the morphine victims to legislate the sale of morphine out of existence.

The women know. They have paid an incalculable price of sweat and tears for man's use of alcohol. Ever jealous for the race, they will legislate for the babes of boys yet to be born; and for the babes of girls, too, for they must be the mothers, wives, and sisters of these boys.

And it will be easy. The only ones that will be hurt will be the topers and seasoned drinkers of a single generation. I am one of these, and I make solemn assurance, based upon long traffic with John Barleycorn, that it won't hurt me very much to stop drinking when no one else drinks and when no drink is obtainable. On the other hand, the overwhelming proportion of young men are so normally non-alcoholic, that, never having had access to alcohol, they will never miss it. They will know of the saloon only in the pages of history, and they will think of the saloon as a quaint old custom similar to bull-baiting and the burning of witches.

*The "white logic" is London's term, elaborated on elsewhere in his book, for the bleak, deceptive, and destructive "truth beyond truth" that alcohol brings, distorting the drinker's entire mode of thought.

# *Brian Moore, from* The Lonely Passion of Judith Hearne *(1955)*

*If drinking in Irish culture has been stereotypically excused as a "good man's failing," it has never been known as a "good woman's failing." The social opprobrium that particularly accrues to drinking women in many societies plays a prominent role in this novel by the celebrated Irish novelist, Brian Moore (1921–1999). The Lonely Passion of Judith Hearne explores a young Irishwoman's descent into drunkenness in mid twentieth-century Ireland, but Judith Hearne's loneliness, her intimidation by the raised eyebrows of others, and her increasing use of drink as a crutch and anodyne reflect problems that appear far beyond the Irish setting of this book. Moreover, Judith Hearne's gender is a key aspect of her particular drinking problems—her increasing rationalization of drinking as "medicinal" and the especially embarrassing, even shocking nature of Judith passing out drunk in her room are directly related to her being a woman. Although recent years have seen far more openness about female drinking problems, historically, the shame associated with female alcoholism has often made it a hidden, even "invisible" condition. Brian Moore's sympathetic yet clear-eyed portrayal of Judith's decay— including the passage below, describing the exposure of Judith's inebriety to her landlady in Chapter X in the novel—strikingly exemplifies fiction's ability to help readers see what otherwise might remain invisible because of social pretense, convention, and unexpressed feeling.*

"Miss Hearne. Miss Hearne. Hello There? Miss Hearne?"

She was on the floor. O my God, where? Where? My room.

She raised herself on an elbow, staring in panic at the shaking door. Och, och, och, it cried.

"Yes," she said. "Yes. Who is it?"

"Mrs Rice. Are you sick? Are you all right?"

"Yes." O, that cracked-sounding voice. She cleared her throat. "Yes, I'm perfectly all right, thank you. I was sleeping."

"Are you sure?" the door said. "Would you like me to get you something? May I come in?"

"No, no, I'm all right. I just want to sleep."

"Well, let me know if you want anything," the door said. It waited.

She waited.

Silence.

Then the footsteps going down the stairs. She dropped her face back on the worn carpet. The trembling started in her arms and spread upwards to her shoulders and face. What did I...? When did it start? How long have I been lying here?

Through the window she saw the night sky silhouette the houses across the street. Her little travelling clock screamed confirmation: eight-fifteen.

And this morning, last night, all afternoon, where and what did I do?

Events unrolled themselves then, like a reel of film spinning backwards in nickering confusion. Mrs Rice, yes, and then this morning, the maid came, last night I drank, I was upset, yes, Mrs Rice and what she said. James Madden a doorman. But what had happened in the lost time, the dead time of drinking? What awful thing? The anxiety of not knowing began, set her trembling, brought sharp needle pains to her forehead: sweat trickled like tears along her cheeks. She stood up, looked at the spilled glass, the empty bottle, the other bottle kicked in a corner (I must have made a noise when I did that) the drink stain on the floor, the rumpled bed, the stale room.

There was none left. She looked at her trunk, but she knew it was hopeless. Both bottles were empty. She must manage the trembling, the nausea, the awful hours of conscience, without any help at all. For the moment, don't think, just get the place tidy.

In her dressing-gown, her hair rumpled and falling about her shoulders, she began shakily to set things to rights. The bottles she wrapped in old newspaper and hid in a dresser drawer. The stain in the floor would not come out. She abandoned it and then, cramming her parched mouth with sweet nauseating cachous, she began the frightening task of dressing.

It took ages. Badly, rouged, over-powdered, her hair done up in a bun, she sat down in her chair at last, and let the shaking take its course. The fears came. How much noise, did I talk to myself the way I did in Cromwell Road, did I go out of the room or let anyone in? Or was it all quiet, sitting in my chair, oversleeping, medicinal drink to help me sleep?

She was so weary, so worn with the ravages of her sin. But God was weary too. He had suffered through her carelessness, her sinfulness. She knelt beside the bed and made an act of contrition.

"O, my God, I am heartily sorry for having offended Thee and I detest my sins above every other evil because they displease Thee my God Who are so deserving of all my love—and I firmly purpose—by the help of Thy Holy grace—never more to offend Thee—and to amend my life."

But this seemed too impersonal. She looked up at the Sacred Heart for guidance and saw with shame that he was turned towards the wall. She stood on the bed and turned him around to face her. His eyes, as always when the sin was committed, were hurt and reproving.

"I am sorry, I am terribly sorry and I promise Thee that it will never happen again."

But he did not believe her. His eyes said as much: she half expected him to shake his head and turn his sad face away.

And who could blame Him? Why should He believe me when I'm such a backslider, such a weak, useless, hopeless sinner?

Useless and hopeless, she straightened the bed, lit the bedside lamp and went to the mantelpiece to stare at the photograph of her dear aunt. A good thing God took you away, she thought, a mercy. For if you could only see me now, how could you have borne the shame of it?

Penitence gave strength. The open admission of error helped to drive it out. Still trembling, but with new confidence, she lit her gas fire. She warmed her hands for some minutes, then went to the wardrobe and put on her old green tweed coat and a dark red hat. She turned the stove and lights out and locked the door. She felt light-headed and terribly weak, it was the want of food, she was sure. If she hurried, the tea-shop at Bradbury Place would still be open. A cup of tea and a sandwich would do wonders.

But there was to be no slipping out. When she reached the hallway, the curtained door opened to reveal Mrs Henry Rice, fat and curious, her bland eyes showing nothing of what went on behind them. She stepped close to Miss Hearne, took her arm and put her face very near. At that moment, Miss Hearne blessed her foresight in eating so many of the nauseating scented cachous.

"Feeling better now?"

"O, yes, thanks."

"Catch a chill or something? You certainly slept a long time."

"Well, I wasn't feeling up to the mark." (Woman to woman, I must find a bond.) "O dear," she said, holding her handbag tight against her stomach to stop the trembling. "We women have to put up with a lot. Men are so lucky."

Mrs. Henry Rice raised her eyebrows. "You feel sick with it? Some do. I used to get awful headaches myself, every thirty-three days, regular as clockwork."

"I know," Miss Hearne said. "Headaches are even worse than being sick. Still, I do feel rotten."

But her lie had not taken. Mrs. Henry Rice had opened a trap for her victim. She closed it now, with a smile of full-bloated malice.

"Well, it seems to affect you pretty merrily. Why, you were singing away all afternoon."

"...No—I mean..."

"Yes, singing and talking away to yourself as happy as a lark. It's a wonder nobody complained, you were louder than the wireless."

"I used to sing a lot. I was—practising. I give music lessons, you know. I'm awfully sorry, I didn't realise I was disturbing anyone. I—I suppose the walls are thinner than I expected."

"The walls in this house are not thin, they're old wads, very thick, as a matter of fact. You'd have to shout at the top of your voice to be heard."

"Well, a person singing—you know the singing voice carries. The tones penetrate. I'm awfully sorry if I disturbed you."

"O, singing's loud, I know that. Why, there was a drunk man in the street last week, you could hear him a mile away. It's terrible the noise a drunk man makes."

She knows. The bad, black-hearted slimy voice of her. O, I could kill her. "Well, I must hurry on out now, Mrs. Rice, if you don't mind. I have an engagement."

"It's a pity you weren't up and about sooner. My brother was asking for you, but he's gone downtown now."

"O, indeed? Well, I must be on my way. Good night, Mrs. Rice."

"Good night, Miss Hearne. And—Miss Hearne?"

"Yes?"

"You will be careful, won't you? About singing. I wouldn't like people to get the wrong impression."

"What do you mean, the wrong impression?"

"Well, people are funny. Even Jim, my brother, he got the wrong idea about it. Why he said to me this afternoon that it sounded as if you were having a party in your room. I said no, that was silly, you were just singing to yourself."

"Good night, Mrs. Rice."

"Good night."

The night air helped. It tasted clean and fresh and she breathed deeply as she walked, trying to stop the trembling which had now become a sort of shivering as the cold crept into her bones. She felt nauseated. Singing, talking to herself, awful, it was awful. And in front of other people. In front of him, what could he think of her? He had waited to see her, his horrid sister had rubbed that in, the sly one.

The Bon-Bon teashop was still open, thank heavens. She picked a table near the radiator. A slow, shuffling waitress took her order and served a pot of tea and an egg sandwich. With her eyes on the slightly soiled tablecloth, Miss Hearne forced herself to get the food down. She drank the tea and when the pot was empty, she asked for more hot water. But the waitress had seen her before and knew that she never tipped. The kitchen was closed, she said, she was sorry, but the teashop closed in five minutes, at nine o'clock.

She paid and went out. The thought of going back to her room was hateful. It was too late to go anywhere else, the pictures, for instance, and besides, even the pictures couldn't stop the shaking. There was only one other place to go, and perhaps an hour there, an hour of quiet prayer, would give her strength to resist the temptation that was coming fast upon her.

It was shameful, shameful. Singing like a crazy woman, lying on the floor of her room, drunken, dirty, sinning, while God in his Heaven looked down at her. And then being forced to humiliate herself in front of a person like Mrs Rice, telling that lie about monthlies *and being caught in it*. Could anybody blame her if she despised me? I deserve it. I'm rotten, rotten, just a useless woman, all alone.

But there in front of her was Saint Finbar's, its Gothic spire uplifted like two praying hands, a grey religious place, the house of God in the peace of night. She went in, dipping her hand in the dirty Holy Water font, making the Sign of the Cross as she pushed open the door leading from the vestibule to the nave.

\* \* \*

The church was dark: here and there, a small lamp or a cluster of candles burned in lonely devotion before a picture, beneath an altar. The church was empty: cleared of its stock of rituals, invocations, prayers, a deserted spiritual warehouse waiting new consignments. One old woman kept watch for the community, sitting in the darkness with her back to a radiator. As she praying as she watched the altar, or had she come in to keep warm?

This quiet, this gloom, this immense repose, soothed Miss Hearne as she stood in the deep shadows at the back of the church. She walked up the highway of the centre aisle, past the side aisles tormented by the Stations of the Cross, up to the great golden and white sweep of the main altar. She genuflected, and sat down in the front bench, feeling faint, weary, but at peace. O Sacred Heart forgive me, she prayed, her eyes on the small golden door of the tabernacle. God sat behind that door, God in the form of bread by the sacrified of the Mass, God sat alone behind that door in His empty church. Deserted God, she thought, You wait alone each night while men forget You.

The tabernacle glowed red-gold from the small light of the hanging sacristy lamp. She remembered that when the lamp is lit, God is in the tabernacle. When it is put out on Good Friday, He is absent.

The sacristy lamp winked. In the shadows the old woman stood up, genuflected, and turned her back on God. Miss Hearne watched the tabernacle, heard the dragging footsteps, the muffled slap of the swinging door, as the old woman went out into the streets. Alone in the immensity of His house, she gazed at the unseen Presence behind the little golden door. Alone with her God, she knelt down and begged Him.

O Sacred Heart, please, I need Your strength, Your help. Why should life be so hard for me, why am I alone, why did I yield to the temptation of drink, why, why has it all happened like this? O Sacred Heart, lighten my cross, You know it was hard, aunt dying after all those years of caring for her and You, only You, know the things I wanted, the home, children to raise up to honour and reverence You. O Sweet Jesus, You have shared my suffering, You know that I love You, please dear Lord, give me a sign, give me strength.

Tears wet her eyes. She raised her head. But the tabernacle was silent. Behind the door, God watched. He gave no sign. And around her the statues, unlit and unlovely, stared coldly across the church, unhearing, uncaring. Our

Lady her eyes and hands uplifted in her own private prayer; Saint Patrick, a gaunt old man in a green chasuble and a golden mitre, his right hand gripping a staff, unmindful of the snakes which coiled around its base; Saint Joseph, his meek eyes downcast, a good grey-beard few people prayed to. Plaster saints, no entreaty could move them. Alone, rejected, Miss Hearne looked again at the tabernacle, behind whose tiny door bread made into the Body of God lay hidden. The Holy of Holies.

Behind the altar an old sacristan appeared a minor mummer on God's stage. Perfunctorily, he paused, genuflected in front of the tabernacle, then mounted the altar steps. His old eyes sought the tabernacle, dismissed it and he went wearily around the back of the altar. She heard him fumble with a switch and the lights in the side aisles went out. Then he came around the front again, walked down the steps and opened the little gate at the Communion rail. He did not genuflect but walked straight down the main aisle.

"Closing now, closing," he said in an angry voice as he passed her bench. But she sat stiffly, terrified by the thing she had felt. For when the lights went out, it seemed as though the tabernacle were empty, a little golden house, set in the middle of a huge mantelpiece. It was as though the old sacristan, keeper of secrets, knew he had no need to genuflect again. The lights were out, the people had gone home, the church was closing. In the tabernacle there was no God. Only round wafers of unleavened bread. She had prayed to bread. The great ceremonial of the Mass, the singing, the incense, the benedictions, what if it was show, all useless show? What if it meant nothing, nothing?

O God, God forgive me! she cried, falling on her knees. Forgive me, O Sacred Heart, for the terrible doubt the devil put in my head. O my guardian angel, shield me, protect me. Forgive me, O God, for I have sinned. I have blasphemed.

The footsteps returned. "You'll have to leave now, missis," the old sacristan said. His soutane was unbuttoned, showing a dirty brown pullover underneath. She looked into his old discoloured eyes, searching for secrets. But saw only that he was tired, that he wanted to close the church, that he wanted her to go.

She sat up then and watched as the old man banged the Communion gate shut, all pretence at devotion gone, as he went to close the side door without bending a knee to his immortal God. She stood up, bowed her head to the tabernacle, genuflected and went quickly down the aisle to the door. She made the Sign of the Cross in dirty Holy Water (if it is only ordinary water and the priest is wrong...?) and went out of the church, hearing the swinging door slap shut.

Outside the church gates, people passed. People busy with the immediate things of life. People making a living, bringing up children, planning, talking, sharing each other. Alone, Miss Hearne looked back at the church, an unhaunted house of God, an empty place, stripped of the singing, the ritual, stripped of men; men who brought it to sudden glorious life. Empty. And above her, the night sky, curved and vast. An empty sky, nothing beyond it but the stars, the planets, with the earth spinning among them. Surely some great design kept it all moving, some Presence made it meaningful. But what if the godless were right, what if it all started back aeons ago with fish crawling out of the sea to become men and women? What if not Adam and Eve, but apes, great monkeys, were our ancestors? In that world, what place had a God who cared for suffering?

She began to walk. Supposing, just supposing, her heart cried, supposing nobody has listened to me in all these years of prayers. Nobody at all up above me, watching over me. Then nothing is sinful. There is no sin. And I have been cheated, the crimson nights in that terrible book from Paris the sin, permissible then. Nobody above. Nobody to care. Whiteness hers, he seized, revelled in. Virile he, his dark flashing eyes, they lifted beakers of wine and quaffed them, losing themselves in the intoxication of love, homage to Bacchus, lusts of the flesh. That handsome boy bathing that day at Greystones, standing up in his tight bathing trunks, his bump of virility sticking out, he would enfold me, he would run gracefully with me up the strand to the dunes. No sin in it. It would be passion, sublime freedom. And my breasts bare, that day in Doctor Bowe's surgery, his assistant, McNamara his name, me lying on the examination couch, my arms hanging over the edge, and he came close, yes, close, his stethoscope cold on my chest, he bent over and against the back of my hand his trousers pressed, I felt it, his thing, swelling there soft, he didn't notice, an accident, but behind the material it was there, soft, swelling, the hot flushes I had, daren't move my hand for fear he'd notice, felt it against the back of my hand, soft, hard, warm, supposing he had noticed, it swelled, all caution gone, he had turned, the rough beast, tearing his clothes off, black hair all over him, lusting after my whiteness, yes, I could too, give myself, gipsy girl, hair about my shoulders, my breasts bare, rolling on the greensward, Romany marriage, blood mixing blood, while he, his male blackness enfolds me. It would be nature, not sin. For remember the night old John Healy said to aunt that if he weren't a Catholic and did not believe, then what would there be to prevent him living as a profligate, cheating his neighbours, owning slaves, living like a great Roman in the golden days of Rome. Rome, Samson and Delilah, his great powerful half-naked body in the picture. What would prevent him, what indeed? No hell, no purgatory, no responsibility to God. If all the priests were wrong and you died and slept into nothingness, what point, then, in all of that? The community, it can go hang, what did the community ever do for me that I should help my fellow man?

No god. But the Protestants would never be saved and still they went on making laws stopping people from doing sinful things, canting about sin and corruption. And if we Catholics were wrong too? she thought. Then we'd be no better off than godless Russia, free love, no morals, rape in the streets, men killing, strangling, defiling women like the sex maniacs in the *News of the World*. Who'd stop them? What use in courts if there was no moral code, no bible to swear on? A woman like me, defenseless against the beast in men, what would I do? No, no, there has to be a god and if there was no god, men would make one.

Idols, like that great idol, in the picture, the Temple of Dagon, Victor Mature pulled it down, a god of clay. And those people back in ancient times, superstitious they were, afraid of the sun, of snakes, of things of clay. Omens and portents. And us? The golden door, the circle of bread in the monstrance. What if...? O forgive me Sacred Heart, the devil's thoughts, forgive me. But—tearing at my dress, ripping it away, his toga thrown aside, his huge hands feel me, press me close, his body, muscled, hard. And drunken, that wonderful cheerfulness, gay laughter, quaffing the wine, forgetfulness. Sweet oblivion. O Thou. A loaf of bread, a jug of wine and Thou beside me in the wilderness. Paradise now.

A car, headlights like yellow angry eyes, brakes screeching in rage. She stumbled, drew back, fell. Strong hands lifted her.

"Are you all right, Miss? You nearly got kilt."

And a man's head from the car window. "The lights were against her. She just walked out, not looking. Get herself killed."

Then the noise of engines backing up, moving again. The passers-by stared, resumed their progress. The man who had lifted her, touched his hat. "Sure you're all right? Are you ill?"

"No, no, thank you. Thank you very much."

Nearly killed, not looking. *I was nearly killed.* Called to meet my Maker. And in mortal sin, sinful evil thoughts, sins of intent. Denying God.

She stood there shaking, saying an act of contrition. Struck down in the midst of my sinfulness, O Sacred Heart, forgive me. You gave a sign, a warning. Your patience will not last for ever. O dear Jesus, the drink, the sin that led to another sin. Hallucinations I had, and shaking like this. O my God, I am heartily sorry. I thank Thee.

Her eyes sought the night sky and she gave thanks. Then she crossed carefully when the lights showed green and continued home to Camden Street. She said a whole rosary on the way. A rosary in honour of the Sacred Heart. He had warned: Repent. Once again He had been merciful, He had shown the way.

# VI. Spirits and the Spirit

## *Li Bo, "Drinking Alone by Moonlight" (8th century)*

Like the earlier selection from Li Bo in this volume (under "Causes"), this poem does not hesitate to praise both wine and even drunkenness. But Li Bo's emphasis here—as is the case with Neruda's "Ode to Wine," found later in this chapter—is on the interpenetration of the natural and the spiritual that the poet finds in wine, reflected in the poem's parallelism between heavenly and earthly love for wine.

After the first section's description of the poet drinking alone and contemplating nature, the poem builds on this to connect drinking to a state of spiritual calm and detachment from earthly concerns; the poem concludes by identifying wine as a vehicle for elevating the drinker into a seemingly mystical union with nature itself: "A gallon, and one is in accord with all nature."

Far more than Neruda's ode, however, Li Bo's poem emphasizes drunkenness as a parallel to visionary enlightenment: "Three cups, and one can perfectly understand the Great Tao." Yet the enlightenment bestowed upon the speaker is of an exclusive, hermetic nature: wine and its ensuing intoxication provide the poet-drinker with a secret knowledge not to be shared with any but those who are themselves drunk. In this way, the poem reveals an affinity with the pervasive tradition of mystical or religious initiates guarding their knowledge from outsiders (e.g., in Christianity and in the earlier Eleusinian mysteries of ancient Greece).

The poem also reflects the extensive cross-cultural associations of alcohol (among other psychotropic drugs) with visionary experience. However spurious or genuine that experience may be is another matter; what is relevant here is the poem's manifestation of these patterns of association in the space of its few short lines.

The translation and notes to the poem are by Amy Lowell, in collaboration with Florence Ayscough.

A pot of wine among flowers.
I alone, drinking, without a companion.
I lift the cup and invite the bright moon.
My shadow opposite certainly makes us three.
But the moon cannot drink,
And my shadow follows the motions of my body in vain.
For the briefest time are the moon and my shadow my companions.
Oh, be joyful! One must make the most of Spring.
I sing—the moon walks forward rhythmically;
I dance, and my shadow shatters and becomes confused.
In my waking moments, we are happily blended.
When I am drunk, we are divided from one another and scattered.
For a long time I shall be obliged to wander without intention;
But we will keep our appointment by the far-off Cloudy River.\*

IF Heaven did not love wine,
There would be no Wine Star in Heaven,†
If Earth did not love wine,
There should be no Wine Springs on Earth.‡
Why then be ashamed before Heaven to love wine.
I have heard that clear wine is like the Sages;
Again it is said that thick wine is like the Virtuous Worthies.
Wherefore it appears that we have swallowed both Sages and Worthies.
Why should we strive to be Gods and Immortals?
Three cups, and one can perfectly understand the Great Tao;
A gallon, and one is in accord with all nature.
Only those in the midst of it can fully comprehend the joys of wine;
I do not proclaim them to the sober.

> \*The Cloudy River is the Chinese name for the Milky Way.
> †The Wine Star is a constellation composed of three stars, to the North of the Dipper.
> ‡The Wine Springs lie, one in Kansu, and one in Shansi. The water of the one in Kansu is supposed to taste like wine, that of the one in Shansi is used in the making of wine.

# *Emily Dickinson,*
# *"I taste a liquor never brewed" (1860)*

*One of the few poems published during her lifetime, "I taste a liquor never brewed" is also one of the best known poems by Emily Dickinson (1830–1886).*

*Intoxication, whether literal or metaphorical, is a prominent theme throughout Dickinson's poetry. This fact should not surprise us, given the general prevalence of three potent intellectual forces in Dickinson's social and intellectual milieu: the imagery of intoxication found in much Romantic poetry that Dickinson would have known (e.g., the work of Coleridge, Keats, and Emerson, among others); the emphasis on uplifting, visionary experience in American transcendentalism, where the transcendent state has obvious parallels to a state of intoxication; and the concern with questions of drinking and abstinence that permeated Dickinson's society, a society in which drink was widespread but which also witnessed the political and social burgeoning of teetotalism in America. In this particular poem, the poet employs drunkenness and drinking in an entirely metaphorical sense: the poem celebrates a state of mind and perception analogous to drunkenness but otherwise unrelated to the ingestion of psychotropic substances. The poem is, thus, at a far remove from the interpenetration of literal and metaphorical or physical and spiritual drinking found in some other passages in this section, such as those by James, Li Po, and Neruda. If anything, in Dickinson's poem we find not a linkage but a demarcation between the spiritual and physical forms of drunkenness. And, though Dickinson herself was no teetotaler, the poem unequivocally prioritizes non-alcoholic intoxication above more mundane forms of drunkenness. That said, the passage emphasizes with equal intensity the prioritizing of a state of non-rational exhilaration and experience above everyday reason, ironically and somewhat humorously describing the poetic speaker as a "little tippler" whose behavior leaves the proper "seraphs" of society aghast at her unconventionality. As is usual with this poet, the poem suggests far more than it states, inviting a speculative, contemplative engagement with its imagery and implications rather than a definitive explication.*

I taste a liquor never brewed,
From tankards scooped in pearl;
Not all the vats upon the Rhine
Yield such an alcohol!

Inebriate of air am I,
And debauchee of dew,
Reeling, through endless summer days,
From inns of molten blue.

When landlords turn the drunken bee
Out of the foxglove's door,
When butterflies renounce their drams,
I shall but drink the more!

Till seraphs swing their snowy hats,
And saints to windows run,

To see the little tippler
Leaning against the sun!

## William James, from
## The Varieties of Religious Experience *(1902)*

*William James (1842–1910) was a luminary in a family of luminaries— his father, the theologian Henry James, Sr.; his sister, Alice James, known today primarily for the vivid descriptions of contemporaries found in her diaries; and his novelist-brother, Henry James. In addition to being a distinguished professor at Harvard University, William James made major contributions to philosophy (especially pragmatism), psychology, and physiology. Although not a work of literature per se, James's influential study,* The Varieties of Religious Experience, *is included here for its remarkably eloquent analysis of the spiritual dimensions of drinking. To be sure, images of alcoholic dissipation, whether humorous or pathetic, are widespread in literature, as many earlier selections in this anthology demonstrate. At the same time, however, the links between intoxication and religion are ancient and profound. In many cultures, intoxication (whether literal or metaphorical) is associated with a liminal state between the mundane and the divine.\* Not surprisingly, alcohol or other psychotropic substances have functioned to enhance altered states of consciousness sought in religious ceremonies; often, a non-rational condition of heightened spiritual excitement or awareness is figuratively expressed through images of drunkenness, even when literal drinking is condemned, as in St. Paul's injunction to the Ephesians: "And be not drunk with wine, wherein is excess; but be filled with the Spirit" (Ephesians 5:18).*

*To William James, however, the link between the spiritual and the material aspects of intoxicant use is far from metaphorical. To put it more precisely, the metaphorical accounts for only part of the intersection of intoxication and spirituality. Despite the debasements of physical drunkenness, the origins of what James calls "the sway of alcohol over mankind" lie in a universal human yearning for transcendent or mystical experience, however unconscious such a yearning can be. As this observation suggests, James locates drinking deep within human nature, just as his entire book emphasizes the inextricability of human nature from all aspects of religious experience.*

*William James also has an important but lesser-known connection to Alcoholics Anonymous. The co-founder of AA, Bill Wilson, drew heavily on* The Varieties of Religious Experience *in establishing the organization's principles, especially the notion of achieving sobriety through a spiritual reorientation. James's theories provided Wilson with a conceptual framework for alcoholic recovery that allowed for a spiritual dimension without involving any specific creed or form of institutionalized religion, which Wilson disparagingly described as the "churchy."†  (At the same time, of course, references to "God," even if accompanied by various qualifiers and disclaimers, appear in most of AA's famous "Twelve Steps.") In any event,* The Varieties of Religious Experience *has relevance both to drinking and to the history of the struggle for sobriety, at least as understood in AA.‡*

\*See Marty Roth's discussion of "spiritual intoxication" in his Drunk the Night Before: An Anatomy of Intoxication *(Minneapolis: University of Minnesota Press, 2005), pp. 77–98.*

†*Ernest Kurtz,* Not-God: A History of Alcoholics Anonymous *(Center City, MN: Hazelden, 1979), p. 177; Kurtz's magisterial study includes extensive discussion of the simultaneous pull toward religion and tension with religion in AA.*

‡*The James passage bears a striking resemblance to a passing comment on drink and spiritual needs by Harriet Beecher Stowe in her novel,* Dred: A Tale of the Great Dismal Swamp *(originally published in 1884). Describing Cripps, a ne'er do well drunkard in the novel, Stowe writes: "He was uncomfortable—gloomy; and every one, under such circumstances, naturally inclines towards some source of consolation. He who is intellectual reads and studies; he who is industrious flies to business; he who is affectionate seeks friends; he who is pious, religion; but he who is none of these—what has he but his whiskey?" Harriet Beecher Stowe,* Writings *(Boston: Houghton Mifflin, 1896), 3: 112.*

In a recital like this there is certainly something suggestive of pathology. The next step into mystical states carries us into a realm that public opinion and ethical philosophy have long since branded as pathological, though private practice and certain lyric strains of poetry seem still to bear witness to its ideality. I refer to the consciousness produced by intoxicants and anaesthetics, especially by alcohol. The sway of alcohol over mankind is unquestionably due to its power to stimulate the mystical faculties of human nature, usually crushed to earth by the cold facts and dry criticisms of the sober hour. Sobriety diminishes, discriminates, and says no; drunkenness expands, unites, and says yes. It is in fact the great exciter of the yes function in man. It brings its votary from the chill periphery of things to the radiant core. It makes him for the moment one with truth. Not through mere perversity do men run after it. To the poor and the unlettered it stands in the place of symphony concerts and of literature; and it is part of the deeper mystery and tragedy of life that whiffs and gleams of something that we immediately recognize as excellent should be vouchsafed to so many of us only in the fleeting earlier phases of what in its totality is so degrading a poisoning. The drunken consciousness is one bit of the mystic consciousness, and our total opinion of it must find its place in our opinion of that larger whole.

## *Pablo Neruda, "Ode to Wine" (1954)*

>   Late in his long and varied career, the Chilean poet and political figure Pablo Neruda (1904–1973) began publishing numerous odes on unusually mundane topics—the tomato, the onion, a pair of socks, a chair. The first volume collecting these odes, which have become among the writer's most popular works, is entitled Elemental Odes *(*Odas elementales, *1954), and includes the "Ode to Wine" ("Oda al vino") reprinted below. This ode parallels Neruda's other poetic tributes to everyday, material objects which become the occasions of metaphysical reflection and celebration.*
>   *Unlike many works celebrating drink, "Ode to Wine" focuses less on altered states of consciousness, or on drinking as a metaphor for such states (as we find in Emily Dickinson's "I taste a liquor never brewed"), than it does on wine itself as a substance that mystically and mysteriously blends the physical and the spiritual. The poem glories in wine as an embodiment of the biological world, the world of soil and sun and fruit that leads to the maturation of grapes and, ultimately, to the production of wine. At the same time, the poem's exultation in the world of physical process modulates into a transcendent exaltation of wine above that world. Yet this modulation involves not a break between the realms of matter and spirit, but rather their coexistence on an ineffable continuum that the poet can describe but never precisely define. The intertwining of physical and spiritual is furthered by Neruda's indirect allusions to the Bible, as in his description of the beloved's body in terms reminiscent of the Song of Solomon, and in his use, in the poem's final line, of the phrase "cantico del fruto" ("canticle of the fruit"); the word "cantico" or "canticle" applies to various Biblical songs, including the Song of Solomon (identified, sometimes, as the "canticle of canticles" or "cantico de los canticos"). Through such Biblically inflected imagery and terminology, Neruda enhances the spiritual implications of his ode—one might almost say his "hymn"—to wine. The translation below is by Margaret Sayers Peden.*

Day-colored wine,
night-colored wine,
wine with purple feet
or wine with topaz blood,
wine,
starry child
of earth,
wine, smooth
as a golden sword,
soft

as lascivious velvet,
wine, spiral-seashelled
and full of wonder,
amorous,
marine;
never has one goblet contained you,
one song, one man,
you are choral, gregarious,
at the least, you must be shared.
At times
you feed on mortal
memories;
your wave carries us
from tomb to tomb,
stonecutter of icy sepulchers,
and we weep
transitory tears;
your
glorious
spring dress
is different,
blood rises through the shoots,
wind incites the day,
nothing is left
of your immutable soul.
Wine
stirs the spring, happiness
bursts through the earth like a plant,
walls crumble,
and rocky cliffs,
chasms close,
as song is born.
A jug of wine, and thou beside me
in the wilderness,
sang the ancient poet.*
Let the wine pitcher
add to the kiss of love its own.
My darling, suddenly
the line of your hip
becomes the brimming curve
of the wine goblet,

your breast is the grape cluster,
your nipples are the grapes,
the gleam of spirits lights your hair,
and your navel is a chaste seal
stamped on the vessel of your belly,†
your love an inexhaustible
cascade of wine,
light that illuminates my senses,
the earthly splendor of life.

But you are more than love,
the fiery kiss,
the heat of fire,
more than the wine of life;
you are
the community of man,
translucency,
chorus of discipline,
abundance of flowers.
I like on the table,
when we're speaking,
the light of a bottle
of intelligent wine.
Drink it,
and remember in every
drop of gold,
in every topaz glass,
in every purple ladle,
that autumn labored
to fill the vessel with wine;
and in the ritual of his office,
let the simple man remember
to think of the soil and of his duty,
to propagate the canticle of the wine.

*This line and the two before it allude to one of the most famous passages in the Rubaiyat of the 11th–12th-century Persian poet Omar Khayyam: "A Jug of Wine, a Loaf/of Bread—and Thou/Beside me singing in the/Wilderness" (translation by Edward Fitzgerald).

†The poem's sensual, figurative association of the beloved's body with parts of the natural world is reminiscent of the Song of Solomon, e.g., in Chapter 7, the Song compares the beloved's navel to a round goblet, her breasts to clusters of grapes, her belly to a heap of wheat, the roof of her mouth to the best wine; similar comparisons occur throughout the Song of Solomon.

## Simon Ortiz, "Woman Singing" (1969)

Early in the American Indian experience with alcohol, drinking began to be associated with magical or religious qualities. As the historian Peter Mancall observes, "Liquor's ability to alter perception led many Indians to consider it a sacred substance. Such beliefs crossed various cultural boundaries in Indian America."* Consequently, it is not surprising that in much Indian fiction, the recovery from alcoholism entails a spiritual reorientation, particularly one that replaces the spurious spirituality offered by alcohol with a return to the genuine spiritual traditions of tribal culture; this pattern appears throughout writing by or about Indians, e.g., in works by such authors as Oliver LaFarge, Frank Waters, N. Scott Momaday, and Leslie Marmon Silko, as well as in the work of Simon J. Ortiz (1941–). One of the most prolific and highly regarded American Indian authors working today, Ortiz is a member of the Acoma Pueblo tribe, and was raised in New Mexico. Currently a Professor specializing in Indigenous Literature at Arizona State University, Ortiz has written fiction, poetry, and non-fiction exploring many dimensions of contemporary Indian life, including the corrosion of native culture as a result of alcohol abuse. In "Woman Singing," Ortiz deals with the way that alcoholic disruption of native life, especially family life, can be healed through what Paula Gunn Allen has described as one of Ortiz's earliest themes: "the restoration of tradition's voice in the lives of modern Indians."† In "Woman Singing," that restoration begins with a reaffirmation of Indian spiritual values that are expressed artistically, through the medium of the ancient Navajo prayer song known as "The Night Chant," sung by the woman of the story's title. Such a restoration can, moreover, begin to take effect even if, as is the case with the story's drunken protagonist, Clyde, a traditional "song of the People" is sung silently, within the mind.

*Peter C. Mancall, Deadly Medicine Indians and Alcohol in Early America *(Ithaca: Cornell University Press, 1995), p. 75; on the use of alcohol among some Indian tribes as "a search for visions and supernatural revelations," see Craig MacAndrew and Robert B. Edgerton,* Drunken Comportment: A Social Explanation *(Chicago: Aldine, 1969), p. 119.*

†Paula Gunn Allen, "Introduction," in Allen, ed., Voice of the Turtle: American Indian Literature 1900–1970 *(New York: Ballantine, 1994), p. 18.*

"Yessir, pretty good stuff," Willie said. He handed the bottle of Thunderbird wine to Clyde. Clyde took a drink and then another before he said anything. He looked out the window of their wooden shack. Gray and brown land outside. Snow soon, but hope not, Clyde thought.

"Yes," Clyde said. But he didn't like it. He didn't drink wine very much, maybe some sometimes, but none very much.

Willie reached for the bottle, and Clyde thought that Willie didn't mind drinking anything. Any wine was just another drink. But he knew, too, that Willie liked whiskey, and he liked beer, too. It didn't make any difference to Willie. Clyde wished he had some beer.

They had come from the potato fields a few minutes before. It was cold outside and Willie threw some wood into the kitchen stove as soon as they came in. He poured in kerosene from a mason jar and threw in a match. After a moment, the kerosene caught the small fire and exploded with a muffled sound. Willie jumped back and laughed. Clyde hung up his coat and then put it back on when he saw there were only a few pieces of wood in the woodbox. He looked over at Willie, but Willie was taking his coat off and so Clyde went on out to get the wood. Willie didn't do anything he didn't have to.

There was singing from the shack across from theirs. Singing, The People singing, Clyde said to himself in his Native Indian tongue. It was a woman. Sad kind of, but not lonely, just something which bothered him, made him think of Arizona, his homeland. Brown and red land. Piñon, yucca, and his father's sheep, the dogs too around the door of the hogan at evening. Smoke and smell of stew and bread, and the older smell of the juniper mingled with the sheep. His heart and thoughts were lonely. Woman singing, The People singing, here and now, Clyde thought to himself. He stood for a while and listened and then looked over at the shack. The door was tightly shut, but the walls were thin, just scrap lumber and roofing paper, and the woman's voice was almost clear. Clyde was tempted to approach the shack and listen closer, his loneliness now pressed him, but he would not because it was broad daylight and it was not the way to do things. The woman was Joe Shorty's wife, and she was the mother of two children. Clyde picked up an armful of wood and returned to his own shack.

"Have some more, son," Willie said. Willie was only a few years older than Clyde, but he called him son sometimes. Just for fun, and Clyde would call him father in return. Willie was married and the father of two children. They lived in New Mexico while he worked in the Idaho potato fields.

"I think I'll fix us something to eat," Clyde said after he had taken a drink. He began to peel some potatoes. Willie's going to get drunk again, he thought. Yessir. They had gotten paid, and Willie had been fidgety since morning when they had received their money from Wheeler, their boss. He had told the Indians who worked for him, "Now I know that some of you are leaving as soon as you get paid, well, that's okay with me because they ain't much to do around here until next year. But some of you are staying for a while longer, and I'm telling those guys who are staying that they better stay sober. Besides, it's getting colder out, and we don't want no froze

Indians around." Wheeler laughed, and Willie laughed with him. Clyde didn't like the boss, and he didn't look at him or say anything when he received his pay. He was going to stay for at least another month, but he didn't want to. But he figured he had to since he wasn't sure whether he could get a job around home right off or even at all. Willie was staying, too, because he didn't feel like going home just yet, besides the fact that his family needed money.

"I think I'm gonna go to town tonight," Willie said. He was casual in saying it, but he was excited and he had been planning for it since morning. "Joe Shorty and his wife are coming along. You want to come?"

"I'm not sure," Clyde said. He didn't know Joe Shorty too well, and he had only said Hello to his wife and children.

"Come on," Willie insisted. "We'll go to a show and then to the Elkhorn Bar. Dancing there. And all the drunks have left, so it'll be okay now. Come with us."

"Yeah, I might," Clyde said. He listened for the woman's singing while they ate, but the fire crackling in the stove was loud and Willie kept talking about going to town. "Isn't Joe Shorty and his family going back home?" Clyde asked.

"I don't know," Willie answered. He pushed back his chair and carried the dishes to the sink. Clyde began to wash the dishes but Willie stopped him. "Come on, let's go."

When they knocked on Joe Shorty's door, a boy answered. He looked at the two men and then ran back inside. Joe came to the door.

"Okay, just a little while," Joe said.

Willie and Clyde sat down on the front step. They could hear movement and mumbled talk inside. Clyde thought about the singing woman again. He felt uncomfortable because he was thinking of another man's woman. It was a healing song, strong mountains in it, strong and sharp and clear, and far up. Women always make songs strong, he thought. He almost told Willie about the song.

Joe and his wife and children, two boys, came out and they all began to walk on the road towards town. It was five miles away, and usually someone was driving into town and would give them a ride. If not, they would walk all the way. The children ran and walked ahead. They talked quietly with each other, but the grownups didn't say anything.

When they had walked a mile, a pickup truck stopped for them. It was Wheeler. "Hey, Willie. Joe. Everybody going to town, huh? Come," Wheeler called. Willie and Clyde got in front with Wheeler, and Joe and his family got in the back.

"Well, gonna go have a good time, huh? Drink and raise hell," Wheeler said loudly and laughed. He punched Willie in the side playfully. He drove pretty fast along the gravel road.

Willie smiled. The wine he had finished off was warm in him. He wished he had another bottle. Out of the corners of his eyes, he searched the cab, and wondered if Wheeler might have a drink to offer.

"You Indians are the best damn workers," Wheeler said. "And I don't mind giving you a ride in my truck. Place down the road's got a bunch of Mexicans, had them up at my place several years back, but they ain't no good. Lazier than any Indian anytime, them Mexicans are. Couldn't nothing move them once they sit down. But you people—and for this reason I don't mind giving you a lift to town—Willie and your friend there do your work when I tell you, and that means you're okay for my farm."

Clyde felt the wine move in his belly. It made him swallow and he turned his head a little and saw that the woman's scarf had fallen away from her head. She was trying to put it back on.

"That Joe's got a pretty woman," Wheeler said to Willie. He looked at Clyde for comment, but Clyde would not look at him. Willie smiled and nodded.

"Yeah, don't get to see too many pretty Indian women around the camps, but she's a pretty one. You think so, Willie?" Wheeler nudged Willie with his elbow.

"Yes," Willie said and he shrunk down in his seat. He wished that Wheeler would offer him a drink if he had any. But he knew that he probably wouldn't.

"Hey, Clyde, you married? A woman at home?" Wheeler asked, but he didn't look at Clyde. They were approaching the town and Clyde stared straight ahead at it but he decided to answer.

"No," Clyde said. "Not yet, maybe when I get enough money." He smiled faintly to show that he was making a minor joke.

"Someday you'll get a woman, maybe a pretty one like Joe's, with or without money," Wheeler said. And he laughed loudly. He pulled the pickup truck over to a curb in the center of the small town. "Well, take it easy. Don't over do it. Or else you'll land in jail or freeze out in the cold or something," Wheeler said with no special concern.

"We're going to the show," Willie said, and he smiled at Wheeler. "Okay," Wheeler said, gave a quick laugh, and turned to watch Joe's wife climb out of the truck. He wanted to catch her eye, maybe to wink at her, but she didn't look at him. He watched the Indians walk up the street towards the town theater. The woman and her children followed behind the men. Wheeler thought about all the drunk Indians he'd seen in his life. He shrugged his shoulders and turned down the street in the opposite direction.

The movie was about a singer. Hank Williams was the singer's name. Clyde knew who he was, used to be on the Grand Ole Opry on radio, he remembered, sang songs he remembered, too. Clyde thought about the singers back home. The singers of the land, the people, the rain, and the good things of his home. His uncle on his mother's side was a medicine man, and he used to listen to him sing. In the quiet and cold winter evenings, lying on his sheepskin beside the fire, he would listen and sing under his breath with his uncle. Sing with me, his uncle would say, and Clyde would sing. But he had a long ways to go in truly learning the songs; he could not sing many of them and could only remember the feeling of them.

Willie laughed at the funny incidents in the movie, and he laughed about the drunk Hank Williams. That made him wish he had a drink again, and he tried to persuade Joe to go with him, but Joe didn't want to leave. Joe's wife and children watched the movie and the people around them, and they watched Willie fidget around in his seat. They figured he wanted to go drink. At the end of the movie, they walked to a small cafe. On the way Willie ran into a liquor store and bought a pint of whisky.

"Come on, son," he said to Clyde. "Help your father drink this medicine." Joe followed along into an alley where they quickly gulped some of the liquor.

"Call your woman and ask if she wants some," Willie said to Joe. He was in good spirit now. The whisky ran through him quickly and lightly.

"Emma, come here," Joe called to his wife. She hesitated, looked up the street, and stepped into the alley. Her husband handed her the bottle and she drank quickly. She coughed and gasped for a moment, and Willie and Joe laughed.

Clyde saw the two children watching them. They stood in the weak overhead glare of a streetlight. Traffic barely moved, and a few people from the movies were walking on the streets. The children waited patiently for their parents.

They ate a quick dinner of hamburgers and Cokes. And when they finished, they paid up and walked to the Elkhorn Bar a couple of blocks away.

"Do se doe," Willie said when he heard the music coming from the bar. Saturday night was always a busy night, but most of the Indian potato pickers were gone now. There were only a few cars and trucks; some men and women stood by the door. A small fire blazed several yards from the bar, and around it were a few Indians quietly talking.

Willie walked over to the fire, and Clyde followed him because he didn't want to be left alone. Joe and his family stood beside the door of the bar and peered in. "Here comes a drunk," someone in the circle of Indians said as

Willie and Clyde walked up. They laughed, but it was not meant in harm. For a moment, as he did upon entering a crowd away from his home, Clyde felt a small tension, but he relaxed quickly and he talked with an acquaintance. Willie passed him a bottle, and he made a small joke, and Clyde laughed. He felt better and took a long drink. Whisky went down into the belly harder than wine but it made him feel warmer. And when he thought that it didn't make any difference to Willie what he drank he laughed to himself. The men talked.

The talk was mostly about their home and about The People at home. Clyde again felt the thought travel into his heart. It made him long for his home. He didn't belong here even though he had friends here, and he had money in his pocket and a job. He was from another place, where his people came from and belonged. Yet here some of them were around this fire, outside the Elkhorn Bar, and they worked in the Idaho potato fields cultivating, irrigating, and picking potatoes. Someone began a song. It was the season for sings back in The People's land. The song was about a moving people.

When no one passed a bottle for a while, Clyde decided to go get a drink at the bar. The liquor in him made him sleepy, but he was getting cold too. There was no wind, but it was getting colder. He remembered Wheeler's words, thought about them for a moment, but he knew it would not freeze tonight. The bar was crowded. Someone was on the floor near the doorway, and others stepped over him without taking much notice.

Clyde met Joe Shorty and his wife, and they drank some beer together. Joe was getting drunk and his wife was drinking quietly. It was too noisy for Clyde to remember the song anymore. The children were standing by the jukebox, watching the revolving discs. Clyde wondered when they were going back to the camp by the potato fields, and he went to look for Willie.

"So there you are, son," Willie said when Clyde found him. He was with the men around the fire. "Come join us." He was drunk, and he handed Clyde another bottle.

The Indians, who were very few now, were singing in the high voice of The People. Like the wind blowing through clefts in the mountains. Clyde wondered if it was only that he was getting drunk with the liquor that he could make out the wind and the mountains in the song. But it was the men getting drunk, too, which didn't make it sound like the wind, he thought. He drank some more, but he was getting tired and colder, and he told Willie he wanted to go.

"No, stay," Willie said. "It is still a long night. These nights are long, and at home the sings last all night long." This Idaho was not where The People's home was, Clyde thought. And he wanted to tell Willie that. He wanted to tell the others that, but they wouldn't pay attention to him, he knew.

The women would sit or stand quietly by the singing men at home. The fire would be big, and when it got smaller someone would bring an armload of wood and throw it in. Children would hurry through the crowd of The People until they were tired and sleepy. Here there were no children except by the jukebox, watching it play records. In the morning, there would be newly built fires before-camps of families. In the mountains of The People. And the light beginning in the East would show that maybe it will snow sometime soon, but here by the Elk-horn Bar there would be no fires and no one to see the light in the East. Maybe, like Wheeler talked, there'd be some frozen Indian left lying around. Clyde walked away. The town was quiet. A police cruiser went in the direction of the bar and the officer looked at Clyde. When he got to the edge of town, he lengthened his stride.

When he had walked for a while, he saw that someone was walking in front of him. He slowed down, and he saw that it was a woman and two children. Joe Shorty's family. Joe must have stayed, drunk I guess, Clyde thought, and his family had left without him. Clyde didn't want to talk with them because they were another man's wife and children. They heard him and one of the boys said loudly, "It's Clyde. Clyde, come walk with us."

The woman was slightly drunk. Clyde could see her smile. She staggered some. "It's cold," she said. "We left Joe Shorty. He's going to come home in the morning."

Joe Shorty's wife and sons and Clyde walked quietly and steadily. The children stepped carefully in the dark. Once, Clyde looked back, and he could barely make out a pale light over the town. He thought about Willie and thought he would be all right. It was cold and Clyde let his hand out of his pocket to test the cold. Willie would be all right. Joe Shorty and Willie would probably come back to the camp together in the morning.

The lights of a truck lit them up and Clyde said, "We better get on this side of the road." The younger boy stumbled and grabbed for Clyde's hand. The boy's hand was cold, and Clyde felt funny with Joe Shorty's son's hand in his.

The truck was Wheeler's. It passed them and then slowed to a stop fifty yards ahead. Wheeler honked his horn. Clyde and Joe Shorty's family walked toward the truck as it backed towards them.

"It's Wheeler, the potato boss," Clyde said to the woman. She did not look at him or say anything. The younger boy clung to his mother's skirt.

The pickup truck drew back alongside of them and stopped. Wheeler rolled down his window and studied them for a moment. He looked at Clyde and winked. Clyde felt a small panic begin in him. He realized that he still held the child's hand in his. What did this mean to the potato boss, Clyde asked himself.

"Well come on," Wheeler said. "Get in, but just a minute," and he got out. He stood by the side of the truck and urinated. The woman and her children and then Clyde climbed into the back of the truck.

When Wheeler saw that they had climbed in the back, he said gruffly, "Come on, get in front." And then with a softer tone, "There's enough room and it's colder than hell out," and he reached out a hand to one of the boys. But the boy hung back. Wheeler grabbed the other and swung him over the side. The woman and the other boy had no choice but to follow.

Clyde felt his feelings empty for a while and then he slowly felt himself burning. He watched the woman climb out of the back into the front. It was not cold as before and it was the liquor, he thought. When he jumped down from the back and got into the front he felt light and springy. He smiled at Wheeler.

Joe Shorty's wife did not say anything. She was looking at the dashboard and her children huddled against her.

"Well, Joe Shorty must be having a good time," Wheeler said. He laughed and steered wildly to keep the truck on the road.

The woman did not say anything. She held one of her children, and the other huddled against her tightly. Clyde was on the side against the door. He could feel her movement and her warmth. But he looked straight ahead until Wheeler spoke to him.

"Weren't you having a good time, Clyde? Maybe there's good times other places, huh?"

Clyde felt a hot liquid move in him. It was warm in the truck. The heater was blowing on his ankles. It's the whisky, he thought. What does this man think of this, he thought. And then he thought of what all the white men in the world thought about all the Indians in the world. I'm drunk, he thought and he wanted to sing that in his own language, The People's language, but there didn't seem to be any words for it. When he thought about it in English and in song, it was silly, and he felt uncomfortable. Clyde smiled at Wheeler, but Wheeler wasn't paying attention to him now.

Wheeler drove with one hand and with the other he patted Joe Shorty's older son on the head and smiled at Joe Shorty's wife.

"Nice, nice kid," Wheeler said. The woman fidgeted, and she held her other son tightly to her.

Clyde felt her move against him and he tensed. He tried to think of the son then. The People singing, he thought, the woman singing. The mountains, the living, the women strong, the men strong. But he was tense in his mind, and there was no clear path between his mind and heart. Finally, he said to himself, Okay, potato boss, okay.

They drove into the camp and stopped in front of Clyde's and Willie's shack. Clyde thought, Okay, Potato boss, okay. He opened the door and began to climb out. The woman and her children began to follow him. "Wait," Wheeler said. "I'll drive you home. I'm going your way." His voice was almost angry.

Wheeler grabbed her arm, but she wrenched away. Clyde stopped and looked at Wheeler.

"She lives over there," Clyde said, pointing to Joe Shorty's shack, but he knew that Wheeler knew that.

Wheeler scowled at him and then he searched for a bottle under the seat. The woman did not move away anymore. She watched Wheeler and then said something to the children. Clyde looked at her. The song, he thought, and he tried very hard to think of the woman singing. The children ran to the shack, and Joe Shorty's woman and Wheeler followed.

For a long time, Clyde stood behind the door of his and Willie's shack. Listening and thinking quiet angry thoughts. He thought of Willie, Joe Shorty, the Elkhorn Bar, Hank Williams, potatoes, the woman and her sons. And he thought of Wheeler and himself, and he asked himself what he was listening for. He knew that he was not listening for the song, because he had decided that the woman singing was something a long time ago and would not happen anymore. If it did, he would not believe it. He would not listen. Finally, he moved away from the door and began to search through Willie's things for a bottle. But there was no bottle of anything except the kerosene and for a moment he thought of drinking kerosene. It was a silly thought, and so he laughed.

When the bus pulled out of the town in the morning, Clyde thought of Willie again. Willie had come in when the sun was coming up. He was red-eyed and sick. "We had a time, son," Willie said. He sat at the table woodenly. He did not notice that Clyde was putting clothes into a grip bag.

"That Wheeler, he sure gets up early. Joe Shorty and I met him outside his house. 'The early bird gets the worms,' he said. Sure funny guy. And he gave us some drinks," Willie mumbled. He was about to fall asleep with his head on the table.

"I'm going home," Clyde said. He had finished putting his clothes in the bag. "You never have a good time," Willie said. Clyde thought about that and asked in his mind whether that was true or not.

When Clyde thought about the woman's singing he knew that it had been real. Later on he would hear it someplace again and he would believe it. There was a larger hurt in his throat and he began to make a song, like those of The People, in his mind.

## Naguib Mahfouz, "Blessed Night" (1991)

*Naguib Mahfouz (1911–2006), born in Cairo, received the Nobel Prize for Literature in 1988. A prolific novelist and short-story writer of enormous distinction, Mahfouz had a career marked by controversy, particularly over accusations that his works were disrespectful of Islamic traditions. The controversy took a violent turn when, in 1994, a few weeks before his 83rd birthday, the nearly blind Mahfouz was stabbed (though not fatally) in a Cairo street, presumably by those outraged by Mahfouz's free-thinking attitudes and his criticism of extremism in the Arab world.*

*In approaching "Blessed Night," readers should remember that, though frowned upon, drinking in Egypt is generally more tolerated than in most Muslim countries. Thus, despite religious injunctions against its use, alcohol is readily available in Egypt, as it is in The Flower, the small back-alley tavern in the story. Although tinged with a sense of the illicit, the alcohol use in this story is less negative and more ambiguous than it often is in Mahfouz's work. The first reference to alcohol in the story is literal, to the actual physical beverage itself. But shortly thereafter, drinking assumes highly evocative, metaphorical connotations of visionary experience, including suggestions that through drink the protagonist has entered a transitional realm between life and death. This treatment of alcohol is in keeping with Islamic mysticism where, in contrast to mainstream Islamic teaching, "wine and drunkenness ... symbolize the yearning for God and mystical trance or ecstasy" (Menahem Milson,* Najib Mahfuz: The Novelist Philosopher of Cairo, *New York: St. Martin's Press, 1998, p. 103). Such imagery is familiar in the traditional literature of the middle east generally, e.g., the poetry of Abu Nuwas Hafiz, Sadi, Rumi and Omar Khayyam.\* Moreover, "Blessed Night" reflects a long-standing association of drinking with death. While alcohol is sometimes linked to life-giving properties (e.g., the word "whiskey" derives from "usquebaugh," Gaelic for "water of life"), it also possesses associations with death. For instance, the distinguished alcohol researcher, E.M. Jellinek, has pointed out that Dionysos, god of wine, "appears to have been one of the few, if not the only, gods in the Greek pantheon who gave a promise of a higher life after death"; in this regard, Jellinek also mentions the image on an ancient sarcophagus "of the deceased being carried to his grave in a drunken condition," a situation that suggests a parallel to that of Mahfouz's befuddled protagonist in "Blessed Night" (see Jellinek, "The Symbolism of Drinking: a Culture-Historical Approach," ed. for publication by Robert E. Popham and Carole D. Yawney,* Journal of Studies on Alcohol *38, (1997), p. 857).*

*The translation of "Blessed Night" is by Denys Johnson-Davies.*

*\*A thorough discussion of the wine-poem tradition in Arabic appears in Philip Kennedy,* The Wine Song in Classical Arabic Poetry: Abu Nuwas and the Literary Tradition *(Oxford: Oxford University Press, 1997).*

It was nothing but a single room in the unpretentious Nouri Alley, off Clot Bey Street. In the middle of the room was the bar and the shelf embellished with bottles. It was called The Flower and was passionately patronized by old men addicted to drink. Its barman was advanced in years, excessively quiet, a man who inspired silence and yet effused a cordial friendliness. Unlike other taverns, The Flower dozed in a delightful tranquility. The regulars would converse inwardly, with glances rather than words. On the night that was blessed, the barman departed from his traditional silence.

"Yesterday," he said, "I dreamed that a gift would be presented to a man of good fortune...."

Safwan's heart broke into a song with gentle lute accompaniment, while alcoholic waves flowed through him like electricity as he congratulated himself with the words "O blessed, blessed night!" He left the bar, reeling drunk, and plunged into the sublime night under an autumn sky that was not without a twinkling of stars. He made his way toward Nuzha Street, cutting across the square, glowing with an intoxication unadulterated by the least sensation of drowsiness. The street was humbled under the veil of darkness, except for the light from the regularly spaced streetlamps, the shops having closed their doors and given themselves up to sleep. He stood in front of his house: the fourth on the right, Number 42, a single-storied house fronted by an old courtyard of whose garden nothing remained but a solitary towering date palm. Astonished at the dense darkness that surrounded the house, he wondered why his wife had not as usual turned on the light by the front door.

It seemed that the house was manifesting itself in a new, gloomily forlorn shape and that it exuded a smell like that of old age. Raising his voice, he called out. "Hey there!"

From behind the fence there rose before his eyes the form of a man, who coughed and inquired, "Who are you? What do you want?"

Safwan was startled at the presence of this stranger and asked sharply, "And who are you? What's brought you to my house?" "Your house?" said the man in a hoarse, angry voice. "Who are you?"

"I am the guardian for religious endowment properties." "But this is my house."

"This house has been deserted for ages," the man scoffed. "People avoid it because it's rumored to be haunted by spirits."

Safwan decided he must have lost his way, and hurried back toward the square. He gave it a long comprehensive look, then raised his head to the street sign and read out loud, "Nuzha." So again he entered the street and counted off the houses until he arrived at the fourth. There he stood in a state of bewilderment, almost of panic: he could find neither his own house nor the haunted one. Instead he saw an empty space, a stretch of wasteland lying between the other houses. "Is it my house that I've lost or my mind?" he wondered.

He saw a policeman approaching, examining the locks of the shops. He stood in his path and pointed toward the empty wasteland. "What do you see there?"

The policeman stared at him suspiciously and muttered, "As you can see, it's a piece of wasteland where they sometimes set up funeral pavilions."

"That's just where I should have found my house," said Safwan. "I left it there with my wife inside it in the pink of health only this afternoon, so when could it have been pulled down and all the rubble cleared away?"

The policeman concealed an involuntary smile behind a stern official glare and said brusquely, "Ask that deadly poison in your stomach!"

"You are addressing a former general manager," said Safwan haughtily. At this the policeman grasped him by the arm and led him off. "Drunk and disorderly in the public highway!"

He took Safwan to the Daher police station, a short distance away, where he was brought before the officer on a charge of being drunk and disorderly. The officer took pity on him, however, because of his age and his respectable appearance. "Your identity card?"

Safwan produced it and said, "I'm quite in my right mind, it's just that there's no trace of my house."

"Well, now there's a new type of theft!" said the officer, laughing. "I really don't believe it!"

"But I'm speaking the truth," said Safwan in alarm.

"The truth's being unfairly treated, but I'll be lenient in deference to your age." Then he said to the policeman, "Take him to Number 42 Nuzha Street."

Accompanied by the policeman, Safwan finally found himself in front of his house as he knew it. Despite his drunken state he was overcome with confusion. He opened the outer door, crossed the courtyard, and put on the light at the entrance, where he was immediately taken aback, for he found himself in an entrance he had never before set eyes on. There was absolutely no connection between it and the entrance of the house in which he had lived for about half a century, and whose furniture and walls were all in a state of decay. He decided to retreat before his mistake was revealed, so he darted into the street, where he stood scrutinizing the house from the outside.

It was his house all right, from the point of view of its features and site, and he had opened the door with his own key, no doubt about it. What, then, had changed the inside? He had seen a small chandelier, and the walls had been papered. There was also a new carpet. In a way it was his house, and in another way it was not. And what about his wife, Sadriyya? "I've been drinking for half a century," he said aloud, "so what is it about this blessed night?"

He imagined his seven married daughters looking at him with tearful eyes. He determined, though, to solve the problem by himself, without recourse to the authorities—which would certainly mean exposing himself to the wrath of the law. Going up to the fence, he began clapping his hands, at which the front door was opened by someone whose features he could not make out. A woman's voice could be heard asking, "What's keeping you outside?"

It seemed, though he could not be certain, that it was the voice of a stranger. "Whose house is this, please?" he inquired.

"Are you that drunk? It's just too much!"

"I'm Safwan," he said cautiously.

"Come in or you'll wake the people sleeping."

"Are you Sadriyya?"

"Heaven help us! There's someone waiting for you inside."

"At this hour?"

"He's been waiting since ten."

"Waiting for me?"

She mumbled loudly in exasperation, and he inquired again, "Are you Sadriyya?"

Her patience at an end, she shouted, "Heaven help us!"

He advanced, at first stealthily, then without caring, and found himself in the new entrance. He saw that the door of the sitting room was open, with the lights brightly illuminating the interior. As for the woman, she had disappeared. He entered the sitting room, which revealed itself to him in a new garb, as the entrance had. Where had the old room with its ancient furniture gone to? Walls recently painted and a large chandelier from which Spanish-style lamps hung, a blue carpet, a spacious sofa and armchairs: it was a splendid room. In the foreground sat a man he had not seen before: thin, of a dark brown complexion, with a nose reminding one of a parrot's beak, and a certain impetuosity in the eyes. He was wearing a black suit, although autumn was only just coming in. The man addressed him irritably. "How late you are for our appointment!"

Safwan was both taken aback and angry. "What appointment? Who are you?"

"That's just what I expected—you'd forgotten!" the man exclaimed. "It's the same old complaint repeated every single day, whether it's the truth or not. It's no use, it's out of the question...."

"What is this raving nonsense?" Safwan shouted in exasperation.

Restraining himself, the man said, "I know you're a man who enjoys his drink and sometimes overdoes it."

"You're speaking to me as though you were in charge of me, while I don't even know you. I'm amazed you should impose your presence on a house in the absence of its owner."

He gave a chilly smile. "Its owner?"

"As though you doubt it!" Safwan said vehemently. "I see I'll have to call the police."

"So they can arrest you for being drunk and disorderly—and for fraud?"

"Shut up—you insolent imposter!"

The man struck one palm against the other and said, "You're pretending not to know who I am so as to escape from your commitments. It's out of the question...."

"I don't know you and I don't know what you're talking about."

"Really? Are you alleging you forgot and are therefore innocent? Didn't you agree to sell your house and wife and fix tonight for completing the final formalities?"

Safwan, in a daze, exclaimed, "What a lying devil you are!"

"As usual. You're all the same—shame on you!" said the other, with a shrug of the shoulders.

"You're clearly mad."

"I have the proof and witnesses."

"I've never heard of anyone having done such a thing before."

"But it happens every moment. You're putting on a good act, even though you're drunk."

In extreme agitation, Safwan said, "I demand you leave at once."

"No, let's conclude the incompleted formalities," said the other in a voice full of confidence.

He got up and went toward the closed door that led to the interior of the house. He rapped on it, then returned to his seat. Immediately there entered a short man with a pug nose and prominent forehead, carrying under his arm a file stuffed with papers. He bowed in greeting and sat down.

Safwan directed a venomous glare at him and exclaimed, "Since when has my house become a shelter for the homeless?"

The first man, introducing the person who had just entered, said, "The lawyer."

At which Safwan asked him brusquely, "And who gave you permission to enter my house?"

"You're in a bad way," said the lawyer, smiling, "but may God forgive you. What are you so angry about?"

"What insolence!"

Without paying any attention to what Safwan had said, the lawyer went on. "The deal is undoubtedly to your advantage."

"What deal?" asked Safwan in bewilderment.

"You know exactly what I mean, and I would like to tell you that it's useless your thinking of going back on it now. The law is on our side, and common sense too. Let me ask you: Do you consider this house to be really yours?"

For the first time Safwan felt at a loss. "Yes and no," he said.

"Was it in this condition when you left it?"

"Not at all."

"Then it's another house?"

"Yet it's the same site, number, and street."

"Ah, those are fortuitous incidentals that don't affect the essential fact—and there's something else."

He got up, rapped on the door, and returned to his seat. All at once a beautiful middle-aged woman, well dressed and with a mournful mien, entered and seated herself alongside the first man. The lawyer resumed his questioning. "Do you recognize in this lady your wife?"

It seemed to Safwan that she did possess a certain similarity, but he could not stop himself from saying, "Not at all."

"Fine—the house is neither your house, nor the lady your wife. Thus nothing remains but for you to sign the final agreement and then you can be off...."

"Off! Where to?"

"My dear sir, don't be stubborn. The deal is wholly to your advantage, and you know it." The telephone rang, although it was very late at night. The caller was the barman. Safwan was astonished that the man should be telephoning him for the first time in his life. "Safwan Bey," he said, "Sign without delay."

"But do you know...."

"Sign. It's the chance of a lifetime."

The receiver was replaced at the other end. Safwan considered the short conversation and found himself relaxing. In a second his state of mind changed utterly, his face took on a cheerful expression, and a sensation of calm spread throughout his body. The feeling of tension left him, and he signed. When he had done so, the lawyer handed him a small but somewhat heavy suitcase and said, "May the Almighty bless your comings and goings. In this suitcase is all that a happy man needs in this world."

The first man clapped, and there entered an extremely portly man, with a wide smile and a charming manner. Introducing him to Safwan, the lawyer said, "This is a trustworthy man and an expert at his work. He will take you to your new abode. It is truly a profitable deal."

The portly man made his way outside, and Safwan followed him, quiet and calm, his hand gripping the handle of the suitcase. The man walked ahead of him into the night, and Safwan followed. Affected by the fresh air, he staggered and realized that he had not recovered from the intoxication of the blessed night. The man quickened his pace, and the distance between them grew, so Safwan in turn, despite his drunken state, walked faster, his gaze directed toward the specter of the other man, while wondering how it was that he combined such agility with portliness.

"Take it easy, sir!" Safwan called out to him.

But it was as though he had spurred the man on to greater speed, for he broke into strides so rapid that Safwan was forced to hurl himself forward for fear he would lose him, and thus lose his last hope. Frightened he would be incapable of keeping up the pace, he once again called out to the man.

"Take it easy or I'll get lost!"

At this the other, unconcerned about Safwan, began to run. Safwan, in terror, raced ahead, heedless of the consequences. This caused him great distress, but all to no avail, for the man plunged into the darkness and disappeared from sight. Safwan was frightened the man would arrive ahead of him at Yanabi Square, where various roads split up, and he would not know which one the man had taken. He therefore began running as fast as possible, determined to catch up. His efforts paid off, for once again he caught a glimpse of the specter of the man at the crossroads. He saw him darting forward toward the fields, ignoring the branch roads that turned off to the eastern and western parts of the city. Safwan hurried along behind him and continued running without stopping, and without the least feeling of weakness. His nostrils were filled with delightful aromas that stirred up all kinds of sensations he had never before properly experienced and enjoyed.

When the two of them were alone in the vast void of earth and sky, the portly man gradually began to slow down until he had reverted to a mere brisk trot, then to a walk. Finally he stopped, and Safwan caught up with him and also came to a breathless stop. He looked around at the all-pervading darkness, with the glittering lights of faint stars. "Where's the new abode?" he asked.

The man maintained his silence. At the same time, Safwan began to feel the incursion of a new weight bearing down upon his shoulders and his whole body. The weight grew heavier and heavier and then rose upward to his head. It seemed to him that his feet would plunge deep into the ground. The pressure became so great that he could no longer bear it and, with a sudden spontaneous burst of energy, he took off his shoes. Then, the pressure working its way upward, he stripped himself of his jacket and trousers and flung them to the ground. This made no real difference, so he rid himself of his underclothes, heedless of the dampness of autumn. He was ablaze with pain and, groaning, he abandoned the suitcase on the ground. At that moment it seemed to him that he had regained his balance, that he was capable of taking the few steps that still remained. He waited for his companion to do something, but the man was sunk in silence. Safwan wanted to converse with him, but talk was impossible, and the overwhelming silence slipped through the pores of his skin to his very heart. It seemed that in a little while he would be hearing the conversation that was passing between the stars.

# Further Reading

The following list includes works of both scholarly and general interest related to some of the topics and texts found in this volume.

Ames, Genevieve M., and Linda A. Bennett, eds. *The American Experience with Alcohol: Cultural Perspectives*. New York: Plenum, 1986.
Barr, Andrew. *Drink: A Social History of America*. New York: Carroll & Graf, 1999.
Barrows, Susanna, and Robin Room, eds. *Drink: Behavior and Belief in Modern Society*. Berkeley: University of California Press, 1991.
Charters, Steve. *Wine and Society: The Cultural and Social Context of a Drink*. London: Butterworth-Heinemann, 2006.
Crowley, John. *The White Logic: Alcoholism and Gender in American Modernist Fiction*. Amherst: University of Massachusetts Press, 1994.
——, ed. *Drunkard's Progress: Narratives of Addiction, Despair, and Recovery*. Baltimore: Johns Hopkins University Press, 1999.
Dardis, Tom. *The Thirsty Muse: Alcohol and the American Writer*. Boston: Ticknor & Fields, 1989.
Douglas, Mary, ed. *Constructive Drinking: Perspectives on Drink from Anthropology*. Cambridge: Cambridge University Press, 1987.
Drowne, Kathleen. *Spirits of Defiance: National Prohibition and Jazz Age Literature*. Columbus: Ohio State University Press, 2005.
Earnshaw, Steven. *The Pub in Literature: England's Altered State*. Manchester: Manchester University Press, 2000.
Galanter, Marc, and Lee Anne Kaskutas, eds. *Research on Alcoholics Anonymous and Spirituality in Addiction Recovery*. New York: Springer, 2008.
Gately, Iain. *Drink: A Cultural History of Alcohol*. New York: Gotham, 2008.
Gilmore, Thomas B., Jr. *Equivocal Spirits: Alcoholism and Drinking in Twentieth-Century Literature*. Chapel Hill: University of North Carolina Press, 1987.
Gusfield, Joseph P. *Contested Meanings: The Construction of Alcohol Problems*. Madison: University of Wisconsin Press, 1996.
——. *Symbolic Crusade: Status Politics and the American Temperance Movement*, 2nd edition. Urbana: University of Illinois Press, 1986.
Haine, W. Scott. *The World of the Paris Café: Sociability Among the French Working Class, 1789–1914*. Baltimore: Johns Hopkins University Press, 1996.
Harrison, Brian. *Drink and the Victorians*. Pittsburgh: University of Pittsburgh Press, 1971.

Heath, Dwight B. *Drinking Occasions: Comparative Perspectives on Alcohol and Culture.* Philadelphia: Brunner/Mazel, 2000.
Herlihy, Patricia. *The Alcoholic Empire: Vodka and Politics in Late Imperial Russia.* Oxford: Oxford University Press, 2002.
Jellinek, E.M. *The Disease Concept of Alcoholism.* New Haven: Millhouse Press, 1960.
Kennedy, Philip F. *The Wine-Song in Classical Arabic Poetry: Abū Nuwās and the Literary Tradition.* Oxford: Clarendon Press, 1997.
Kurtz, Ernest. *Not God: A History of Alcoholics Anonymous.* Center City, Minnesota: Hazelden, 1979.
Lender, Mark Edward, and James Kirby Martin. *Drinking in America: A History.* New York: Free Press, 1982.
Levine, Harry Gene. "The Discovery of Addiction: Changing Conceptions of Habitual Drunkenness in America." *Journal of Studies on Alcohol* 39 (1978), 143–74.
MacAndrew, Craig, and Robert B. Edgerton. *Drunken Comportment: A Social Explanation.* Chicago: Aldine, 1969.
Mancall, Peter C. *Deadly Medicine: Indians and Alcohol in Early America.* Ithaca: Cornell University Press, 1997.
McGovern, Patrick E. *Ancient Wine: The Search for the Origins of Viniculture.* Princeton: Princeton University Press, 2007.
Murdock, Catherine Gilbert. *Domesticating Drink: Women, Men, and Alcohol in America, 1870–1940.* Baltimore: Johns Hopkins University Press, 2001.
Plant, Moira. *Women and Alcohol: Contemporary and Historical Perspectives.* London and New York: Free Association Press, 1997.
Reynolds, David S. *Beneath the American Renaissance: The Subversive Imagination in the Age of Emerson and Melville.* New York: Alfred A. Knopf, 1988.
Rorabaugh, William J. *The Alcoholic Republic: An American Tradition.* New York: Oxford University Press, 1979.
Roth, Marty. *Drunk the Night Before: An Anatomy of Intoxication.* Minneapolis: University of Minnesota Press, 2005.
Santora, Patricia B., Margaret L. Dowell, Jack E. Henningfield, eds. *Addiction and Art.* Baltimore: Johns Hopkins University Press, 2010.
Segal, Boris M. *Russian Drinking: Use and Abuse of Alcohol in Pre-Revolutionary Russia.* New Brunswick, CT: Rutgers Center of Alcohol Studies, 1987.
Taylor, Anya. *Bacchus in Romantic England: Writers and Drink, 1780–1830.* New York: St. Martin's Press, 1999.
Warner, Nicholas O. *Spirits of America: Intoxication in Nineteenth-Century American Literature.* Norman: University of Oklahoma Press, 1999.
Wilson, Thomas M. *Drinking Cultures: Alcohol and Identity.* Oxford: Berg, 2005.
Yip, Wai-Lim, ed. and trans. *Chinese Poetry: An Anthology of Major Modes and Genres.* Durham: Duke University Press, 1997.

www.ingramcontent.com/pod-product-compliance
Ingram Content Group UK Ltd.
Pitfield, Milton Keynes, MK11 3LW, UK
UKHW041951140426
5217IPUK00014B/742